Praise for *What Happy Companies Know*

"These concepts link to executive health, organizational wellness, and the impact of rising health care costs because of stress in the workplace. Better understanding of such concepts may lead to a healthier, high-performance workplace, and possibly a happier overall work environment for human flourishing."

—Vice Admiral Richard Carmona,
United States Surgeon General

"Everybody who wants to make their organization the best organization it can possibly be should read *What Happy Companies Know*. Let Dan Baker, Cathy Greenberg, and Collins Hemingway guide your journey to becoming a happy company."

—Ken Blanchard, author of *The One-Minute Manager*

"*What Happy Companies Know* will be one of the most important business books in our time. The science of happiness is a crucial strategy for the health and wellness of both leaders and their organizations if they are truly capable of 'leading beyond the walls'—getting the best from people both within and beyond the organization."

—Frances Hesselbein, founding president and
current chairman, Leader to Leader Institute

"...Relevant to both the CEO concerned with motivating workers and the employee figuring out how to improve personal coping skills."

—*Publishers Weekly*

"As a former U.S. Secretary of Labor, I've been involved in countless business and labor negotiations. I've generally witnessed situations when companies were at their worst, and can't help but think that if they were 'happy companies' things might have been less stressful. *What Happy Companies Know* is filled with brilliant and original ideas that can improve the health of any company—big or small. The executive health and business culture principles are applicable to all areas of labor relations. This book provides the tools necessary to assist companies in the planning and organization essential for profitable and positive negotiations."

—W.J. Usery, Jr., former U.S. Secretary of Labor

"The authors' central concept that 'happiness' is not a *result*, but rather the *cause* of success, will change basic business thinking. Instead of ROI, they focus on ROP, return on people, and encourage applying the techniques of the human potential movement to the process of doing business. This book should be on the reading list of every executive and every board member of every type of organization."

—Jonathan Estrin, executive vice president, American Film Institute

"Filled with practical ways to master 'the softer side' of business, this guide will help employers effectively implement change and produce more cooperative, innovative, and dedicated employees...Thanks to the authors' thorough research and accessible style, readers will understand not just how to improve their companies, but *why* it's necessary."

—Kirkus Reports

What Happy Companies Know

What Happy Companies Know

How the New Science of Happiness
Can Change Your Company for the Better

Dan Baker, Ph.D.
Cathy Greenberg, Ph.D.
Collins Hemingway, MA

PEARSON
Prentice
Hall

An imprint of Pearson Education

Upper Saddle River, NJ • Boston • Indianapolis • New York • London
San Francisco • Toronto • Sydney • Tokyo • Singapore • Hong Kong
Cape Town • Madrid • Paris • Milan • Munich • Amsterdam

Vice President and Editor-in-Chief: Tim Moore
Acquisitions Editor: Paula Sinnott
Editorial Assistant: Susie Abraham
Development Editor: Russ Hall
Associate Editor-in-Chief and Director of Marketing: Amy Neidlinger
Cover Designer: Nina Scuderi
Managing Editor: Gina Kanouse
Project/Copy Editor: Deadline-Driven Publishing
Indexer: Angie Bess
Compositor: Jake McFarland
Manufacturing Buyer: Dan Uhrig

© 2006 by Dan Baker, Cathy Greenberg, and Collins Hemingway
Published by Pearson Education, Inc.
Publishing as Prentice Hall
Upper Saddle River, New Jersey 07458

First Printing June, 2006

ISBN 0-13-185857-2

Pearson Education LTD.
Pearson Education Australia PTY, Limited.
Pearson Education Singapore, Pte. Ltd.
Pearson Education North Asia, Ltd.
Pearson Education Canada, Ltd.
Pearson Educatión de Mexico, S.A. de C.V.
Pearson Education—Japan
Pearson Education Malaysia, Pte. Ltd.

Library of Congress Cataloging-in-Publication Data

Baker, Dan.
  What happy companies know / Dan Baker, Cathy Greenberg, Collins Hemingway.
    p. cm.
  Includes bibliographical references and index.
  ISBN 0-13-185857-2 (hardback : alk. paper)
  1. Organizational effectiveness. 2. Organizational sociology. 3. Leadership. 4.
Corporate culture. I. Greenberg, Cathy. II. Hemingway, Collins. III. Title.
  HD58.9.B343 2006
  658.3'14--dc22
                        2005035713

Table of Contents

To the memory of Peter Drucker

Who, long before anyone else, advocated the central role of moral vision in organizational life and understood the way in which business could promote human dignity and change human lives for the better.

From Dan Baker

To my wife Amy, who has consistently been there as my most important partner in the business of life; and to my six children, Steve, Susie, Brett, Laurie, Joe, and Jeremy, who have taught me the finer points of servant-based leadership.

From Cathy Greenberg

To my daughter, Elisabeth Oriana, for the never-ending joy and happiness she brings to my life and for showing me how gratitude and appreciation round out better leaders—and mothers.

From Collins Hemingway

To Wendy Alden Hemingway, who gives me all the reasons to smile; to Joshua and Matthew, the best sons a man could have; and to Kyle, the best stepson a man could want.

Acknowledgments

From Dan Baker

To my mentors: my grandfather, Cletus Baker, who taught me the meaning of appreciation; my uncle, Donald White, who was a model of fair competition, sportsmanship, citizenship, and courage; my high school chemistry teacher, Conrad Florida, who guided me through adolescence; Benjamin Center, Ph.D., who turned my life in the right direction and taught me that the only real failure in life is to give up and that success comes from perseverance and leading with strengths; Clay Gerken, Ph.D., who helped me face my own fears and taught me that the world belongs to risk takers; and Robert Eliot, M.D., who taught me about the science and nature of the human heart.

To those who helped make this book possible: Mel Zuckerman, co-founder and chairman of Canyon Ranch, and Enid Zuckerman, co-founder of Canyon Ranch, the platform that has allowed me to meet some of the most incredible business minds of our time; Jerry Cohen, CEO of Canyon Ranch, whose support allowed me the time so necessary for laying the foundation of this book; Herman Gyr, Ph.D., who introduced me to IDEO and Tom Kelley; Larry Sternberg, who introduced me to Talent+, Doug and Kimberly Rath; and Horst D. Steklis, Ph.D., and Netzin Steklis.

To all the "C" officers and incredible entrepreneurs I have had the privilege of meeting in more than 20 years of service to Canyon Ranch. Finally, to all the people I have met in my many years of consulting and coaching that taught me first hand that work without meaning is drudgery, but that work with meaning defines purpose and generates energy for living.

From Cathy Greenberg

To my mentors: Warren Bennis, my guardian angel and mentor, who inspired me as a woman to become a leader and also made me feel that I could be a leader of leaders; Marshall Goldsmith, for always being there with his "life is good" insight and loving direction in life to help me become an executive coach; Frances Hesselbein, who believed in my voice and included my thinking in Drucker Foundation publications over the years; Noel Tichy, who taught me how to think strategically and apply good insight when working with all leaders; John R. O'Neil, who involved me with the World Economic Forum; Rosemarie Greco, for her faith, fortitude, and personal leadership; my parents, Barbara and Bernard, who gave me the courage to reach for my dreams; and my brothers, Fred and Phillip Greenberg.

Throughout my professional career as both a consultant and executive coach, so many "C" suite executives have taught me about creating happy companies by their own leadership that it is impossible to name them all individually without the danger of overlooking someone who deserves mention. You know who you are. Please take this as generous thanks, particularly to those of you who took the time to help a young executive grow and learn by your example.

I also must cite a number of organizations that enabled the testing of values, ideas, models, and processes that underlie much of this book: Accenture, Aetna, Allied Signal, Anthem, AMP Australia, Andersen Consulting, AT&T, AXA Insurance, Bank of America, Bell South, BOC Gases, Boeing, BP, Center for Applied Research (CFAR), Central Penn National Bank, CIGNA, Citizens Bank, Commerce Bank, Computer Sciences Corporation, Corning, CSC/Index, Dell, Drexel University, Endo Pharmaceuticals, First Union Bank, GE, Goldman Sachs, Harvard University, HEB, Independence Blue Cross, The JFK School of Public Policy, John Hancock, J.P. Morgan, Livingston College, Lockheed Martin, Mando Machinery, the Mann Center for the Performing Arts, Merck, Meridian Bank, Merrill Lynch, Navimedics, Ontario Department of Defense, PECO, the Philadelphia Zoo, PNC Bank Corporation, PP&L, Rutgers University, Rutgers University Medical School, SAP, Sovereign Bank, Starbucks, Toshiba, Toyota, United Healthcare, United States Army War College, University of Australia, University of Pennsylvania, and Vanguard.

Personally, I must thank Carol Stern Switzer, Alan Markovitz, Rick Cairns, Beverly Rowen, Kevin Wilson, Jonathan Landers, Tim Hilbert, Michael L. Spekter, Elaina S. Spilove, Scott Harrison, Jay Weinberg, Greg Hoy and Josh Lane of Pixelworthy, Johanna and Harold Hambrose of Electronic Ink, and my tech team at Data Doctor, Greg, Jeff, Rob (and George) for their kindness in helping me run my own happy company, h2c.

And last but never least, thanks to my new life partner, Tim. He provides both generous love and appreciation for the many talents I have as a woman—and yet his true measure of my worth comes down to how good I can bake a chocolate-chip cookie. Now that's the kind of happiness I can live with!

From Collins Hemingway

To my mother, Billie Hemingway, and my brothers, Chuck and Mac, who taught me the straight and narrow as well as to strive, to seek, and not to yield; to Jerry McConnell, whose moral and intellectual guidance has shaped my outlook since I was 17 years old; to Jo McConnell for her generous heart; to Jim Allen, Wally Hall, Randy Hankins, Patsy Lewellyn, Deb Mathis, and Russ Mathis for their lifelong friendship; to Don Riggin and Dave Emery for their examples; to many, many teachers, particularly Mrs. Phelps, who believed and encouraged; to Don and MaryBeth Bishoff for their many years of kindness; to Bunky and Ted Baker, who ran the first happy company I ever worked for; to Bruce Campbell and Tom Hanrahan, whose intelligence and generosity of heart make them friends that I admire as well as appreciate.

From the team

To Tim Moore, vice president and editor-in-chief of Prentice Hall Business, who saw the potential for a book on business and ethics that did not just point fingers but provided real, positive solutions that leaders could implement; to agent Richard Pine, who saw the same potential; to editor Paula Sinnott, who helped bring the team together, enthusiastically supported the book during development, and set into motion the many marketing efforts; to Russ Hall, whose early insight helped us take the project in the proper direction, whose careful review of draft after draft ensured that we properly developed the themes, and whose shepherding in the final stages put us over the top; to Cynthia Smith, who critiqued the text with great care and thought; to Ginny Munroe, the production editor, who shepherded the text through the production process with her usual care and precision.

Also, other people gave willingly of their time and insight in direct support of the project: Julie Allport, Doug Bates, Gaby Boehmer, Jim Bradshaw, Chris Baréz-Brown, Leslie Copland, Bruce Cryer, Nancy Drozdow, Pam Edstrom, Jan Fisher Chernin, Kathleen French, Mark Goulston, Kevin Gregson, Wendy Alden Hemingway, Charlie Horn, Daniele Joudene, Jennifer King, Harvey Mallement, Emily Masters, Robert Mayo, Mario Moussa, Peter Papadogiannis, Jim Palmer, Joe Phelps, Susan Priddy, Melissa Roadman, Michael Sheehy, Cindi Sparks, Mary Sutton, Amanda Trosten-Bloom, Melissa Waggener Zorkin, R. William Whitmer, and Col. Thomas J. Williams.

Other Resources and Further References

Our goal being a work easily digested by the business community, we sought to have a footnote-free book. Anyone familiar with positive psychology, emotional intelligence, and motivational profiling will recognize our debt to research done by, among others, Richard Boyatzis, Ph.D.; David Cooperrider, Ph.D.; Daniel Goleman, David McClelland, Ph.D.; Rollin McCraty, Ph.D.; Alastair Robertson; Steven J. Stein, Ph.D.; George West, and Diana Whitney, Ph.D. In addition to their many publications, we have also benefited from direct conversations and interviews, joint projects and programs, and even coursework with several of them. We have mentioned these people and other sources by name (and usually by book) in the text, at the point in which a particular topic is treated in depth. Internet searches on the people or subject will turn up a wealth of relevant and fascinating information on human behavior and motivation in organizations.

Corporate behavior (and misbehavior) has been broadly treated in the news media; most details here came from the online version of *The New York Times*. As the stories of corporate malfeasance continue to unfold, some particulars may change. Health and related statistics came from the National Institutes of Health website, links from there, or via Internet searches of reputable medical, health, and wellness sites. New studies on the rising toll of stress-related illnesses and their costs produce fresh or updated data on virtually a monthly basis. The history of Sam Walton came from Walton's autobiography, *Made in America* (with John Huey), the *Sam Walton Story* by Austin Teutsch, and an interview by one of the authors with Sam Walton in 1974. *A Carrot A Day* by Adrian Gostick and Chester Elton provided several examples of positive recognition techniques and one vignette on positive employee behavior. General encyclopedia-style references came from Microsoft Encarta.

All of the examples in this book are real. Most of the positive examples are identified. At request, a few are not. Negative examples are identified if they were already public knowledge. Other negative examples are disguised in various ways to protect the privacy of individuals, but the central matter being discussed did happen. All of the opinions expressed, positive or negative, regarding all of the organizations and people mentioned here are those of the authors. The opinions are based on direct experience, detailed research, or considered reading of multiple news accounts.

About the Authors

Dan Baker, Ph.D., a licensed psychologist, is founding director of the Canyon Ranch Life Enhancement Program. Since 1988, his mission has been to engage guests of Canyon Ranch—some of the world's highest-achieving people—in emotionally connecting with their well being. Dan often coaches and consults with CEOs, corporate officers, and their organizations.

Baker wrote the best-seller *What Happy People Know: How the New Science of Happiness Can Change Your Life for the Better*, a *Reader's Digest* pick of the month and the subject of a *Time* Magazine special issue cover story. His articles have appeared in publications ranging from *O* Magazine and *Prevention* to *Fast Company*. An adjunct lecturer at the University of Arizona Medical College, he has also facilitated and taught at Harvard Business School.

Cathy L. Greenberg, Ph.D., is an internationally recognized authority in leadership effectiveness and optimizing workforce performance. She specializes in executive coaching, eLeadership, and personal and organizational transformation.

Greenberg served as a founding partner of Accenture's Institute for Strategic Change, leading a multi-year research effort to examine the behaviors and competencies required for success as a global leader. A sought-after speaker, contributor to more than 50 articles, contributor to *The Future of Leadership* edited by Warren Bennis, and co-author of *Global Leadership: The Next Generation* with Marshall Goldsmith, Cathy and her work have been featured in media ranging from *Fortune* to *The New York Times*, CNN to the BBC. She was the founder and executive director of the Institute for Strategic Leadership, LeBow College of Business at Drexel University, one of only two nationally recognized leadership institutes headed by women.

Greenberg and Baker are co-founders of h2c—Happy Companies, Healthy People—the first organization to specialize in coaching leaders and their teams on the art and science of positive psychology to build happy, high-performance teams.

Collins Hemingway, MA, is the "practical business guy" and one of today's leading business writers. Best known for partnering with Microsoft CEO Bill Gates to co-author the #1 best-selling book

Business @ the Speed of Thought, he is also co-author of *Built for Growth,* the most thorough and compelling book yet on creating, establishing, and renewing retail brands.

Hemingway served as director of business development and international marketing for Microsoft's fastest-growing division. Through his own company, Escape Velocity Ventures, Inc., he now consults with businesses on marketing and technology, and lectures and writes on diverse topics, including management, aviation, medicine, technology futures, and the importance of conscience in creating profitable enterprises. He is also an executive coach.

Foreword

When Sigmund Freud was asked what constitutes a successful life, he answered, "Lieben und arbiten"—*love* and *work*. Taking his concept into business, what constitutes a successful organization? The answer is, people who *love* their *work* and who love the organizations they work for. Business success depends on highly motivated employees. Highly motivated employees multiply in organizations whose missions, leaders, and inner workings provide profound meaning and inspiration.

Yet many companies plod along with uninspiring leaders and uninspired employees. Many companies provide little motivation or the wrong motivation. They make short-term decisions, undermining employee morale and the organization's future. The worst of them stampede into the kind of misdeeds and corruption that have been trumpeted in many news stories. These ongoing corporate debacles have had devastating impacts on the people in the organizations and repercussions that ripple through society as a whole. The damage is more than economic. It is also the loss of public trust in business and its leaders. Consumers, regulators, and business leaders are searching for ways to change such unhappy behavior, which expresses itself in everything from dreary work for individuals to personal conflicts between individuals and teams to outright criminality by the organization as a whole.

My own half-century sojourn of inquiry, study, scholarship, and practice in business has led me to understand a compelling paradox. When business leaders focus strictly on the bottom line, they are more likely to misbehave in an effort to achieve results, and they are also less likely to achieve good results even if they do *not* misbehave. Business leaders who address more than the bottom line avoid ethical lapses and are also far more effective at maintaining healthy bottom lines. They make their organizations ones that employees are proud to be a part of. They make their organizations a positive part of the overall community.

Such exemplary leaders have similar attributes. Driven by character, great leaders create meaning and trust, hope and optimism—and results. Three authors—Dan Baker, Cathy Greenberg, and Collins Hemingway—have combined their considerable talents to write a book that describes how you can develop such capabilities for yourself and for employees at all levels within your organization. They show how "mastery of the softer side" of business—my own phrase for people skills, good taste, judgment, and character—can improve business performance. They give practical examples of how to develop such attributes and apply them in the many situations that businesspeople confront every day. *What Happy Companies Know: How the New Science of Happiness Can Change Your Company for the Better* examines the underlying motivations and psychologies of outstanding companies and demonstrates how those positive mindsets can take hold in other organizations to transform their character and their fortunes.

Together, the three authors—Baker, a medical psychologist and a pioneer in applied positive psychology; Greenberg, a former partner in two of the world's largest consulting organizations, an anthropologist, and now a respected executive coach; and Hemingway, a seasoned business professional and author—show the enormous potential that comes when businesses, indeed all organizations, adopt a "happy" mindset. As they define it, happiness is a mature, considered, positive outlook coupled with a search for meaning and self-fulfillment, the same sense used by America's founding fathers when they established a new country dedicated to "life, liberty, and the pursuit of happiness." Happiness creates enormous potential such as that unleashed when companies switch from trying to fix what is wrong within their operations to discovering the possibilities that emerge from what is right within their operations.

For many decades, business schools and business organizations have focused on numbers-oriented disciplines, such things as production and finance and return on investment. The authors propose that the new science of happiness adds a missing dimension that enables organizations to fully realize their return on people—on their talents, their passion, their interests, their knowledge. Far from a frivolous or secondary concern, happiness is the secret sauce to success that so many businesses seek everywhere except within the human beings inside their walls.

Among the elements of the new science of happiness, first and foremost is positive psychology applied to organizations—the study of strengths, best practices, character, and virtue in an organizational setting. Bio-evolutionary theory provides new insight into why humans react as they do under stress and how proper leadership can alter human behavior from the most self-serving to the most civil, noble, and altruistic. From organizational development comes the application of appreciative inquiry, a process that delves into the question of what gives life to an organization.

Among many new psychological instruments are the Benchmark of Organizational Intelligence (BOEI), which gauges the emotional intelligence of an organization as a whole, and various motivational profiling tools that evaluate not only how people function in organizations but also why—and how people with differing motivations can learn to work harmoniously together. Also, the latest in neurology and a fascinating new science known as cardio-neurology show how the coherence generated by positive emotion and positive thought unleashes creativity and imagination in ways that dramatically improve personal health and corporate productivity.

Although covering these topics in depth, *What Happy Companies Know* is no dry scientific treatise or abstract psychological discourse. The new science of happiness is always presented in a lively discussion of the real things businesses do: the real-world concerns, the day-to-day emotions, the hard decisions, and the tough actions. Baker, Greenberg, and Hemingway, with unique yet interlocking skills, bring nearly 80 years of accumulated experience to guide the reader in understanding how to create a constructive corporate culture in meaningful, measurable, and practical ways.

What Happy Companies Know takes you on a journey that describes human behavior and how it typically manifests itself in business, describes how that behavior can be changed for the better, and culminates in numerous examples of how that better behavior leads to improved financial results. The early chapters explain the behavior of unhappy people and unhappy business cultures through examples, many of which are "ripped from the headlines." Showing that reactive, short-term decision making is hard-wired into us as an early biological adaptation that kept us alive in a hostile physical world, the authors demonstrate how such fear-based behaviors cause disaster after disaster in modern business.

Succeeding chapters contrast the self-limiting nature of reflexive behaviors with a myriad of healthy and happy behaviors that successful companies exhibit in outperforming their more macho counterparts. Because happy companies work from the highest level of consciousness and cooperation, they show consistent patterns of innovation, creativity, and strong financial postings. Chapters 12 and 13 in particular provide the more rigorous data supporting the thesis that "happy" means profitable.

The authors show how the values, visions, ethics, and cultures of such businesses call upon what is best and highest in human conduct, what is most moral, and what most unlocks the creativity and talents of their employees. They show how to engage the "whole-brain" functions that are at the disposal of every person in every organization. From these examples, the book develops the principles, practices, and tools that enable every company to become a happy one.

Several years ago, I wrote that effective leaders understand that there is no difference between becoming an effective leader and becoming a fully integrated human being. *What Happy Companies Know* extends that idea to the entire organization. It demonstrates the power of an entire organization whose people have become fully integrated human beings working cooperatively. The authors demonstrate that the real power of good business goes beyond the creation of jobs, products and services, and consumer value. A happy company transforms its people in ways that benefit them as individuals and society as a whole.

Dr. Warren Bennis
Distinguished Professor
Marshall School of Business, University of Southern California

1

The Naked Ape Dons the Designer Suit

What follows, with only a touch of dramatic license, is a true story. The details have been changed to protect the not-yet-indicted.

Three days remain in the quarter. You stare at the clock as if pure concentration can reverse the ticking of the minutes and hours until the reporting period closes. The cold, hard lump of dread settles in your belly: You will not make your numbers. This is not a fact that Wall Street will want to hear, not after your optimistic projections just six months ago that shot up the stock price four and a half points. Bad results now, barely halfway into the fiscal year, and the Street will hammer the stock. Never fool Mother Nature, or stock analysts.

But Wall Street will not be the worst problem. The board will ask probing questions. Your hard-won performance bonuses will be out the window. The board's executive committee might dig into the sales analyses and realize that not only have sales *not* been increasing, but they also have been on a slight *decline.* Truth be told, you made your numbers the first quarter of the fiscal year only because of the heroic efforts of the sales staff. But those efforts to bring sales forward have left the pipeline empty. No amount of haranguing the vice president of sales or his staff will generate any more bookings.

Your head hurts. You feel a fluttering in your chest, a bit of constriction when you breathe. Just a little stress-related hypertension. ("Nothing serious," the doctor said, "at least not in the short term.") You go to the executive washroom and splash cold water on your face. There are dark circles under your eyes.

This is what it's like at the top, you think. The loneliness of leadership. Just at the point when you have achieved your dream of running a company, at the point when all your striving and sacrifice have finally paid off, the tail end of the recession is going to cost you everything. To come this far and end up the victim of a lousy sales environment (or so you tell yourself). You look out the window. It's a beautiful day, but the campus lawn could be a wasteland for all that you can appreciate it. Your mind is whirling and blank at the same time. Neither a cloud in the sky, nor an idea in your head. 30 years in the business, and you see no way out. Except one. A little trick you used a time or two when you were in sales. A little trick that you suspect your VP of sales has used a time or two himself. Why 'fess up to the shortfall when you know you can turn things around, given enough time? Why let some other schmuck come in and take credit just at the moment when things would have turned around for you? You have worked too hard, come too far to lie down and quit. You are going to fight for your job and your company.

You get the VP of sales on the line. And the chief financial officer. They are both long-time associates. Their careers are as much on the line as yours.

*   *   *

24 months later

Three days remain in the quarter. Your VP of sales is in your office, along with the CFO. When they're not yelling at each other, they're yelling at you. You will not make your numbers this quarter. The nothingness you felt—it seemed like only a few weeks ago—has turned into a brick wall, one that you're hurtling toward at a hundred miles an hour. A couple of months before, several unidentified employees alerted the board to potential "irregularities" in the financial reporting. The board has launched an investigation. The problems began with your "trick," when you called up a couple of big customers and sweet-talked them into placing orders in exchange for hefty discounts. That saved one quarter's results. But in succeeding quarters, the discounts became more common and grew larger. Funny how fast the customers caught on. Just delay orders until the last week of the quarter and the customers would get a call offering the latest "one-time-only special." Then it took discounts *plus* extremely lenient credit terms. Then it took off-the-books deals with distributors (another form of discounts) to keep the sales flowing.

When those tactics were not enough, you began to book sales that were not quite "done," back-dating documents as needed. "What harm was there in advancing a real sale by a few days on the books?" you had thought. First it was a few days, then it was a few weeks, and then it was creating entirely faux sales to cover the ever-widening deficit. By now, the discrepancy between the reality of sales and the fiction of the financial statements has become what the CFO calls an "arbitrarily large number." The results of the board's investigation will not be known for a few more weeks, but you know in your heart the game is over. Check and mate. The issue is no longer the stock price or bonuses or even keeping your job. It is the hope that the board will not turn over its findings to the authorities.

"What are we going to do?" the VP of sales asks. "They've got all of the records. It's only a matter of time." He suggests another set of transactions that will put off the reckoning until you all can come up with a better plan.

Your CFO observes his shoes as if they have disappointed him in some way. "It's over," he says. "There's no more robbing Peter to pay Paul. Peter is broke. Peter and Paul are both going to jail."

You feel the urge to go over by the window, to find relief in the scenery. But you're wound so tight that it's an effort to stand. One quick move, you think, and you'll pull every muscle in your body. The two others take your movement as a decision. They look to you for advice, for a way out. You've never failed them before. You are the leader, but this time you have taken your troops down a blind alley. Before you turn to them, a phrase pops into your head: *survival of the fittest*. This is what the game has always been about.

Once again, you stare at the clock. Once again, you wish you could turn back time. You collect your thoughts, face them, and begin to speak.

"Let me understand what you are saying. You're telling me that for the past two years you've been taking shortcuts to run up the value of your stock options? All because you thought we could make up for the shortfall with additional sales? Are you crazy? Cooking the books—what am I supposed to tell the board?"

"You're kidding, right?" the VP of sales says, frozen in place by your words.

"So you're going to leave us holding the bag?" the CFO says. His eyes follow you with the coldness of a snake's. "You think you can get away with that?"

"I have no idea what you are talking about," you say. "Get out of my office, both of you, before I call security."

Cooking the Books a Common but Deadly Recipe

This day-in-the-life rendering is the slightly cloaked story of an actual accounting fraud involving a small manufacturer in the American South. A handful of people have pleaded guilty to various offenses; other people are standing trial. All of the accused face jail terms. Even those who escape legal censure will have lost their jobs, sullied their reputations, and humiliated themselves and their families. Fortunately for this company, scrupulous employees alerted the board of directors. Unlike other boards of directors, this one launched a serious investigation before the "cooking of the books" boiled over into bankruptcy. It was a close call, however. Another year of such behavior and the company would have gone out of business, costing hundreds of people their jobs. The criminality not only stained the company and its innocent employees and board members, but also adversely affected many others connected economically to the company. Customers remained wary for some time of buying products from a "bad" company. It took more than a year for the firm to recover its momentum, not to mention its repute.

Because of its size, this particular company and its felonies have not been splashed across the front pages of any national newspapers, or warranted coverage by the major news networks, or raised the ire of the Internet gossips. If this scenario seems familiar, it is because it is a template for the behavior of senior executives at companies such as Enron, Arthur Andersen, HealthSouth, WorldCom, Global Crossing, Adelphia Communications, Italian-based Parmalat, Swedish-Swiss Engineering, ABB—these and all the others, the corporate transgressors you *have* heard about. This particular series of actions has been repeated over and over again in the corporate world for many, many years. Next to direct employee theft, cooking the books is the most common white-collar crime behavior in the business world. It is particularly insidious because, whereas employee theft consists of people stealing from the company, cooking the books consists of the company stealing from everybody: employees, investors, and consumers.

The number of dollars involved and the complexity of the accounting shell games vary according to the size of the enterprises, but the conduct is the same: a rash act to cover a shortfall triggers another rash act to cover a bigger shortfall, eventually setting off an avalanche of fraud that takes the company to its knees. Sometimes, as at Enron, the participants become so caught up in the make-believe that they not only inflate sales, but they also siphon off sizable funds from the company for themselves. Andrew Fastow took $60 million from

Enron; the Rigas family took hundreds of millions from Adelphia. The primary motivator is an unwillingness to face up to immediate short-falls in the business plan: to face the consequences of a bad month or quarter, to deal with hard times, and to admit failure.

Corporate wrongdoing has wrought serious damage to the econ-omy as well as to many personal lives. Various mismanagements have caused bankruptcies and collapses that cost tens of thousands of peo-ple their jobs. About 20,000 people lost their jobs at Enron alone. Close to 40,000 people nearly lost theirs as the result of the $11 billion accounting fraud at WorldCom. Many innocent people have lost col-lege funds, retirement funds, and sometimes, entire life savings. Years of hard work and future prosperity for thousands and thousands of people evaporated, not just at the individual companies but also in the business networks of which they are a part. As just one example, about six months after Enron collapsed, a business author gave a speech in Tulsa, Oklahoma, in the heart of oil country. In casual con-versations with many of the attendees, followed by a question from the podium, the author discovered that *every one* of the people among the 300-plus attendees, representing a hundred or so businesses, had suffered because of Enron. Some had been Enron employees who lost their jobs. Some had been employees of successful businesses bought by Enron, only to have Enron fail and take their unit down with it. Others were suppliers to Enron, left with unpaid invoices and unsold goods and no way to pay for them, or people who provided profes-sional or other services and were never paid. Others were customers who, having lost access to Enron energy sources, had to pay inflated prices elsewhere. Still others held company stock that was worthless or bonds that were nearly so.

Aftershocks continue years after the original crimes. At WorldCom, CEO Bernie Ebbers was sentenced to 25 years in prison for 9 counts of fraud and agreed to turn over more than $40 million to investors, for-mer CFO Scott Sullivan was sentenced to 5 years in prison, 290 of the top 300 executives lost their jobs, WorldCom directors agreed to pay $18 million out of their own pockets, and J.P. Morgan Chase paid $2 billion to settle claims that it did not adequately research WorldCom before marketing company bonds. At Enron, CFO Fastow pleaded guilty on conspiracy charges and faces 10 years in prison, treasurer Ben Glisan pleaded guilty and is serving 5 years in prison, Enron faces $1.7 billion in fines for fixing energy prices in California, and the pres-ident and CEO are awaiting trial at the time of this writing. Arthur Andersen, Enron's accounting firm, collapsed because of the scandal, throwing many hundreds of people out of work, and also paid $25 million because of its involvement with Global Crossing. CitiGroup,

Global Crossing's banker, agreed to pay $75 million. Adelphia's John Rigas was sentenced to 15 years in jail, his son Timothy was sentenced to 20 years in jail, and the family was fined more than $750 million. Tyco International CEO Dennis Kozlowski and CFO Mark Swartz were convicted of looting more than $600 million from their company, sentenced to 25 years each in jail, and between them ordered to pay $134 million in restitution and $105 million in fines.

The dubious behavior that brought on the convictions, fines, and lawsuits is in no way limited to high-growth or freshly deregulated industries where a "cowboy" mentality might prevail. In the past few months as of this writing, a financial services company paid an $850 million fine for fixing prices and taking kickbacks. A major computer company, a major pharmaceutical company, and a major insurance company piled up hundreds of millions of dollars in fines and dozens of lost jobs for overstating revenue, and a doughnut purveyor's internal audit found similar problems. A music company paid a $10 million fine for paying radio station programmers to play songs. A well-known lobbyist was indicted on fraud charges involving his purchase of a fleet of gambling boats. A newspaper executive pleaded guilty to hiding million-dollar payments to himself. The KPMG accounting firm paid $456 million in fines related to questionable tax shelters, and eight former executives were indicted. Time Warner agreed to set aside $3 billion to settle lawsuits over its merger with AOL, which was financed by overinflated AOL stock.

These and other miscreant behaviors have repercussions far beyond the individual company. Such misdeeds have put entire business sectors out of favor with the stock market and have stoked distrust of corporations in general. For several years after such debacles, senior corporate executives would not identify themselves to strangers as "CEOs" because of the virulent response by average citizens, who assumed that they too were criminals. Cumulatively, corporate wrongdoing in the past decade has caused more total economic harm than terrorist attacks against the United States. Only the direct human death toll of 9/11 makes the terrorist actions more grievous or horrifying.

After the fact, ordinary people—consumers *and* businesspersons—scratch their head and wonder how anyone could get caught up in such self-destructive acts. The easy answer is, "These guys are crooks." And, of course, they are. But to label the people responsible for these events as "greedy" or "arrogant" does not provide insight into the complexities behind these debacles. Unless we understand what motivates that crooked behavior, no number of ethics courses in school or ethics seminars in the workplace will ever stand a chance of correcting it. What emotions and dynamics drive the already rich and powerful to behave with such destructive actions? Although not overtly evident to the casual observer, the driving factor is *maladaptive coping strategies of misplaced fear*. Fear is a great actor. It appears in many forms, expresses itself in many ways: greed, arrogance, anger, short-sightedness, and insecurity. These are some of the masks of fear. However different they look on the surface, these external behaviors track back to the fear centers in the brain, the result of a person feeling threatened. The threat may be real or imagined, may be the result of lifelong behavior or behavior learned in business. However it originates, the fear is real. The fear drives human behavior in predictable, unhealthy ways.

What triggers crooked behavior in business, then, is the oldest human emotion, the one most connected to survival. However much they may posture or strut, these guys are *scared*. That much may be obvious in retrospect. What may not be obvious is how deeply fear is rooted in human behavior, how deeply that behavior is rooted in the biology of the brain, and therefore how quickly fear can be activated in the business environment—or in any social context for that matter.

As we will show, this pattern of behavior is nothing more than a modern expression of a survival behavior, the fight, flight, or freeze response done up in pinstripes. Although biologically simple, this fear response is so compelling that it can override the moral and ethical conduct of the people involved. The fear is also contagious, in a cultural sense that is strongly driven by biology. Fraud at a big company requires complicity of many people. At least 15 people were involved at HealthSouth, including 5 different chief financial officers. Fear can also make people delusional. HealthSouth initially fabricated $50 million in earnings to meet profit projections in 1996, with expectations of erasing the shortfall later. Instead, quarter after quarter the deficits piled up. Each time, the company convinced itself that next time would be better. The company ended up creating $2.7 *billion* in fraudulent bookings before being unmasked. Three decades earlier, Ford's fear of missing the small-car market created the delusion among a dozen executives that they could hide the fact that rear-end collisions caused its Pinto sedans to explode.

Other Expressions of Damaging Unhappiness

When discovered, outright fraud is the most visible form of unhappy companies, but corporate fraud is rare. Unhappy corporate cultures in general are common, however, and they have many other costs. Some costs are direct. High absenteeism and high turnover are two obvious ones. Far more often, the costs are hidden. Deriving from the same fear-driven actions that can lead to fraud, these behaviors can damage the company nearly as badly. The following two unhappy companies serve to show how corrosive fear and mistrust can become.

Demonstrating the problem of personal divisiveness, the first example involves a mid-level information systems manager at a major bank. Needing to take down the computer system for urgent maintenance, the IS manager had received approval from the most senior executive in the division. She issued a memo to all department heads alerting them of the shutdown the next day and the need to schedule important bank transactions around it. Shortly before the scheduled maintenance time, one of the department heads came to her office door and complained that the shutdown was going to seriously affect his department's work. He was a large, physical man, and he reached up to grab the top of the door frame, blocking entry to her office—as well as her escape. Growing ever angrier, he insisted that the younger manager reschedule around his needs. Through her office window, the IS manager was able to catch the eye of the more senior executive. This individual sauntered over as if he just happened to be passing by. His appearance caused the department head to back down. Having lost the fight he had picked, the department head promptly returned to his area and spent the afternoon screaming at his staff.

Demonstrating the problem of corporate divisiveness, the second example involves a Japanese manufacturing company and its American subsidiary. In the early 1990s, the company developed a reputation for not being able to meet product demand in the United States. The parts were manufactured in Japan and assembled in the United States, so that the machines were officially "made in the USA." To solve the problem of product shortages, the manufacturer brought in an outside consultant to improve its supply-chain management.

Before long, the consultant recognized that the problems were not technical but relational. The American subsidiary had the habit of placing a large number of orders, then canceling the orders months later—*after the U.S. salespeople had received their bonuses for the sales.* When the Japanese headquarters realized what was going on, the senior executives there arbitrarily cut ongoing U.S. orders by 50 percent.

In other words, rather than tackle head-on the subsidiary's bogus bookings, headquarters guessed at what the actual orders were so as not to over-manufacture parts. A bizarre dynamic emerged: When the orders were fake, salespeople received undeserved bonuses. When the orders were real, the arbitrary cutbacks meant that salespeople were unable to deliver sufficient product, which cost them bonuses and future sales. The supply-chain management project was Japan's way of solving the difficulty without creating a conflict. It took months before the consultant could bring the two sides together to confront the unsavory behavior of the American subsidiary as well as the enabling behavior of their Japanese counterparts.

Almost every office has at least one bully, and most people learn to work around such individuals; but corporations seldom consider how much corporate time and energy is absorbed in those accommodations. The bank bully would have gladly disrupted operations for several other departments to suit his needs and to hide the fact that he had not bothered to read a time-critical memo. Instead, he had to be satisfied with disrupting productivity in his own department for much of the day. A single tantrum could easily have cost the bank $10,000 in lost time. A similar bully at an R&D company left not one but *two* successive departments in such shambles that the entire staffs of both groups had to be reassigned and entirely new teams brought in. *The loss set back the company more than a year in two key technology areas.* Higher-level bullies can bring entire companies down. Subordinates have testified that Richard Scrushy, the former CEO of Health-South, and Bernie Ebbers, the former CEO of WorldCom, used intimidation and manipulation to get underlings to cook the books. One HealthSouth employee said that Scrushy exploded in a rage at him when confronted about accounting irregularities. (The employee who left the company was one of the few in the department not indicted. Scrushy avoided a criminal conviction but faced civil charges for his actions.)

The conflict between organizations at the Japanese manufacturer took the company into the red for that product line. In most cases, companies are unwilling to confront either personal or organizational conflict in a constructive manner. In fact, few companies will acknowledge that social conflict exists, seeking answers in numbers analysis, reorganizations designed to shake up the group's performance, or misapplied technology such as the Japanese company's supply-chain solution, which would have glossed over deep human issues rather than addressed them.

How a Happy Company Would Operate

All of these companies are unhappy—dysfunctional, in the word of the day. A return to the small company in the American South shows how a *happy* company would have responded to the same slipping financial situation that bedeviled the preceding management. The behavior serves as a *positive* template in contrast to the leadership of the scandal-ridden companies mentioned. The difference could not be any more clear or more telling than that shown in the behavior of the leadership team that followed the unhappy CEO and his cohort at the small manufacturer.

Consider that the new CEO had an even more serious problem than the previous one. Not only were sales down, but the corrected financials of the company were also now abysmal, and the company's credibility with all constituents was shot. Employees were dispirited, themselves fearful—legitimately so—that they might soon be out of jobs. Yet the new leadership refused to act on fear or panic or short-term expediencies. Indeed, the near-collapse of the company had left the new team with no choice but to act in a way that would put the company on a secure, long-term footing. A curious effect of brain wiring is that short-term problems often trigger the fear response because a reflex action might fix them, whereas deep, evident structural problems cause humans to step back and proceed sensibly because no amount of hysteria can solve them. You would be tempted to jump a 15-foot gap, but you would look for an entirely different way to cross a 100-yard chasm.

The new leadership began by carefully studying the problem with sales. The analysis quickly revealed that there were too many products in the product line. The old 80/20 rule applied: 80 percent of the sales were coming from 20 percent of the product line. By paring the product mix, the company trimmed costs in a hurry and was able to focus more effort on the profitable lines. In addition, the company discontinued the discounting. The new CEO and his senior executives met with all the important customers and said, "This is the right price. It's a fair price. If you want us to supply the equipment, we have to be in business. To be in business, we have to make a decent profit." Most of the customers stayed with the company, because the list prices were in fact quite reasonable, the products were solid, and customers understood that the firm had to operate on a sound financial basis. The new leadership's calm, no-nonsense approach also gave the customers confidence.

Eliminating the discounts solved another major problem: the bottlenecks in manufacturing that occurred at the end of each quarter. Putting the pricing on a rational basis caused orders to arrive in more regular fashion, as customers needed product. The company required less overtime, employees were less stressed, mistakes were made far less frequently. The company was able to linearize shipments to roughly one third each month rather than two thirds in the last two weeks of the quarter. Manufacturing and shipping costs plummeted.

After a while, the company was profitable again, as it had been for two decades before the unhappy CEO took over.

From a social standpoint, the outgoing regime's crime was fraud, and the perpetrators deserve whatever legal punishment they get. From a business standpoint, the real crime of succumbing to the "shell-game ploy" is that the focus on pumping up the short-term financials served to create and mask *poor operating performance*. The focus on the short term and the need to cover up the first one or two fraudulent acts became so intense that the discounts alone were enough to ruin the company. Tens and tens of millions of dollars were given away in discounts—effectively all of the company's profits! (As common as quarterly discounts are in some industries, they are the bane of a well-run company.)

While senior managers kept thinking that they could somehow beat the odds and "win the lottery"—have a truly outstanding quarter that would square accounts—they failed to address the hidden issues that kept them from having that same outstanding quarter. They were so focused on the target of making sales that they never addressed the weaknesses in the business model or other fundamentals. They attempted to cover up their weaknesses rather than build on their strengths, such as a good core product line and sound customer base, as the successor management did. The tragedy is that a single, relatively small act of fear quickly corrupted the entire management culture and took the concentration away from the right business issues.

That tragedy is an order of magnitude larger at a company the size of Enron. An outsider has to marvel at the complexity of the fake deals, the ingenuity of the sham accounting, the creativity of the nonexistent entities, the sheer audacity of the swindle. An outsider also has to wonder: If Enron's senior executives had taken all that energy and put it into addressing the real business opportunities of the company, wouldn't they have made just about as much money and felt a whole lot better about themselves? And tens of thousands of employees and other stakeholders would be far better off. If it had behaved honestly, Enron probably would have shown less growth early on, as it built its fundamentals, and more growth later, as it capitalized on those fundamentals. This comparison assumes that the self-styled "smartest guys in the room" actually had some level of basic business skills.

If the company had faltered honestly at some point, recovery would have been far more likely because the losses would not have been so staggering and many more productive assets would have been available to rebuild the company or to repay creditors. Interestingly, the first legal maneuver of the three top executives at Enron was to request a change of venue from Enron's hometown of Houston, Texas, a flight response not too much different from that which got them in trouble in the first place—fleeing from bad numbers by covering them up rather than addressing them.

The approach taken by the new management at the southern manufacturer shows that the answer is to never let fear drive business decisions. The new management at the small manufacturer showed good old common sense. They practiced sound business; they did the right blocking and tackling. This makes them a good business, but how does that make them a "happy" business? Well, honesty and health are two great predictors of happiness. (Later, we show how health and happiness interweave biologically.) The new managers created a healthier emotional environment by reestablishing an atmosphere of trust, both within and without the firm. They created a healthier economic environment by giving the sales force products that would sell. (The sales force had healthier psyches as a result.) The new managers created a healthier physical environment through regularizing shipments and by reducing fatigue, stress, and the job hazards that stress created. At every level and in every sense of the word, they turned a culture that was insane into a culture that was sane.

This book is about happy companies and how to become one. A happy company is not a giddy company, any more than a happy person is someone who runs around with a smile plastered on his or her face all the time. Happiness is an attitude rather than emotion, a prevailing way of life, an overriding outlook composed of qualities such as optimism, courage, love, and fulfillment. Corporate happiness has the same composition at the organizational and social level. Happiness is not a mood (moods are biochemically regulated) or an emotion (emotions are subject to situational influence), but an approach toward life. Happiness is knowing what is truly important and living in accordance with what is important. On an individual level, happiness is developing your potential and engaging your life to make a difference for the better. A definition relevant on an individual level must be at least as relevant in organizations that are made up of a multitude of individuals. As happiness applies to the psyche of an individual, happiness applies to the culture of a company.

Developing potential invariably involves making emotionally mature choices. If the need for immediate gratification is the mark of a child and the ability to wait for delayed gratification is the mark of an adult, so too is short-term thinking the mark of an immature company and long-term thinking the mark of a mature one. Short-term thinking is fear driven, which means that it is not *thinking* at all but a gut-level *reaction* to a threat; long-term thinking is conscious, proactive contemplation of what truly matters to the company and where its future truly lies.

For the purposes of this book, then, the definition of a happy company is this: *an organization in which individuals at all levels of authority exhibit a diversity of strengths, constructively work together toward a common goal, find significant meaning and satisfaction in producing and providing high-quality products and services for profit, and through those products and services make a positive difference in the lives of others.*

Although we expect satisfaction from work, we do not associate "happiness" with it. If you ask senior executives or mid-level managers or blue-collar workers if they expect to be happy at work, they would likely scoff, or even feel a little embarrassed for you. At the highest levels of a company, leaders may feel the pressures so greatly—and take themselves so seriously—that they do not think of the fun that should accompany the job. Fun is not the goal, yet fun naturally arises when people do work that they enjoy and find meaningful. Typically, people spend one third to one half of their adult lives at work. They have most of their social interaction at work. They most commonly meet future spouses at work. Who in their right mind gets up in the morning hoping to have a miserable day in the vast majority of their personal interactions?

Yet countless people react negatively to the idea of going to work. They know that the company is not succeeding or that their own work has little to do with what makes the company succeed. Because work is no fun, they do not want to go. Often, people have personal animosities toward peers or superiors. The bank bully mentioned previously illustrates a frightening fact: The biggest reason most people quit their jobs is not the company or the nature of the work but the hatred they have for their boss. Their *hatred*. In his book on toxic managers, Roy Lubit even suggests that symptoms of serious personality disorders are often mistaken for "leadership" in today's aggressive marketplace.

Most people know when there is something wrong in their work environment, but they often are not aware of how caustic it is until after they have left. Conversely, just about all of us can remember the job that had us bouncing out of bed in the morning and that completely engaged us all day long. Companies that have such engaged, enthusiastic CEOs and employees tend to do extremely well. Such jobs are happy occupations. A reason exists for the folk saying, "Find a job you love, and you'll never have to work."

By exploring the social and biological origins of fear-based behavior, we can learn not only how to avoid major ethical lapses but also avoid other fear-driven actions that cause companies to collapse or that otherwise hinder their success and keep them from sprinting to the front of their industry. More than that, leaders can create a positive climate that generates creativity. Organizations can create more profits, more opportunity for market growth, and more personal satisfaction for employees. They can blow by their competitors. They can establish a solid foundation for long-term growth. All it takes is one thing: a little organizational happiness. Not more fiscal discipline. Not better change processes. Not better technology. Not an expanded product portfolio. Companies just need to foster happiness. By happiness, we do not mean an immature giddiness, the corporate equivalent of puppy love, which might come from some short-term win. We mean instead a deep, mature delight that comes from a committed group of people energetically engaged in a fulfilling corporate mission. Some call this a state of "flow."

Through real examples of the principles and practices of leading companies, in-depth research, and the application of years of business experience, this book contrasts the negativity that haunts struggling organizations with the positivism that imbues successful organizations. Any leader, any employee, any organization can grasp and apply the lessons.

What happy companies know, other companies can learn.

2

What Is a Happy Company and Why Do I want One?

Most people would call the southern manufacturer that opened Chapter 1, "The Naked Ape Dons the Designer Suit," crooked, corrupt, or dysfunctional. The company was all these things. Few people would want to use the correct descriptor for the underlying cause. The company was unhappy. So were the other companies that misbehaved in less egregious ways. *What Happy Companies Know* is about how these and other companies can make the single greatest transformation possible to improve their competitive position: going from being unhappy to being happy.

If the phrase *happy companies* seems slightly out of key in the hard-nosed, number-crunching world of business, then prepare to sing in a new register: Happy companies are those best prepared to succeed long term. Several in-depth statistical studies plus an exhaustive survey of the practices of successful companies prove the point conclusively. If the phrase *happy company* makes you squirm for fear that it means a place of excess or inappropriate emotions, or a place where everyone is supposed to be happy all the time, then relax. A happy company is not a company that is devoid of challenge or conflict. It is not a place in which employees seek the kind of emotional validation that best comes from their family and friends. It absolutely is *not* an environment in which all the employees hold hands in front of the campfire and sing "Kumbayah"—although not a few companies might benefit from that exercise.

Instead, a happy company is one that distinguishes reality through a positive lens and a positive mindset. It perceives its universe as a marketplace with a multiplicity of opportunities rather than as a marketplace with a thicket of problems to be fought through. It is one in which optimism pervades the attitudes of leaders and is not squeezed from the culture when the going gets tough. Leaders *choose* optimism over pessimism, making a conscious decision to maintain an atmosphere that inspires creative, pragmatic approaches rather than reactive, unthinking measures to their ever-changing business environment.

A happy company intuitively knows that positivism rather than negativism is the way to pull the best out of its employees during crises. It understands how to effectively balance all the demands on its resources and people while continually developing new products and services. It is honest at all levels, and it has a culture in which personal respect, appreciation, and trust become a major reason for its business success. A happy company is respected and appreciated by all of its stakeholders and by its community, which perceives the organization as a pervasive, constructive force that contributes to an enhanced quality of life.

All of us want to work in an organization like this. With the prospect of spending approximately one third of our adult lives in the workplace, we all want to wake up every day looking forward to going to work, eager to meet with like-minded people who tackle their projects with obvious enthusiasm—with *smiles*. Undoubtedly, every businessperson sets out to create a happy company, one that he or she wants to enjoy as much as any associate would. Yet many organizations fall short of achieving these goals; still others are the antithesis of the qualities just described.

Yet few business leaders understand the importance of "happiness" within their organization. Few leaders know how to recognize whether their company is happy or how to create a happy workplace if it does not exist. Everyone wants to work in a happy, healthy, highly productive organization, and nobody wants to work in a toxic workplace. Yet few employees or mid-level managers know how to create a positive environment within their own teams and work spaces, or the benefits to their own health and psyches—not to mention to their company's productivity—that such a change would create.

Why are there so few happy companies?

Most people would probably blame competitive pressures. Conventional wisdom would say that competitive pressures cause companies to take shortcuts, such as shipping products before they are ready or promising service levels that cannot be delivered. Conventional wisdom would say that financial pressures twist and collapse the company's collective will, forcing short-term financial maneuvering to maintain an air of profitability until the profits actually arrive. Conventional wisdom is right, but for the wrong reason. "Pressure" will not make a happy company unhappy or a good company bad—unless the company is already "unhappy" at its core. Unless that company is a *fear-based*, reactive operation.

Most companies, in fact, *are* unhappy. Without a "happy" frame of reference, too many leaders do not perceive the negative atmosphere. Employees may be extremely unhappy, but management may not recognize that unhappiness exists or may assume that "disgruntled workers" are unavoidable. Managers may not know that unhappiness severely impedes performance. Leaders are not geared to look for either happiness or unhappiness or to think about what either means with regard to success. Leaders of unhappy companies know only that they are struggling. Despite their best efforts, they cannot bring products to market as fast as competitors can. Employees work harder—they try to work smarter—but they see only the adage that "the faster I work, the behinder I get." Such companies are able to sustain positive energy for only short bursts, and even in the best of times they are often beset by internal dissension.

The leaders of these businesses have not learned the most important lesson that a leader can learn: You cannot run a successful, dynamic business on fear. Yet fear may be the single most motivating emotion in any organization. There are personal fears: of missing an opportunity, of losing a sale, of the boss even if you make the sale, of losing your best person, of losing your own job. There are business fears: of the competition, foreign and domestic, of the high-quality or low-price alternative to your product, of a hostile takeover, of missing Wall Street's profit projections, of success and growth that may prove more than the company can handle. There are financing fears: of interest rates, bond rates, exchange rates, a downturn in the capital markets just as you need to raise money. There are cost fears: of materials, health care, energy. There are technology fears: of a competitor's disruptive technology, of your own unproven, bleeding-edge technology. There are conflicting fears: management's of spiraling wages and a possible strike; labor's of abusive management and insufficient raises. There is even fear of the weather, which might disrupt your production, your delivery, or your customers' buying patterns. There are fears that haunt us all: of terrorism and the outbreak of war.

A scan of the media for any one week will turn up 50 *serious* things for any business leader, manager, or associate to fear. And many of us consciously or subliminally do. It does not matter what the fear is, it matters only that fear is the underlying emotion. Fear is as much a part of our lives as the air we breathe. It imbues our spirit and the cultures of our organizations, so much so that we come to accept that this negative state of affairs is "normal." As many people live lives of quiet desperation, many companies live lives of quiet apprehension. Some of these companies fail. Many others survive but fail to live up to their potential. Others live up to their potential—to the instant that key employees burn out, the leadership takes its money and runs, and the company collapses.

Fear is a limited motivator. In companies as well as individuals, fear triggers one of three basic responses: freeze, flight, or fight. Companies may freeze by failing to respond to market changes, hoping that a new competitor will just go away. They might flee overseas to avoid regulation or high wages. They might throw up financial smokescreens to run from the disclosure of financial problems. Of the three choices, however, businesses inevitably fight. That is what competition is supposed to be about, different companies battling it out to the customer's benefit. When companies respond aggressively toward competition, they assume that this response is positive. It can be, if the response is a thoughtful answer to a change in circumstance. Too often, however, the reaction is fear-based hostility, as primal, reactionary and unimaginative as when our ancestors confronted marauding animals a hundred thousand years ago. Fear is a great mechanism for split-second survival, but it is self-limiting for long-term prosperity. Fear short-circuits higher thought. Fear shuts down the consciousness that enables the pursuit of any possibility except that which is *immediately apparent this instant*. However subtly, fear permeates far too many business cultures. Fear drains the individual and collective psyche of energy and imagination. Fear becomes the heavy steel chain that yanks the aggressive dog well short of its long-term intentions.

When to React, When to Think

The statement that "fear short-circuits higher thought" is more than a figure of speech. The analogy of fear-based boardroom behaviors to caveman savagery is more than a wry jest. The behaviors are biologically identical. You cannot change prevailing business attitudes unless you understand how deeply and quickly primal emotions operate in people. Fear and imagination operate in different parts of the brain. Not surprisingly, evolution has wired our brains to give fear precedence. If you are being charged by a lion, you need to *react*, not to contemplate the possibilities of peaceful coexistence with nature's abundant fauna. Those humans who did ponder such abstractions during crises did not live long enough to contribute their DNA to the gene pool. No one can flip a switch between fear and conscious thought. If fear is activated, fear wins. Every time. The secret is to learn to recognize the fear response and to condition yourself and your organization to pause long enough to enable conscious thought to have a say. The only exception is the rare occasion when a real rather than symbolic beast is coming at you, red in tooth and claw.

Further, our day-to-day business behavior is far more laden with emotion than most people want to admit. Even if an office features shouting matches between company principals, backstabbing between departments, tension between bosses and subordinates, vicious e-mail exchanges between rivals seeking a promotion, salary gossip over the water cooler, or illicit affairs between co-workers, the mindset is that "work" is somehow supposed to be less emotional than "life." When negative emotions permeate, fear-based behavior thrives. Creativity shrivels. When people say, "It's a jungle out there," or "it's hard to be optimistic when you're up to your rear in alligators," they may think that they are using metaphorical language. But their psychological attitudes have very real *physical* effects on their own biology and on the biology of the people around them. From the standpoint of human and organizational behavior they might as well be fighting for their lives in the forest or the swamp.

What Happy Companies Know expands into the social and organizational realms the psychological principles first expounded in the best-selling book *What Happy People Know: How the New Science of Happiness Can Change Your Life for the Better*. In short, these principles state that primal emotions, although necessary for survival, short-circuit the higher human emotions that enable us to bond with others. Brought into play by conscious thought, higher emotions are the ones that enable humans to find strength in numbers, to feel appreciation, to achieve creativity, to create a sum that is greater than whole of the parts. These capabilities, which arrived by way of neocortical and frontal lobe development, differentiate humans from all other species. These capabilities are what created human culture, human civilizations—human commerce!

By delving into the depths of our human biological and cultural past, and by calling on in-depth behavioral research from the new initiative of positive psychology, we can apply the knowledge of human personal dynamics to the dynamics of the corporate world. The premise of this book is that human emotions and human thought are more closely entwined than most people realize. This close twining means that fear can drive us down and optimism can lead us up. Maladaptive, fear-driven emotion, inherent in each and every human being, is at the root of the failings of corporations. Fear is the root cause for the failure of corporations that have succumbed to greed, malfeasance, or plain old competition. The antidote to a fear-based organization is a happy company in which individuals at all levels engage with positive, reinforcing emotion to make the best use of a diversity of strengths, constructively work together, find significant meaning and satisfaction in their work, and consequently deliver high-quality service and products that positively contribute to their society. And, not least, deliver profits to the company and its shareholders.

Going to the Source for Ethics

In the wake of the many corporate scandals over the past few years, business schools are emphasizing ethical training more than ever. But unless educators comprehend the fundamental difference in fear-based responses versus higher-brain responses, no amount of ethical training will reshape corporate behavior. The biological approach to business behavior is the one approach that can actually explain why people in stressful business situations behave as they do. The solution is for business schools to teach students new ways to analyze behavior—their own and others'—and to use new techniques to instill optimism instead of fear as the fundamental approach to managing people.

If no pessimist ever made an investment, why do business schools fail to develop people who can manage through optimism? Answer: They do not know how optimism fundamentally reshapes behavior. Optimism, hope, and courage are the rally points for business as much as for society as a whole. When a writer describes courage as "grace under pressure," or when a president says that "one man with courage is a majority," both are describing the victory of the conscious mind over the primal reaction. Courage is the ability to think and act clearly during uncertain or dangerous times. Courage is the ability to use fear to intensify perception without letting fear overwhelm thought. The mark of a good leader has always been the ability to consciously choose to do what is right despite being afraid.

In *What Happy Companies Know* you will learn how organizations can make the cultural transition from destructive, fear-driven decision making to healthy, thoughtful—happy—choices with all their constructive attributes. You will learn how constructive attributes help companies to prosper—and employees to prosper, even if they cannot directly affect the overall direction of the enterprise. Whether involving a business, nonprofit, educational, or community enterprise, the principles outlined in this book will lead organizations and their members to greater understanding of happiness at a group level.

At the heart of our approach are the five general attributes of positive companies grouped together under the acronym of (surprise) HAPIE:

H	Humble, inclusive, inspirational, innovative, and heartfelt leadership
A	Adaptive, enthusiastic, emotionally intelligent employees
P	Profit for all who contribute to the company's success, with the focus being ROP (return on people) in addition to usual metric of ROI (return on investment)
I	Invigorated stakeholders, vendors, and clientele who serve as first-line marketers for the company
E	Engaged, constructive community citizenship

From the five broad traits emerge a set of specific behaviors that cascade through the organization to create a positive, transformational culture. No one attribute defines a happy company. In fact, companies with only one positive attribute often fail. Successful companies have most of these attributes along with cultures that drive the attributes from top to bottom. We explore each attribute, the companies that best exemplify them, and the success that results, in great detail.

The result is that HAPIE companies are able to transform the mindset of corporate governance from an energy-draining, deficit-focused orientation, resulting from the chronic vigilance of looking for what's wrong and who's to blame, to an energizing, positive orientation that focuses on what is right about the company, its practices, and the strengths of its people. This book identifies previously unidentified sources of organizational unhappiness and the suboptimal outcomes that unhappiness creates. More important, it identifies principles, practices, tools, and real-life illustrations of individual leadership and corporate behavior that, when made the basis of organizational culture, become pleasantly self-reinforcing and therefore self-perpetuating.

Among the real-life examples there are companies large and small, public and private, representing a number of industries. A few example companies, in particular Wal-Mart and Microsoft, have at various times and in various ways been both praised and condemned. This dichotomy proves that corporate happiness has many facets. Companies may be happy in some areas and not in others, and public perception may differ from actuality or may shift over time. We do not claim that any one company today is totally happy. We claim that the many different positive behaviors exhibited by all these different organizations *do* create a composite view of what a completely happy company can be. Your challenge is to apply that composite image to all the aspects of your own organization.

The purpose of our book is threefold. The first is to help people learn about and prevent large-scale, fear-driven, human-induced personal and organizational crises. The second is to manage and bring about creative, large-scale change and enhancement to work culture. The third is to design moral and ethical work environments so people at all levels of the organization have a passion and desire to go to work and to be the most productive possible. Through stories, examples, and illustrations, we demonstrate that companies with a "dog-help-dog" mentality can succeed in a "dog-eat-dog" world.

By examining the patterns of behavior in the leaders and employees of happy companies and investigating what energizes and drives these organizations, we show:

- How happy companies are more capable of bringing about creative, large-scale organizational change needed to succeed in today's highly competitive world.

- How happy companies are culturally far more *possibility* oriented than they are *problem* focused and how this fundamentally different mindset enhances their ability to survive, adapt, and succeed through the challenges of the new global economy.

- How their leaders create an environment conducive to collaboration, cooperation, creativity, and personal responsibility.

- How positive emotions and a positive environment reset the human brain biologically and reset group dynamics culturally.

- How a positively charged group sets about transforming possibilities into real solutions that carry a company into the future.

We provide a roadmap that organizations, management and employees alike, can follow to steer their organizations from point A—fear, with all its limited and counterproductive attributes—to point B—happiness, with all its creative, unifying, and productive attributes. We provide a process and set of tools by which organizations can shift their culture from the negative to the positive.

To succeed in the twenty-first century, every company will have to evolve into a more advanced corporate organism. Regardless of its organizational structure, product portfolio, cost structure, change processes, or underlying technology, a company must change its psychological mindset and culture to prosper. Successful businesses are ones that can adapt to change quickly, and the ability to adapt comes not from fear but from higher brain functions. Shifting from fear to positivism is well within the grasp of *all* companies, if they follow the principles outlined in this book and avoid the pitfalls and snares of reactive, fear-based thought.

Our ancestors never actually outran the lion or individually outfought the bear. Our ancestors *outsmarted* them. Collectively. They pulled together to create social entities that more than compensated for humanity's physical shortcomings. If primitive humans had the good sense to thrive by higher thought and cooperation, shouldn't businesspeople today do the same?

3

The Nerd from the Mists

When modern humanity emerged from the mists of history a few thousand generations ago, we were the nerds of the Paleolithic age. Gorillas could kick sand in our face and take our banana money. The major predators could see, hear, or smell their prey from a distance and could chase them down and kill them with a single snap of the jaw or swipe of the claw. Humans were puny and slow. Our vision, hearing, and smell were limited. Our teeth and claws were the laughing stock of the Predators' Country Club. With all of our physiological limitations, we were far more likely to *become* dinner than to *enjoy* dinner. In this bloody, hostile world, survival remained Job Number 1, and humans seldom lived beyond the age of 30. All we had to differentiate us was the latest in "wetware," a thin new layer of brain tissue at the very front of the skull that, for the first time on this planet, provided executive functions to a species on the make.

This new area, the frontal lobes, coordinated all of the other areas of the brain, gave us the ability to think, and led to the rise of consciousness. It functions today very much as it did in our earliest days. It directs, but does not *control*, all of the preexisting parts of the brain that kept us alive. The understanding of how the frontal lobes functioned came late. Until recently, they were considered the "silent lobes" because they didn't seem to *do* anything. Traditionally, scientists divided the brain into three parts: the cerebrum, the locus of thought; the cerebellum, the locus of refined movement; and the brain stem, the locus of reflexes and autonomic processes such as breathing. Discoveries in the past 40 years have greatly complicated that picture.

The brain has at least a dozen major structures, all of which communicate by a labyrinth of cabling, the neurons. The brain's left and right hemispheres replicate many capabilities but specialize in ways we are only beginning to understand. For example, the right side tends to activate for novel situations, whereas the left side activates for routine situations. Memory and other capabilities appear to be distributed throughout. Visual memory is stored near the optical processing parts of the brain, for example, and auditory memory is stored near the auditory processing part of the brain. Further, cognition appears to blend from one area to another, so that one cannot always state explicitly where one brain structure ends and the other begins. Rather than consisting of three separate computers handling clearly defined functions, the brain is a neural net, with many parts, front, middle, and back, being activated *together* according to context and need.

Equally important from the standpoint of social behavior and leadership, the modern brain evolved from the bottom up. The oldest layer, the base of the brain, contains the necessary command centers for living and the most primitive emotions; later layers added social behavior and conscious thought. This first layer, the hind brain or "reptilian brain" as neurologist Paul MacLean called it, addresses functions such as sleep and waking, respiration, temperature regulation, and basic automatic movements, plus the split-second reactions to sensory input that ensure physical survival. The layer also includes the limbic system, which houses the earliest and most powerful emotions, and the amygdala, which as the center of emotional memory is the brain's "red alert" button for fear. The next level, the mid-brain or "mammalian brain," generates the social drive to create families and to be a member of groups beyond family, whether such groups are herds of ungulates, packs of predators, tribes of early hunter/gatherers, or today's corporate organizations.

The final, most recent part of the brain is the forebrain or neocortex, particularly the frontal lobes. Only higher mammals have frontal lobes, and only humans have frontal lobes of any appreciable size. The frontal lobes comprise only 3.5 percent of the cortex for a cat, 7 percent for a dog, 17 percent for a chimpanzee, and a whopping 29 percent for a human. This rapid increase implies that explosive growth occurred very late in the evolutionary cycle, especially in humans. MacLean called this last development the higher-order, moral brain because the development of the frontal lobes provided humanity with intellect, imagination, spiritual sensibilities, and art, and the ability to ponder our feelings as well as just *feel* them. Although other primates show some rational and emotional capabilities once thought to be the exclusive preserve of humanity, no one can deny that human intellectual and psychological capacity far outstrips that of any other species.

This chapter describes the three broad functional areas of the brain, how they evolved, and how they function to help humanity survive and thrive, and the particular importance of working together. A coordinated response by both logic and emotion can be called "whole-brain function." The text details three important approaches to ensure that you, as an individual, use whole-brain function to take personal responsibility for your work environment. A series of personal and organizational examples contrast the way fear responses have led to a failure of responsibility and to the stalling or collapses of careers, in contrast to whole-brain responses that have created personal and business discipline and shifted people and groups from firefighting symptoms to solving underlying issues. The many scenarios establish the groundwork for other "whole-brain" responses taken up in later chapters.

Wiring That Protects, Wiring That Serves

For our purposes, and defined in terms of function rather than precise anatomy, the brain's three major divisions can be considered the "personal survival brain" (hindbrain and limbic system, the reptilian brain), the "social survival brain" (mid-brain or mammalian brain), and the "executive brain," (the forebrain, which gives us advanced human capabilities). Although an oversimplification from a technical point, for our purposes we can map human emotion against these functional areas in this way:

- **Self-preservation (fear and sexual drive)**—The personal survival brain is very little more than reflex. It causes an animal under assault to react first and think later, whether the reaction is to fight, flee, or freeze. Other basic biologic drives, such as reproduction, are also centered here.

- **Personal and group bonding**—The social survival brain enables humans to survive hostile environments through strength of numbers and cooperative behavior. Bonds are strongest between individuals (mates and friends), then between small groups (families and clans), and then villages and tribes.

- **Moral awareness, inspiration, creativity, and awe**—What makes humans uniquely human, and not merely a slightly evolved form of another mammal, is the forebrain, specifically the frontal lobes, which house consciousness, orchestrate the activities of the rest of the brain, and provide the ability to understand right from wrong and humane from inhumane. The frontal lobes create the capabilities of leadership and creativity, the essence of an executive position in a social or business organization. The lobes create the ability to project possible futures out of experience of the past and the ability to perceive reality from the outside looking in. Such capabilities are the foundation of creativity as well as the capacity for spiritual sensation. Whether it is a religious person pondering God or an atheist pondering the universe, humans can think and feel about issues beyond themselves. If you look up at the stars at night and contemplate your place in the universe, you have an emotional reaction as well as an intellectual one.

Our discussion uses the phrase *emotional brain* (from Daniel Goleman) to describe the more primitive and reactive parts of the brain, and the phrase *executive brain* (from Elkhonen Goldberg) to describe the frontal lobes, which are the center of conscious thought and logic. Thus, when fear clutches the stomach of the senior executive who sees sales numbers well below forecast, his reaction is as old as humankind. In fact, his reaction is older than humankind, older than any of humanity's direct ancestors, and probably older than any mammal. His perception of danger (to his career, his well-being), his desire to smash a competitor, his fury at a subordinate bringing him troublesome news: Any *gut reaction* comes from the circuits of his emotional brain, literally his prehuman brain. Conversely, when a businessperson feels remorse at an emotional outburst, deliberates a complicated business plan, or contemplates the ethics of a difficult personnel decision, his distinctly human executive brain rules.

Humanity has two sets of linked circuitry: the ancient wiring that protects and the modern wiring that serves. In business, too often the default is to the "early circuits" rather than to the "late circuits," and that is where trouble starts. The reason is this: The executive brain has not subsumed the emotional brain and its survive-first reactions. Quite the contrary is true. The programmed reactions at the reptilian level and the highly emotional traits and tendencies at the mammalian level are alive and very much kicking in humanity today. The executive brain can conduct the orchestra only with the orchestra's consent. If the orchestra flees over an actual fire or a rumored mouse, the conductor is likely to be trampled in the panic. The emotional brain is very much the child. The executive brain is the parent. Like too many parents, the executive brain cannot always obtain obedience.

Our emotional brain remains essential to our biological survival. The driver swerving to avoid an accident on a rain-slick highway or the Marine fighting house to house in Fallujah needs reptilian reflexes. The girl walking down a lonely street needs her amygdala to provide an instant, intuitive interpretation of the shadowy figure in the doorway. Even in a civilized world, humans benefit from the ability of the more primitive areas to react first. Because the original wiring is simpler and more direct, the response is faster but is also based on fleeting information. Any time the amygdala senses a threat, for instance, it speed-dials a reaction, bypassing the information-processing parts of the brain. Such speed is a virtue in life-and-death situations but can be problematic in "normal" life. Vietnam vets suffering post-traumatic stress disorder is an overblown cliché (most Vietnam vets survived their service with their psychic health just fine), but they can still react at the deepest survival level long after their service. A person was standing at the 18th hole of a golf course on the Fourth of July one time when a string of celebratory firecrackers went off, sending one of his playing partners headlong into a sand trap. For a millisecond, the limbic system of this one veteran read the firecrackers as machinegun fire, and his reflexes took over. A 79-year-old veteran of World War II recounts that he still has a literal knee-jerk reaction whenever he hears any sharp noise similar to a gunshot.

A more common behavior is seen in adults who were often struck as children. *Any* sudden movement near them causes them to jerk their arms protectively over their face. One man who was often and unpredictably whipped with a belt by his parents would uncork a vile stream of profanity at anyone who sneaked up and surprised him from behind. 50 years later, the reflex remained incorrigibly in force. The emotional brain never forgets.

Usually in such instances, the executive brain comes along a few milliseconds later and begins to sort things out, real threat from false alarm, like the cop who steps in to calm everyone down and break up a potential riot. The rational brain collects more information and sorts it logically, sometimes reaching a different conclusion than the freaked-out emotional brain. In the case of the golf-course vet, he made a joke of always ending up in the sand and proceeded calmly to putt. The figure in the doorway may turn out to be a harmless old man, but it doesn't hurt that the girl has raced away before making that determination. The curse-spewing adult can stifle his invective after a second or two and is always abjectly apologetic.

But when the emotional brain reacts too strongly and too often over too long a time, the highly emotive, survival-based emotions become the brain's preferred response. The brain is efficient if nothing else, and over time the synapses reconfigure to give preference to the most commonly traversed pathways. After a while, the emotional brain hijacks the brain. The executive brain can no longer keep the emotional riot under control. Overwhelmed, the rational cop cannot prevent the city's burning. The corollary with the civil riot is intentional, for the riot is a group acting through its emotional brain, a mob versus democracy.

As long as fear dominates the mind, the brain centers for creativity and high-level thought are constrained, and appreciation is physically shut down. As we will see, appreciation is the center from which creativity and imagination arise. From a neurological standpoint, the lesson to take away is this: *The human brain cannot process fear and appreciation simultaneously.* The bank executive who screamed at his staff whenever he was thwarted was creating a fear environment in which his staff would be biologically unable to come up with the great new ideas he needed to advance his own career.

The takeover of the executive brain by the emotional brain is why some people who were abused as children become the worst abusers themselves. Confronted with a screaming, out-of-control child and in a mirror situation of what they once faced, they suffer a "limbic insurrection," responding primitively and viscerally to a perceived threat. Only now, they are big, and they strike out at their own children in a perverted effort to make their own pain stop. Thus the sins of one generation are too often transferred to the next. This is a description of the behavior, not an excuse for it. Other people do not let abuse freeze their emotional development. Instead, their experience takes them 180 degrees. They become compassionate protectors of the young.

As some of these situations show, humans are wired for hard times, but sometimes that wiring creates the perception of hard times when they are not there, or should not be there. Because of its automatically evoked nature, fear frequently pops up during situations and in contexts in which its reactivity and limited repertoire are very maladaptive. Never is this more true than in business, where an emotionally charged workplace can create the fear reactions that short-circuit higher and more effective business thought.

Hardwired for Hard Times

Survival functions are automatic. No conscious thought is required. The drive to survive is not given to consideration of good or bad conduct or to the consequences of any action. The only goal of the survival brain is preservation of the biological self or of progeny. The predominant driving emotion for survival is the very reactive phenomenon of fear. We are by design, through the evolutionary process and our DNA, hardwired for hard times. For the better part of 200,000 years, the problems faced by humankind were life threatening. It was only about 150 years ago with the advent of the Industrial Revolution, and 20 to 30 years later with the advent of modern medicine, that the majority of problems plaguing humans were transmuted into something less than life endangering.

Even as fast as humanity's executive brain has evolved, however, the bio-evolutionary process and the advancement of neurological wiring are progressing at a far slower rate than technological transformation. Humans went from the first powered airplane ride to a safe round trip to the moon in 66 years, yet written and archeological records show that human behavior, both good and bad, both cultured and cruel, is largely unchanged over at least the span of our written history and possibly much longer. Cultural change also takes time. It requires only 18 to 24 months for new technology to be implemented, but it requires at least two to three generations for human behavior to change. We learn technology from direct experience, but we learn behavior from other humans. A snapshot of a three-generation American family today could have a grandparent who is prejudiced against a minority, a parent who has rejected those ways but whose friends do not include minorities, and a grandchild who has friends of a variety of ethnic backgrounds. The grandparent may still act and speak upon those prejudices; the parent probably behaves "neutrally" on ethnic issues while struggling with buried prejudices learned at the grandparent's knee; although distanced from that prejudice, the grandchild is not be entirely free of it until the grandparent dies and the reinforcement for that behavior disappears entirely. (This assumes that society does not reinforce that prejudice in other ways.)

Much as we would like to distance ourselves psychologically from our Neolithic forebears, the fact is that the "caveman" is just us with early technology, politically incorrect clothing, and bad haircuts. We are still built and wired for biologically hard times, when scarcity prevailed. One anthropologist has suggested that women carry more body fat than men to provide the extra calories necessary to keep a nursing child alive over the typically lean winters of humanity's past. Although of little comfort to a modern woman bemoaning the cellulite in her mirror, the biology has relevance for a nursing mother enduring a famine in Africa or trying to keep her child alive in the first terrible weeks after the tsunami of 2004 or the hurricanes of 2005. This identical biology carries over in the brain, too.

The Irrationality of Logic

This long prehistory prior to the rise of the executive brain remains an intrinsic part of humanity and of what it means to be human. Although the thrust of this chapter is the importance of the executive brain as it differentiates our potential from the potential of our ancestors, the point is not to clone Mr. Spock and his "that's not logical" attitude from the *Star Trek* franchise. In fact, the emotional brain constitutes a far larger percentage of the brain than the executive brain, and the executive brain is intricately linked with all of the emotional centers. As a result, *the brain processes more emotion than it does cognitive activity.* It is not neurologically possible to be exclusively logical when so much of your brain is dedicated to processing emotion. Nor should you be. According to *Star Trek* mythology, Mr. Spock and his fellow Vulcans use meditation and logic to keep their highly emotional selves in check. Or as the Earthling Emerson said, "I am cold precisely because I am too warm." Balance is the byword.

When people suffer injuries to the executive brain, they lose executive abilities. They cannot think long term, they cannot evaluate the consequences of decisions, they cannot edit what they say or do, and they cannot balance risk and reward. Alcohol and drugs disable the executive brain, creating the same effects and leading to risky behaviors. Corporate leaders acting on fear impulses lose their judgment on business matters in the same way. On the other hand, when people suffer injuries to the emotional brain, they lose emotional context, which turns out to be at least as important as cognitive ability and IQ in making good decisions. People with impaired emotional circuits loop endlessly over simple things, such as choosing a meeting time. They cannot cope with choices carrying heavy emotional freight. They could never hope to decide between two potential mates who are "objectively" equal (same height and weight, same financial status). As Goleman points out in *Emotional Intelligence*, the emotional brain provides the first rough cut at decision making, emphasizing some choices and de-emphasizing others based on the emotional lessons a person has learned in life. The executive brain then applies logic to refine the choice. The lack of either capability cripples the overall mental capacities of a human being.

We all know individuals who are scarily intelligent and yet have no social skills or make bizarre and seemingly illogical life choices. Their emotional brain is immature or malfunctioning. We also know individuals who are charismatic, are highly intuitive about others, are great seducers in positive and possibly negative ways, and are prone to temper tantrums or other outrageously selfish acts. Their executive brain is immature or malfunctioning. In both cases, the imbalance is ultimately self-sabotaging. Good decision making, as well as a healthy mental life, comes from the right proportion of emotion and positive thought.

To achieve real happiness, or real success in a social or business context, you have to make full use of your entire brain and the capabilities of all its functions. Indeed, several parts of this book emphasize the importance of calling upon intuition and other emotional capabilities to make the most "rational" decisions. The point is to know which part of your mind is leading. If the emotional brain is leading, you have to learn how to change leads so that the emotional brain informs the executive brain rather than bullies it. The essence of healthy mental behavior and of modern leadership can be described as "whole-brain function:" the appropriate use of all the brain's abilities, mediated by the executive.

Stepping Beyond Fear

The first step in whole-brain function is to learn how to move beyond fear, and as always in human behavior the effort begins with the individual. Later chapters describe how fear-based responses manifest themselves within organizations, and how a variety of tools and procedures can help organizations develop cultures and processes based on whole-brain function rather than on the emotional brain. From an individual standpoint, regardless of where you are in the organization, the single most important mindset comes down to personal responsibility. Regardless of the chaos around you, you have to be accountable for your own emotion and intentionality in the workplace. Three simple—but by no means easy—approaches are these:

1. Establish personal mastery of your work environment, particularly the mental aspects of it. Don't let anyone psyche you out or put you down.

2. Lead from your strengths.

3. Act upon projects according to priority rather than urgency.

Personal mastery does not mean to control every aspect of your job. That is impossible. Instead, it means to define yourself as the master of your own psychic destiny, a personal equal to those around you regardless of your position in the hierarchy. As identified in *Global*

Leadership: The Next Generation, personal mastery of the work environment is one of the 15 critical dimensions that will determine success in the twenty-first-century business environment. Personal mastery means taking responsibility for your behavior, thoughts and emotions. You would probably agree that all mature adults should be responsible for their actions. They are also responsible for their thoughts and emotions. Being responsible for managing *yourself* is the real foundation for personal empowerment. Equally important, personal mastery can be learned and practiced by anyone at any level.

Consider the tale of two women, both low in the organization, both hard workers, and both seldom treated well. The first woman, a secretary, took dictation home for extra pay to help make ends meet. Better-paid male higher-ups often got the credit and the rewards for her work. She complained bitterly to her family about inequities but never asked for a raise. When her boss gave her a raise, she faulted the small amount. If she got sick, she took her vacation days first in order to "save" her sick days in case she really got sick, and groused about the lack of time off. She remained at the same company for 30 years, afraid to seek another job because the company might find out and let her go.

The second woman, a low-level clerk for a small business, worked for the owner, a proverbial battle-ax. This boss was condescending, rude, and frequently nasty. One day Ms. Battle-Ax came flying out of her office to chew out the clerk for some minor mistake. She didn't care that she was in the middle of the office, in front of customers as well as other employees. The clerk took the rant cheerfully and promised to correct the mistake forthwith. When the boss stormed away, another employee asked the clerk how she could put up with such outbursts. "Easy," she said. "I was looking for a job when I found this one."

That one phrase set her free. She gave herself permission to leave anytime she wanted. She did not allow herself to feel trapped. Even making minimum wage in a job in which she was not appreciated, she gave herself control over her destiny. The anecdote is not intended to suggest that people should put up with abuse from a malignant supervisor. Rather, the suggestion is that, short of physical assault (for which you should call the police), you have control over your own emotional and psychological destiny in any work setting.

Both women in these scenarios were children of the Depression who grew up in poverty. Both lived in the time before any notion of women's rights in the workplace. Both just scraped by. But because the secretary submitted to her fears, she allowed her situation to foreclose any sense of other choices and to embitter her toward her employer and life in general. In contrast, the clerk's willingness to walk out if matters got too bad gave her conscious control of the situation, calming her emotional mind and enabling her to make rational choices about her future. After a time, the boss's rants became comical. Other employees hoped to see the boss blow up and the clerk to cheerfully deflect the energy. Despite her lack of status in the organization, the clerk was the one who had the power.

Lead from your strengths so that you do not become frozen by fears about your weaknesses. A mid-level marketing executive used to worry about not being as creative as some of his counterparts. His growing anxiety led him to become cynical, which expressed itself as sarcasm toward "creative types." A period of introspection led him to realize that he had two important strengths. He had a practical and financial grasp of business issues, and he was outstanding at synthesizing the ideas of others. He was invariably the person who found common themes in seemingly disparate matters and who pulled all the strands together in plans and projects. Going forward, he chose to build on those strengths. Rather than quarrel with creative talents, he made a point of bringing them into brainstorming sessions. Knowing that his strength lay in seeing the best practical applications of their ideas, he no longer viewed them as threats. Soon, his managers viewed him as a "star" for having the good sense to think "out of the box." By leading from his strengths, he did not need to focus on problem solving, the subject of Chapter 5, "Aggression, Target Fixation, and the Crashes They Cause." By leading from his strengths and confidently filling in with other resources as needed, his lack of creativity led to creativity!

One caution: Overplaying a strength can turn it into a weakness. An outstanding businessperson who ignores exercise, has a poor diet, neglects personal relationships, or who refuses to take time off for personal replenishment will find her business abilities fading or her life unrewarding despite career progress. The marketing manager just mentioned could easily slide into just a "numbers guy" or a memo writer if he over-exercised his demonstrated strengths.

Act upon projects according to priority is a way of inserting conscious decision making into the work environment. Because humans slide so quickly into reactive, firefighting mode, we invariably end up defining our jobs in terms of deadlines instead of priorities. In his book *First Things First*, Stephen Covey insists on reversing that mindset. He identifies four quadrants according to combinations of priority and urgency. Quadrant I consists of those things that are both important and urgent, for example a major presentation to the CEO tomorrow morning on your division's strategy. Quadrant II consists of those things that are important but not urgent, such as a major product introduction sometime later in the year. Quadrant III consists of those things that are not important, but are urgent, such as responding to people who need your input regardless of whether the matter is strategic or not. Quadrant IV consists those things that are not important and not urgent, such as reviewing business or marketing plans from teams that are only tangentially related to yours.

Most executives have no trouble focusing on Quadrant I (important, urgent). If you are presenting to the CEO in the morning, you are going to be focused on that target. Nor do most executives have a problem in not focusing on Quadrant IV (unimportant, not urgent). Those matters end up in the "to be read" pile and eventually land in the recycle bin. It's the other two quadrants that deadline-driven people reverse. They work on the *urgent-but-not-important* matters rather than on the *important-but-not-urgent*. One executive began to get so far behind that his longer and longer hours were unable to catch him up. After tracking every moment of his day, he realized that he had fallen into the habit of answering e-mail as it came. Although the asynchronicity of e-mail enabled him to respond at a time of his choosing, he had become addicted to the instant gratification of its arrival and his reply. At times, he would even reply to e-mail while other people were in his office. His only productive time was at the end of day, when the e-mail quieted down.

E-mail, in fact, goes through a predictable cycle at all businesses. First, people jump on it because there isn't much of it and a quick response speeds work along. Next, the volume of e-mail becomes so great that it begins to drag productivity down, but people feel compelled as good business citizens to respond to it. Finally, the volume swamps people to the extent that they have to become extremely disciplined to avoid its siren song. Our executive instituted some simple practices: He came in a bit early and reviewed the overnight e-mail, mostly from Europe, over a cup of coffee. He checked e-mail again at 10:30 and 2:30, responding only to time-critical matters. He ran through the rest of e-mail at the end of the day, focusing only on projects that he could help move along overnight in offices in other time zones. He learned the importance of the "Delete" key in place of the "Reply" key.

Our natural tendency is to manage our time based on the urgency of things. E-mail is the exemplar in today's connected world, as some other technology will become the exemplar in the future. However, the important-but-not-urgent must take precedence over the urgent-but-not-important, Quadrant II over Quadrant III. The reason might be dubbed the Firefighting Law of Business: *You fight fires over symptoms today because you failed to address a fundamental issue earlier. Therefore, address fundamental issues today to reduce firefighting tomorrow.* Two examples, one negative and one positive, illustrate the importance of this point.

One individual had come up through the ranks at a major company as a respected individual contributor, with great marks for everything except the tendency to become overextended. His supervisor invested considerable time in helping him prioritize responsibilities and emphasized that his evaluation would be structured around completion of the highest-priority tasks. All outward signs indicated that he was making progress, but one day the supervisor received a phone call. His manager had failed to appear at a local conference at which he was to speak to customers on behalf of another division in the company. Someone else had to step in as a last-minute replacement. The other division was the department's top internal customer, and the conference was for their top external customers.

Not believing that he could have missed such a critical assignment, the supervisor first feared that he had been in an automobile accident, especially because the weather that day was stormy. When the supervisor found the manager in his office, he learned that the individual had spent the morning working there and had left so late that he would barely have been on time even if the weather and traffic had been cooperative. But traffic that day was snarled, a common occurrence in that area and quite predictable given the storm. When he arrived at about the time his speech would have ended, the vice president of the other division had angrily sent him away.

When the supervisor grilled his report about how he could have missed his number one priority, the individual offered multiple reasons. It had taken longer than expected to get through e-mail, voicemail, the daily calls; there were a couple of "crises" to attend to with other internal customers; one of his staff was having difficulties on a project; he had not expected the slow traffic, and so on. "Was there anything you worked on this morning that was half as important as your talk?" his supervisor asked. "No," he replied. "Then why didn't you arrive at the conference an hour or two ahead of time and do your calls from there? Why take any chances?" Pressed, he repeated the long litany of things that had kept him in the office.

"Don't you realize that you have no credibility left? I can never involve you in that division's work again, and they're the reason your team exists!" Finally, it dawned on the employee the damage he had done to his own career. Shortly after, he sought a position in another group, and the supervisor approved the transfer with the proviso that he first complete his personnel reviews, because it was near the end of the review period. He made the transfer, became absorbed in his new work, and never completed the reviews of his old team. In less than a month, he had failed to do the most important priority he had as an individual contributor (the talk) and the most important priority he had as a manager (the employee reviews).

Now for the counter-example.

When Microsoft's Business Systems Division, which produced software for the enterprise, grew from $115 million to $1 billion in business in less than 18 months in the mid-1990s, the marketing vice president, Rich Tong, led an effort to regularize product introductions for the half-dozen new products the division was shipping every year. Until then, the division had managed product launches by brute force, applying hustle, brains, all available bodies, and money to release and market products. Tong scheduled a two-day meeting in which each team broke down each product launch day by day from 120 days prior to launch to 60 days afterward. Each team identified all the elements that needed to be done, including such activities as preparing software for physical manufacture, developing training materials, creating marketing materials, creating advertising and public relations programs, developing technical demonstrations, and engaging the retail channel. Particular emphasis was placed on elements that crossed group lines or that cost a lot of money. Part of the brainstorming focused on ways to improve coordination and reduce expenses.

Within a week, the division had created a "black book" for product launches that covered everything required to release any new product. The most revealing thing to come out of the analysis was that the most expensive items, and the ones requiring the most cross-coordination and therefore had the greatest chance for error, were those things that were done last minute that could have been handled earlier—had people done what was important instead of what was time critical. For example, the shipping manager pointed out that because nobody could ever get the product demonstrations done until the night before an event, the division spent an extra $50,000 a show to ship the demo computers by air at the last minute. Tong decreed that "the night before" was now "the night before minus seven days," so that computers could be trucked inexpensively to events.

Despite complaints by the managers that their groups were already oversubscribed, Tong was firm. All of the steps in the black book, including the timely completion of demos, were made part of the review process and its attendant salary, bonus, and stock. Tong never had to dock anyone any review points because of late demos. Somehow, this high-energy but exhausted band of marketing warriors all managed to finish the technical demonstrations according to the new schedule. The change came once they got their priorities straight. The change came once the company began to reward the behavior it sought to instill.

This one change created ripples of positive effects. The division saved enough money in reduced equipment costs over a year *to stage one extra show annually*. The shows and events themselves had a huge uptick in quality. As one senior executive told Tong, "We still work the last 48 hours straight, but now we do it to make the event perfect, not just to get things to work." To their surprise, the product teams found that the new schedule made their life easier. By being more systematic and beginning earlier, they had more time to develop demonstrations, they made many fewer mistakes, and they had time to polish the presentations.

More important than any specific gain, however, Tong succeeded in changing the mindset of his managers. Facing constant competitive pressure in a rapid-change environment, they had perceived everything as being out of their control. All they and their staff could do was react. Tong's goal was to insert conscious decision making into his team's pell-mell but sometimes undirected efforts. He used the analogy of the ski slalom, in which snow skiers have to pass through a series of right and left gates on their way down the hill at high speed. The champion skiers are the ones who anticipate their entry point not only for the next immediate gate but also for the two or three beyond that. If you miss one gate a little, you miss the next gate by a lot and soon you run off the course. By hitting each gate properly set up for other ones farther ahead, you are doing more work but the effort feels easier. Without having to constantly make high-speed corrections at the last second to stay on track, you get into a smooth rhythm. The change Tong sought had much less to do with detailed schedules than it did with removing fear from a launch, convincing his reports that they held their destinies in their own hands, and getting them into a rhythm of constantly looking ahead. He showed them how to be as disciplined in managing priorities as they had been in fighting fires.

Both the case of the time-driven manager and the case of the priority-driven vice president provide the same lessons. Both were dealing with a firefighting mentality. The first individual succumbed to the emotional drama of helter-skelter daily tasks. He could not calm himself long enough to see that the fires he fought were symptoms of a single, bigger, underlying cause. It was easier and more emotionally satisfying for him to put out the individual flames than to determine the source and figure out how to save the barn. He became so mesmerized by the symptoms that he could not turn away from them even to save his job. His compulsion to firefight sent him spectacularly down in flames.

Microsoft's Tong, however, recognized that every underlying cause produced a dozen different symptoms. He went to the source, cut off its oxygen, and eliminated a lot of problems that would have surfaced later. With less firefighting to do, his teams had more free time to spend on other important-not-urgent matters. Slowly, the division was able to shift the balance of time significantly toward important issues rather than daily crises. Over the next several years, his division was able to go from frenzied individual product launches to coordinated launches of multiple products, something that would never have been possible until his teams managed toward priorities, not urgency. When focus is on priorities, urgency takes care of itself.

You will never eliminate all firefighting, of course. Urgent, unpredictable, and important matters arise in business all the time. But you will eliminate enough firefighting to reclaim a huge hunk of time and energy. In general, you will be able to use "above and beyond" efforts to improve results, not merely to survive. When legitimate crises erupt, you have the mental and emotional reserves to respond to them.

What these examples show is so simple that many people miss the point all together. Businesspeople frequently complain about not having enough time, but time is the great equalizer. We all have precisely 24 hours in our day. Knowing how to properly prioritize projects separates the effective from those that work with great energy but seldom achieve lasting success. An ounce of prioritization is worth a pound of time-criticality.

The Dance of Intentionality and Emotion

Brain evolution created an executive capacity in humans that is lacking in other species. But because the emotional centers are so powerful, make up such a large proportion of the brain, and are so easily triggered by any sense of "hard times," people are subject to emotional takeovers by the survival-oriented parts of the brain. If you've dealt with an angry person who screams that he is being "perfectly reasonable," you know how hard it is for an individual in a heated state to perceive a relapse to primitive behavior. This emotional state is simply too much a part of us. Once called into play, it *is* us. This dichotomy between real and perceived behavior is particularly true in business, where the relative formality, structure, and decorum of the environment leads us to assume civilized, rational behavior. In actuality, most business dynamics, within or without the company, are highly emotional, and the stress of competition defaults humans into those centers wired for hard, fear-reactive times.

At the same time, humans need their emotional centers both for response to genuine emergencies and for the proper evaluation of relationships. A genuine emergency is the need to save your physical life in the next two seconds. It is *not*, however, the loss of two points of market share this quarter, although you and your boss will probably *act* as if your life actually does depend on changing the trend. Nor does a proper evaluation of relationships come from a screaming or cowering emotional mind. The emotional mind should inform the conscious mind of the emotional subtexts of a situation, enabling you to read the other person's emotional state and adjust accordingly. In business and politics, which ultimately rest on relationships, such intuition is an invaluable asset. President Reagan, one of the great "Communist bashers" of our age, nonetheless agreed with the Soviet Union on major reductions in nuclear arms after meeting Prime Minister Gorbachev and thinking, "I can do business with this guy." Reagan's intuition took him where his political philosophy would not have, to the benefits of both nations.

Humanity's frontal lobes invest us all with judgment, with the ability to imagine the future and foresee consequences. Simply put, our executive brain provides our sense of identity as well as our *intentionality*. To function to the highest of our abilities, however, we cannot be rigidly logical any more than we can be hysterically emotional. We must combine intentionality—one of the great gifts of the frontal lobes—with the subtle, intuitive, and insightful capabilities of the emotional brain. Without the mediation of the executive brain, fear can lead to a failure of personal responsibility or to a misdirection of attention to short-term firefighting instead of long-term solutions. Without the humanizing effect of the emotional brain, a failure to read emotional clues can impair your ability to work with others. Beginning with the three steps described in this chapter and more formal approaches and tools described later, the individual can achieve harmony between the executive and emotional centers to achieve whole-brain function, the path to success in business, not to mention life.

4

Scarcity Behavior in the Modern Tribe

Because of the ongoing function of the brain's fear and emotional centers, direct and distinct parallels exist between our behavior and that of our ancestors. To know and understand these dynamics provides powerful insights into the worst and best of human nature, especially within the corporate culture, for the simple reason that humanity's inherited bio-evolutionary predispositions and traits express themselves predominately in a social context. By nature (the brain) and necessity (humanity's physical deficiencies), modern humans became more and more social creatures. We survived not because of *strength of numbers*, but because of *strength of social cohesion*. Herd animals, schools of fish, and any number of insects survive by strength of numbers; they out-produce the capability of predators to eat them all. Humans survived by creating social organizations far beyond the ability of any potential predator to penetrate. Before long, our social structures turned us from knock-kneed weaklings into the most feared predators on the planet. In a variety of evolving family, social, and organizational systems, humans created a whole that was greater than the parts, a whole that enabled us to surmount the greatest challenges of primordial times.

The same social organization that gave us an advantage over other species also provides the template for modern organizations, particularly business organizations. The first issue is that humans, having lived in small groups for almost all of our existence, still do best in small groups. Fear-dominated small groups, however, quickly develop xenophobia—the fear of others—and this fear can trigger all manner of calamitous behavior in society at large, as well as in business. Also, the sense of scarcity, which aided survival for ancient tribes, leads to harmful behavior for modern business tribes. Scarcity's fear-based expressions, typically *the fear of not being enough* or *the fear of not having enough*, account for many of the corporate excesses already summarized. The subject of this chapter is the way such behaviors play out to the detriment of organizations, beginning with some background on the social groups of olden days.

In a hunter-gatherer society, social cohesion applied foremost to the hunt, which provided probably the first important division of labor in human society. All the members of the hunting party had to be skillful, they had to be reliable, and they had to function cohesively. A typical hunt for large game involved driving the animals into a swamp, where their mobility was hampered, or cornering them where multiple spears could do their work, or stampeding them over a cliff. Beaters had to drive the animals in one direction; runners had to contain them on the flanks. If a herd of animals doubled back, or a single large beast turned to charge, the hunters had to maintain their ranks and to at least wound the prey to slow it down. For such a perilous task, members needed to know and understand one another's strengths in order to survive—and to eat. A small miscalculation meant injury or death to one or more of the hunters, as the broken bones and other traumas show in the human remains that have been found of ancient past. Knowing where to place the strongest hunter, the fastest hunter, the one most adept with a spear: These were life-and-death matters that make today's business decisions tame in comparison.

Inherent in the pursuit were strategic, logistical, and tactical planning. The strategy would involve what to hunt, where to seek the prey, the likely length of the hunt, the overall game plan, and the defense of the kill from other predators and scavengers. Logistical planning would involve the amount of food and other support to bring along—a quick day hunt would differ considerably from a weeklong trek into the mountains—how to cut up, preserve, carry the meat, and similar "quartermaster" chores. The tactical planning would vary depending on the terrain, wind and weather conditions, time of day, and the presence of other predators. You can see in all of these activities straightforward parallels with today's business behavior, the difference being in the level of abstraction required in execution. When a sales manager today talks about developing prospects and converting them to sales, she might say, "You bring the bear to the door, and we'll skin it," but she is speaking about closing a deal, not fancy knife work. Indeed, you can imagine the tribal elders (ancient at perhaps age 40 and too crippled for major hunts) advising the CEO and his team (many in their teens) on the long-term strategies for economic success, defined as whether they hit their mastodon as opposed to profit targets; and the team refining their tactical strategies according to "competitive" issues on the plains, whether these issues are uncooperative prey or another band of four-legged or two-legged hunters.

You can also imagine the excitement of an early entrepreneur who finds a way to flake a stone to a sharp point with less waste, or who figures out that if you wet the leather before binding a stone point to a spear, the leather will shrink and bind more tightly, or who finds that using a separate stick to launch a spear will increase its velocity and distance. (For most of humanity's existence, the phrase *throw weight* had to do with obtaining food, not annihilating the enemy with a nuclear payload.) You can imagine, too, the difficulty of inventions taking hold in a conservative culture, especially if early models tested poorly during an animal charge. Still, the rewards were bound to be great: more food, higher status in the tribe, more interest by the tribal lasses in a guy who can literally as well as figuratively bring home the bacon. (Business language uses hunting and military terminology to describe the modern analogue to ancient activities.)

As brain form and function evolved toward abstract reasoning, the interaction between brain, language, tool development, and cultural adaptation led to better personal communication and coordination, more efficient tools, and more complex social structures; and improved language capacity, more sophisticated social interaction, and more complex tools stimulated ever-higher brain functioning. The brain has a high degree of plasticity, and its highly developed circuitry does not fully mature in a normal developing human until the person's early 20s, no doubt aiding the feedback cycle of all these stimuli. We probably will never know the primary driving force, if there was one. All of these capacities seemed to occur simultaneously, creating the presumption of strong reinforcement among them all. Over time, we developed complex languages and became highly skilled craftsmen and artisans, sending technology on an exponential climb. In our predecessors, archeologists have found identical tools in layers separated by hundreds of thousands of years. As modern humans spread, new tools began to show up in layers separated by thousands of years. By the Iron Age, technical advances such as the wheel and metal fabrication occurred on the scale of hundreds of years. Today, major technical advances occur in terms of decades, if not sometimes years. Today, human knowledge doubles every five years.

Beyond the enhanced technical competencies, humans were beginning to grasp intangibles such as good and bad, right and wrong, civil and uncivil conduct, love, loyalty, appreciation, and other "modern" attitudes. The rise of the first agricultural and trading communities helped cement these attitudes. From these communities, the first civilizations arose, and the first moral values became inscribed in written form. However, if there was a Golden Age, it was short and sporadic. Until the Industrial Age, life in any human era was boom or bust. Even as agrarian cultures began to take hold, diversifying labor still further, humans continued to hunt and collect. A collapse of hunting stock or a crop failure could easily wipe out a tribe. Archeology has found many fledgling civilizations that died out because of starvation or disease, because of soil exhaustion, or because of a shift in rainfall. Even when there was enough today, there was no guarantee that there would be enough tomorrow. Scarcity remained an underlying component in the intricate functioning of the brain, and in the continuing evolution of culture.

Tribes: The Best and Worst of Human Organizations

For 99 percent of humanity's lifetime, we lived in small family groups or bands and foraged in small hunting bands. Among humans, these informal collections of two or three nuclear families eventually evolved into tribes, which were larger, usually less mobile, and had some kind of formal leadership. Westerners have sometimes used different names, such as extended families, clans, or small towns, but their organization and social dynamics are similar to these early human groups. In a small group where you know everyone, you can personally assess the strengths and weaknesses of people, and you can have confidence in the group's understood social structures and laws.

It should not surprise us that small-group behavior remains deeply ingrained. Certain "magic numbers" in group size occur with regularity. Most sports teams have 9 to 12 players; military squads have 10 to 12; most organizations believe 8 is the maximum number of direct reports a manager should have. Ancestral bands ranged in size from 10 to 50 people—roughly the size of the bands of humanity's closest relatives today, chimpanzees and bonobos, to give an idea of how ancient this group size is. This number is also usually the size of sports teams, including substitutes; military platoons (30 people); and branch offices. Tribes equate with 100 to 150 people, which is also the size of military companies and mid-size offices. Whether this is the maximum number of faces a human can recognize or the limit of delegated leadership that can be based on personal loyalty, somewhere around a 100 and seldom more than 150 seems to be the top limit for effective working social groups.

In smaller groups, people can work together on the basis of personal contact and personal leadership. Personal strengths are most readily identified; personal accountability is strongest; social structures depend on direct contact. You feel that you belong, that your concerns are heard, and that you can make a difference. Even today, people feel more loyalty and involvement in civic and school affairs in smaller communities than in large. Almost all of us who have worked at a small company will say that we prefer it over a large company; many old timers at a big company look back nostalgically to "when we were small." Gore-Tex, the fabric manufacturer, specifically organizes its operating groups to remain under that magic number of 150 people so that all interactions can be personal.

People identify with the nation-state whenever the population is homogeneous, but nations with more than one ethnic group often have difficulty maintaining cohesion. Humans have to consciously override the emotional brain's desire for a smaller, more easily identifiable tribe. (Henceforth, the word *tribe* is used to refer to any generally small group of people.) In peaceful countries, the tribal instinct may manifest itself in innocent activities such as sporting contests and elections, where people cheer for such things as red or blue uniforms, or red or blue voting patterns, or in good-natured ribbing with people who have regional accents. If you doubt that such tribal instincts remain intact, watch the World Series, tune in to a college football game, follow the Olympics, or read a *Wall Street Journal* account of two competitors brawling in the marketplace.

Fortunately, most of these examples of "controlled" tribalism can be quite enjoyable, but fear-driven tribalism can be extremely destructive. The emotional brain can convert "opponent" to "enemy" faster than you can say "hooray for our side," and both sporting events and elections have led to violence or corruption, and adults and children alike find it easy to ridicule people who look or talk differently. Under John O'Neil's concept of "leadership aikido," which stresses victory without harm, the higher-order approach is to use competition to learn. Your competitor is not your opponent but your teacher! Top-notch coaches understand this principle well. They study opposing teams in order to improve their own. Sam Walton of Wal-Mart never wanted to hear what a competitor was doing wrong. He wanted to know what the competitor was doing right, so that Wal-Mart could learn from it. Calling Kmart the laboratory for Wal-Mart's business, he wanted to meet them and other competitors head-on because the competition would make Wal-Mart a better company. Kimberley-Clark was "exhilarated" at the idea of going head to head with Procter and Gamble. Businesses are too easily derailed into treating the competition as the enemy, leading to often disastrous approaches, as described in Chapter 5, "Aggression, Target Fixation, and the Crashes They Cause." The natural reaction to an encounter with enemies is to strike them down before they do the same to you; but what worked in primordial times will not likely work today. The reactive archetypal belief that one can gain from a competitor's loss is often not the case and can misdirect corporate efforts.

The reason for attack postures in business is that it takes precious little stimulus for the emotional brain to label unrelated groups as outsiders. Tribal instinct plus fear causes teenagers to form high-school cliques such as the preppies, the jocks, and goths—or greasers and freaks. The names of teenage cliques change over the generations but the instinct to create tribes remains. Tribal instinct plus fear drives street gangs. Tribal instinct plus fear explains why it is so easy for humans to quickly perceive any situation as "us versus them" and to discriminate against those of different skin color, economic status, or religious belief. In fact, the most technically correct definition of bigotry might be "tribal instinct plus fear." The emotional brain's interpretation of "different" to mean "threat" leads to ethnocentrism, the assumption that our culture is better than yours. People who are different are conveniently viewed as being unimportant, possibly subhuman, competitors for resources, and therefore dangerous. In many tribes all over the world, often the only word for *people* is the name of that tribe.

Fear in its raw animal form can be so powerful that it swamps our sense of morality, creating a disregard for other human beings and all manner of moral, civil, and legal consequences. We like to think that our legal structures, our legal codes and doctrines, our "civilization," will prevent the brutality of ancient times. However, *xenophobia*, the fear of those who are not of our group, remains ingrained in the human psyche. Opposing sides that view the world as a place of scarcity continue to view one another with suspicion for *fear* that the other will take something away from them. Union workers fear that nonunion workers will take away jobs. Nonunion workers in a developed country fear workers paid even less in undeveloped countries. Immigrants flowing into the United States and Europe from other nations trigger a fear reaction, ostensibly because they take jobs, but also because of evident "tribal" differences in language, color, and economic status.

Although few people really worry about their biological existence, economic fears come close, triggering deep and volatile anxiety. The United States considers itself a nation of laws, but mineworkers, civil rights workers, and other organizers have been murdered in our life-times for challenging the status quo. Xenophobia and perceived scarcity have triggered most other modern violence. Europe considers itself the epitome of culture, yet it was the site of the two bloodiest wars in history and the mass murders of minorities and dissidents by Hitler and Stalin. Asia boasts the oldest civilizations but is home of genocidal Pol Pot and the Myanmar dictators; Japan is only a genera-tion away from a brutal feudal society that considered all other peo-ples inferior. Tribal massacres mark every continent on a regular basis: the Catholic-Protestant wars in North Ireland, the Sunni-Shiite con-flicts in the Middle East, the Christian massacre of Muslims in the Balkans, the Muslim massacre of Christians in Darfur, the dispiriting tribal genocide in almost every other part of Africa. Many Americans remain in full-fear react mode over the terrorist attacks of 9/11, and the American military response to those attacks has triggered a counter-fear reaction among many Muslim peoples, even those glad to see the Taliban and Hussein regimes driven from power.

Fear-driven emotions lurk barely beneath the surface among indi-viduals and among the highest levels of social organizations, the nation-states. It is hardly radical to say that fear plays a major role in organizations within society, particularly business, which functions as today's mental version of yesterday's hunting party. In this context, sociopathic business behavior is comparatively mild, more of a panic attack than the sophisticated brutality to which entire societies can be so easily turned. Enron committed accounting fraud and manipulated energy prices in the West, leading California to the brink of bank-ruptcy. The company might have inadvertently caused the deaths of people who could not afford high prices for air conditioning. But at least the company did not open fire on its employees or other protes-tors, as other organizations have done in modern times.

Tribes, of course, have their laws and customs, or "norms," for dealing with transgressors. In times long past, a serious infringement of a group norm would lead to banishment from the tribe, which either would bring the outcast to his senses or ultimately result in his demise. A few years ago, a Native American tribe in the state of Wash-ington reinstituted the practice with two out-of-control teenage boys, banishing them to a small island for several months where they were forced to learn survival skills and do some serious growing up. Many outdoor schools use a similar approach, taking young people at risk away from the comfortable, lazy, and unreal cynicism of contemporary teenage life and forcing them to come to grips with physical reality. By stripping away the veneer of teenage culture, young people can develop personal self-confidence and learn to function appropriately within a small tribal group of peers. From time to time, businesses have tried outdoor exercises to strengthen teams, but too often they become competitive instead of cooperative, reinforcing the dominance chain rather than building trust. (Such things happen when an unhappy culture wants to pretend at changing without actually changing.) For many years, judges often gave the choice of prison time or the army to young offenders, recognizing that most would choose military service that could provide the proper coming-of-age rituals for undirected young males. In business, banishment occurs with the words *You're fired*. In essence, "go out and starve, or find another tribe." Television shows such as *The Apprentice*, *The Mole*, and *Survivor* capitalize on the fear of banishment that is part and parcel of all healthy human beings.

As a sober attempt to correct personal misbehavior, banishment can be a positive. At best, the individual learns to appreciate the benefits of his tribe; at worst, a disruptive influence is removed. Driven by fear, however, banishment can be tragically negative. Threatened by "free thinking," rigid communities have run decent but nonconforming individuals out of town. Churches have excommunicated followers who question norms or official history or who expose misbehavior by officials. Corporate whistleblowers are seldom treated well by their organizations or by society at large, even when their stories are found to be true and their intentions honorable.

Take, for instance, the case of Roger Boisjoly, who predicted the O-ring failure that destroyed the space shuttle *Challenger*. The veteran expert in mechanical design and structural analysis, a technical troubleshooter on the shuttle's solid rocket boosters, had warned his bosses at NASA and at contractor Morton Thiokol that the space shuttle was not ready for launch. They not only failed to listen to him, but after investigations found NASA and Morton Thiokol guilty of mismanagement in the death of the crew, both organizations carried out reprisals against Boisjoly. Years later, he still suffered from post-traumatic stress disorder. Another long-time NASA veteran, Don Nelson, tried to alert the White House about lapses in NASA's approach to flight safety just prior to the *Columbia* disaster some 16 years later. Nelson's complaints were not just ignored. He received two reprimands for going outside channels.

Other whistleblowers have suffered similar fates. Even *Time* magazine's "Persons of the Year" in 2002, Cynthia Cooper of WorldCom, Coleen Rowley of the FBI, and Sherron Watkins of Enron, risked their jobs, health, privacy, and sanity to publicize the problems within their troubled organizations. When asked whether anyone at the top had thanked them, they all burst out laughing. As *Time* reported, Cooper said that there were times when she could not stop crying. Sociologically, it is interesting to note that all of *Time*'s honorees were women. One reason is that women still remain largely outside the sanctum sanctorum of business; none of the women were in the highest or innermost circles of the businesses. At least as important is that, across the board, women exhibit a stronger social conscience than men. They are more likely to define the "tribe" more broadly than the half-dozen or so individuals who make up a CEO's trusted advisors.

Tribal behavior is intrinsic to every human organization, particularly business. The key is to derive the best from tribal culture—the team play, the cohesion, the emotional connections—while eliminating the self-destructive fear mechanisms. This is harder than it may sound. Sophisticated social behavior is the essence of civilization. Not "sophistication" having to do with fancy dress or artificial mannerisms, but the ability of individuals to successfully engage with other people in a variety of group settings, to weave their way through the complicated interactions of any social structure to meet their physical, emotional, and (today) financial needs. For leaders, the sophistication shows in the ability to obtain the maximum capability of all the others in the group. These skills reside in the interplay between the emotional and executive brain: the emotional brain obtaining the read on other people and the executive brain creating a strategy (conscious or unconscious) of how to guide them toward a goal.

Dominance, Backstabbing, and Other Scarcity Behaviors

Because we are still biologically so close to a life of scarcity, however, oft times the leadership and individual behavior revert to reactive behavior more at home on the precarious savannah than in the corporate suite. "Leadership" becomes the dominance of the alpha male, and "team play" becomes the reactivity of the dominated pack members. A trained anthropologist can observe senior executives seating themselves in a room and quickly determine the power structure. In a fear-based organization, the dominant person (usually a male) might splay himself across several chairs, showing that he has the right to more territory than others. His top assistants spread out so that they can see him and he can see them. The assistants effectively project his power while also protecting his back. The alpha male might further show his dominance by cutting off others when they speak or by insulting them. One CEO keeps a basketball in his office and is fond of playing with it in the presence of his subordinates, sometimes dribbling the ball to drown out what they have to say. Another CEO keeps a hammer on his desk that he is fond of pounding to make a point. Anthropologists sometimes see more civility in a gathering of gorillas than what humans show in a "thoroughly modern meeting."

Some businesspeople have used the Darwinian notion of survival of the fittest and bad-tempered behavior by some of our ape brethren to justify aggressive alpha-type behavior as the "natural" way to acquire resources. In actuality, humanity has two equally close relatives, the chimpanzee and the bonobo. The chimp can be brutally power hungry, but the bonobo prefers to "make love, not war," in the words of Frans De Waal, who has studied all three species, including us. Female bonobos dominate as often as males, and females cooperate in a manner closer to human interaction than to chimp interaction. Bonobos are sexually active for pleasure more often than for reproduction, and females use sex to restore peace and create alliances. Sound like any other species you know? (Bonobos, who can easily walk upright, bear a striking physical resemblance to Australopithecus, one of the earliest of humanity's ancestors, and bonobos have been trained to understand simple human speech and to communicate by using abstract symbols. Sadly, habitat loss threatens them with extinction.) De Waal calls humans "bipolar" in having the political and military skills of the chimp, the easy sexuality of the bonobo, and other traits in common with both. Chimps and other apes show empathy and altruism too. One zoo chimpanzee carried a stunned bird to the top of a tree and tossed it into the air to try to help it fly. Gorillas have been known to sacrifice themselves to save a wounded mate. Although the strongest ape dominates, other apes often form alliances to oppose a despot.

These examples show how deep certain "human" behaviors go. At the very minimum, the complexity of our biology challenges male-biased assumptions that progress comes from aggression. Most often, aggression is a sign of fear, just as it is with other apes. Whether displayed as hostility or arrogance, fear-based leadership behavior is an expression of the *fear of not enough*. If you can convince yourself that someone else is going to take something you need (food, mate, land, job, power, prestige), your emotional brain sets you free to wreak havoc no matter the cost to others or ultimately to yourself. The fear of not enough expresses itself in two ways: 1) *the fear of not being enough* (not being swift, strong, or skillful enough, not being accurate with the spear, not being cunning enough to lead the pack); 2) *the fear of not having enough* (not enough food, shelter, sex, and other basic needs).

In the work environment, the fear of *not being enough* manifests itself in the new leader who immediately begins dismissing other people who might have gotten the promotion, the leader who constantly belittles subordinates, or the executive who surrounds himself or herself with sycophants. In a *Saturday Night* live comedy skit, a caveman explains to his clan the hunting strategy for tomorrow. Another caveman gets up repeatedly to explain a better way. The clan leader welcomes the first suggestion, accepts the second with less enthusiasm, and shows annoyance with the third. When everyone goes to sleep, the leader bashes his clever clansman in the head with a club, then faces the audience and says, "Now me strong *and* me smart!" Instinctively, the leader does not want his performance held up in comparison to a possible challenger. Further, the reaction is emotion-based ("because I'm afraid, I have to get rid of you") rather than intelligence-based ("as the leader, I can use a smart guy like you"). The comedy skit does more than a shelf of books on management to explain an entire class of executive misbehavior.

In the work environment, fear of *not having enough* expresses itself in a drive for power. The person fears not getting the job, the raise, the promotion, the recognition, the title, or the corner office. A desire for some power, some recognition, some rewards is a reasonable and happy trait. A person with executive abilities wants to exercise them. From a social standpoint, a skilled person cannot shape the world for the better from the bottom. Power shaped by the executive brain, by reason and ethics, is a *powerful* good. Fear-driven power, however, leads to duplicitous behavior, to sabotaging other individuals and teams, to putting the person's career above the good of the company. One senior executive, commenting on a talented but power-hungry confederate who had tried to take her job, described the person quite succinctly: "As long as you understand that it's *all about Joe*, then you're okay." The first executive had thwarted the takeover attempt by sitting down with the CEO and laying out Joe's strengths and weaknesses next to her own. "You want Joe? Here's what you get. You want me? Here's what you get. Take who you want, just don't play games." By directly confronting the threat calmly, the first executive created an atmosphere in which the CEO could consider the situation objectively. The decision to retain the first executive had a lot to do with her cool-headed lack of fear and her personal mastery of the threat, which put Joe's aggressive me-first power play in unprofessional and rather-sad contrast.

Less-driven people often wonder what continues to compel individuals to seek more power after they have reached a seemingly safe level in the corporate or political world. In actuality, power breeds its own fear. For lower-level employees, the fear is never acquiring enough, or the need to acquire enough to live on in case they lose their jobs. For leaders, the fear is losing what they have: money, power, status. Russia's Stalin, Iraq's Hussein, and North Korea's Kim Il Jong are just three dictators who emptied their country's treasury to create a police state that would keep them in power rather than building roads and bridges or feeding the poor. North Korea's family dictatorship has built one of the world's most powerful armies on the backs of one of the most impoverished peoples, all ostensibly against the fear of attack from South Korea and the United States. In actuality, the fear is that the North Korean people will compare their meager existence to the high standard of living in the democracy just to the south. An increase in power corrupts more and more because it increases the level of fear. The more you have, the more you have to lose. That's fear reinforcing itself in terms of scarcity.

Compounding the fear is a concept known as *accommodation theory*, which says an increase in wealth creates an increase in satisfaction for only a short time. Then the proverbial "bar" as to what constitutes adequate wealth resets even higher. In common parlance, power-hungry people must always "keep up with the Joneses." Except for the one richest person in the world, somebody else will always have a bigger house, bigger boat, nicer car, prettier wife, or more expensive country club. The effect of accommodation is literally the same as the effect of an addictive drug, for the same centers of the brain are affected in the same way. With every dose of additional power and its trappings, the power-driven personality needs a bigger hit to get the same high. This is the only explanation for the behavior of someone such as Martha Stewart, the wealthy decorating maven. Stewart, who originally trained as a stockbroker and sat on the board of the New York Stock Exchange, was accused of insider trading and coercing a young stock broker into falsifying records, and was convicted of lying and sent to prison. A "not-enough" reflex kicked in to save a comparative pittance, and then drove another and another such reflex until she had landed herself in jail.

For when you add the *fear of not having enough* together with *accommodation*, you get *greed*, another powerful emotion. In the movie *Wall*

Street, the Michael Douglas character, Gordon Gecko, pays fascinating and oily homage to greed as he lays waste to companies for his own ego satisfaction. The fictional *Wall Street*, based on the corporate intemperance of the 1980s, now seems almost quaint before today's excesses, such as the way in which CEO Dennis Kozlowski plundered Tyco's assets to support his extravagant lifestyle, including a $6 million birthday party on the island of Sardinia. This was a guy on one helluva high, his executive brain so addled by power and accommodation that he could not foresee the most obvious fact that one day, *somebody* would notice that he had misappropriated *$600 million* from his company. When accommodation is carried to an extreme, it becomes *morbidly obese consumerism*, a modern phrase for what our elders called *gluttony*.

Another fear-related emotion intrinsic to human nature is a sense of *territorial imperative* (proprietary right). On one level, protecting your turf is perfectly reasonable. A hunter-gatherer clan has the right to defend its hunting territories from outside tribes. Farmers have the right to prevent their crops from being stolen at harvest time, and cattle ranchers have the right to protect themselves from rustlers. You have a right to protect what is truly yours. However, the *fear of not having enough* causes the emotional brain to define anything within reach as "mine." Talk to one of the Neolithic bands invading another tribe's territory, and they would *assure* you that these were really *their* hunting grounds, based on some ancient precedent. This very argument is the basis for many contemporary clashes, including the bloodiest ones in the Middle East and Africa.

Even if these were not their grounds, they would justify the taking on the basis of their survival. That they might well be right is one reason that "fear-taking" remains so strong among humans in a variety of contexts despite the emergence of ethics. In business, appropriate protection of turf is inscribed in laws involving such matters as contracts, antitrust behavior, trademarks, copyrights, and patents. "Fear-taking" can come in many ways, ranging from a hostile takeover, such as Oracle buying PeopleSoft to reach a new market, to predatory pricing to drive competitors from business—or worse. Early in the twentieth century, Sinclair Oil constantly warred with aspiring competitors, not hesitating to use violence or sabotage to protect its territory. The unscrupulous tactics by Sinclair and other major corporations of the day led to the enactment of antitrust legislation, but not before the monopolies had killed a number of would-be competitors.

Fight, Freeze, or Flee: The Only Fear Behaviors

Fear manifests itself in three reactions: *fight, flight,* or *freeze.* The primary function of fear is to *preserve life.* Fear is necessary any time our physical survival is at stake, but numerous examples will demonstrate that fear's extremely *reactive* and *limited repertoire* is of little benefit in business situations and is often detrimental. Business requires the functioning of the executive brain for optimal performance, however much our emotional reflexes may want to take us down a *fearful* path.

Flight and freezing can be grouped together in a business context. Fighting is discussed in Chapter 5. Flight and freezing are attempts to avoid dealing with the challenges of work or a maladaptive way to cope with change in the business environment. A salesperson joined a struggling company that had not defined its sales needs well. Instead of digging into prospect lists or cold-calling potential customers or otherwise figuring out how to at least try to do the job, the individual merely sat at his desk, reading the *Wall Street Journal* and waiting for the phone to ring. He left within a couple of months, having made virtually no sales. As he departed, he sent e-mail to "all" castigating the sales manager, the marketing staff, and the company in general for being poorly run. His critique may have been correct, but he took no responsibility for his own passivity in the face of his personal sales objectives.

It is not uncommon for "a suit" such as this to join a company in some capacity, stay a relatively brief time, and then move on without having made any noticeable impact. Another individual was hired in an organization in which individuals served on a variety of teams. After a while, a manager of several such teams noticed recurrent mistakes and oversights. The only pattern was that this individual was part of each team. As the manager began to scrutinize the situation, he noticed that this one individual's apparent failure to follow up on tasks was the root of the problems. In a discussion of the situation, the individual claimed that he had never promised to do any of the assignments. In reviewing meeting minutes and e-mail, the manager realized that the person was right: The employee would phrase things in a way that *implied* a commitment but would not actually *be* a commitment. He would say things such as, "Don't worry about it." Or "That'll be handled." Or "That'll be taken care of." He never said, "I'll handle it" or "I'll take care of it."

In the next team status report, the manager found another of this person's noncommittal commitments. Innocently, the manager did a routine follow-up asking for clarification about that task. By return e-mail came an additional obfuscation. Back and forth the exchanges went, the manager getting more and more specific, and the team member becoming more and more vague. Finally, the manager queried, "Are you *personally* committed to delivering this task by such-and-such a date?" The individual never responded—had to make a meeting, he said. It was not long before he was shown the door.

Perhaps the world's best at this particular kind of flight was a bright, energetic, personally engaging vice president of marketing at a Fortune 500 company, hired after a fast upward track at one hot company after another. Then a new senior vice president asked the advertising team about the VP's performance, and they said he spent all of his time on public relations. Curious, the president then asked the public relations team about his performance, and they said he spent all of his time on advertising. When the VP got wind of the senior vice president's inquiries, he jumped ship to still another hot company. His pattern was not to leap *toward* one opportunity after another but to leap *away* from one responsibility after another. His behaviors were highly skilled but highly maladaptive responses, in which he first froze at responsibility and then fled the consequences.

Freezing also may be an appropriate response in some situations. Commonly, employees freeze when being lambasted by a boss. They might also freeze when a panicked executive initiates yet more change after earlier change was unproductive. Employees may also want to fight back against an unfair action or unethical demand by management. Humans cannot simply shut off biological responses to actual aggression by another. Nor should they. The problem is that unless people understand their reaction, they may be unable to change it. Employees who have frozen in a sudden conflict may not come out of shellshock later to address whatever concerns were raised, or to explain why some changes may not be needed. People who are in a fighting mood may erupt at the boss in a way that makes things worse rather than using a calm reply to bring the boss back to a rational state.

Employees need to understand their reaction to aggression to restore their equilibrium enough to work and determine a lucid response. Managers need to understand that repeated aggressive behaviors can train employees either not to act (behavioral freezing) or to rebel in secret. After meetings in which the boss pounded on the walls, one manager reported that he spent 20 minutes going around to his staff, calming them down and refocusing them. Otherwise, he said, he would have "deer in the headlights" for an entire day—an apt metaphor for maladaptive behavior, because freezing is the correct behavior for deer in the forest, so that a predator will pass them by unnoticed, but the wrong behavior for deer on a busy highway—or an employee in a business setting.

Freezing is also the result of a defensive reaction to unexpected or unwelcome advice. How many times have you been on the receiving end of a memo from "corporate" that describes how a certain task should be accomplished or that outlines a change in strategy that will cause a shakeup in your department? The emotional brain reacts by thinking, "How dare they tell us what to do? They have no idea what it's like down here in the trenches!" Sometimes the emotional brain is right, but the reaction is anything but productive. Many corporate change efforts have been thwarted by resistance of departments or even divisions at approaching business in a new way. This is freezing at the group level.

Companies become frozen in other ways, too. They retain ill-suited employees because they fear wrongful discharge suits, they rest on past successes out of arrogance, and they stop learning and growing because they fear change. A dozen books have been written on companies in the 1970s, 1980s, and 1990s that rode one technology wave to the top, only to ignore the next one and get washed away. While Bethlehem Steel dallied with ornate new buildings, elaborate golf courses, and a corporate air force, competitors turned the fundamentals of the steel industry upside down. The major airlines developed all kinds of elaborate fare programs that did everything except to change the actual business model, which in plain language was to grossly overcharge business customers. The majors did not react until Southwest, Jet Blue, and other discount providers drove them to bankruptcy. It is bad enough to have a business model of "pillage your best customer." It is worse to maintain that model year after year while revenues plummet.

Social Path Follows Biological Path

Corporate organizations are the present-day version of hunting and gathering groups. The instincts, fears, and survival tactics of our earliest hunter-gatherer ancestors, living tens of thousands of years ago, directly influence our thinking, decision making, and behavior. A straightforward connection exists between the hunter-gatherer group's drive to acquire food and a modern corporation's desire to turn a profit. It is the same endpoint, achieved by different methods. The difference, however, is that businesses are not in a literal survival mode, although they convince themselves that they are. As the beneficiaries and heirs of our ancestors' adaptation systems, we need to understand that operating from the instinctual survival mode manifests one of the great contradictions of our time. What was absolutely necessary for survival 80,000 years ago—or 80 years ago—can be extremely detrimental today in a business organization. Survival mode impedes our capacity to thrive.

Until recently, survivability was the only "work" that one could find. This is true still in some undeveloped regions, but it is not true in the social structures (business) that the developed world uses to feed, clothe, and house our families. The survival instinct that might have caused our ancestors to raid another tribe is the same instinct that might cause a man to steal bread to feed his children today, but neither of these behaviors is the same as that of a business professional who steals from his company or whose company steals from others through various forms of ethical misconduct. The first is eating to survive; the second is gluttony. A fear of scarcity, a *fear of not having or being enough*, distorts business behavior. A sense of scarcity sends individuals, teams, and entire companies into fight, freeze, or flight modes that shut down higher thinking. Invariably the behavior diverts huge resources from the company's future needs, in the form of actual money misappropriated, resources misapplied, or precious human energy drained by unproductive habits and mindsets.

Even though it is not overtly evident, the motivating factor for all of the unprofessional examples described in this and earlier chapters is maladaptive, misplaced *fear*. We often do not recognize fear because it cloaks itself in attitudes such as arrogance, greed, turf-ism, backstabbing, lying, cheating and manipulation. A fear of scarcity also drives today's compulsion to a one-dimensional, workaholic lifestyle. People who would be ashamed to acknowledge alcohol or drug addiction can boast about working 60 hours a week as if it were a testament to their manhood or womanhood. Workaholism may be the only behavioral dysfunction that is socially sanctioned in our society.

People resort to these behaviors because in the short term they provide an antidote to the stress of fear. However, on all but the shortest of time scales (the time it takes to reflexively react in fear), all of these strategies are distractions and diversions that take away from group cohesion, performance, productivity, effectiveness and profitability. Workaholism is a bit different in that it tends to burn out the individual so that the loss of performance and productivity may not be as obvious as other fear-driven actions.

If the previously mentioned individuals and companies had a strong and clear sense of "having enough," they would not have felt compelled to act in unscrupulous ways. Unfortunately, human beings do not come with meters or gauges that indicate when they are sated as organisms or as consumers. We are left with more abstract or metaphysical indicators of values, such as good and appropriate and sufficient, to regulate our decision making and conduct.

Although the hunting and gathering efforts of our ancestors predisposed us to a contemporary fixation on acquiring power, status, and wealth as ends unto themselves, businesspeople can do better than behave as "survivors." Faulkner once said that humanity must do more than survive, it must prosper. People must do more than survive the onslaughts and hard times of life; they must take steps to improve humanity's lot. The search for prosperity, the pursuit of happiness, the desire for spiritual enlightenment, the longing for higher-order ethics: These are the social and psychological paths of humanity that parallel the inward physical development of the brain.

Human social organization gave us an advantage over other species, and our knowledge and culture give us advantage over our earlier counterparts. The first human social structures in particular enabled us to exploit brains over brawn. This same organization is a model for modern organizations, particularly business, only now social structures enable us to exploit conscious behavior over fear. The vicious cycle of fear-based reactivity severely limits our opportunity to develop a corporate vision, to conduct business in an effective, proactive, constructive, and productive way. We do have safety in numbers, and we should act in business from the mental and moral strength that safety provides. The only wolf at the door is our own fear. We can choose to take the best of our inherited traits, particularly our cohesion and creativity in small groups, without being stunted by scarcity-driven fears or lapsing into xenophobia. We can use the tribe to our advantage to enable us to think from our higher centers of reasoning.

But first we have to face the most deadly and destructive of the fear responses: not to freeze or to flee, but to fight.

5

Aggression, Target Fixation, and the Crashes They Cause

Of all the human fear reactions, aggression (the fight response) is most dangerous. When a person cannot safely flee or safely freeze, the person attacks. The expression is "fight like a cornered rat," but a cornered human is far more deadly. In a physical fight with a wild animal or another human, aggression is the one thing that can keep a person alive. Until the invention of modern weaponry changed the nature of battle, kings were the warriors who personally led their tribes into battle from the front. In small-unit combat, that kind of courage, skill, and aggressive instinct still makes a difference. Soldiers learn to charge machinegun nests, even though some of them will die, because otherwise the machine gun will kill them all as they flee. Aggression in combat puts the other side on the defensive, confuses them, demoralizes them, and ultimately routs them.

Along with aggression is a related mind state called *target-acquisition fixation*. Target-acquisition fixation occurs when the brain focuses on a target to the exclusion of everything else. This phenomenon, which has a unique brain signature as demonstrated in advanced brain scans, is another example of a survival mechanism from humanity's past. To the hunter stalking an animal and needing every sense, nerve, and muscle coordinated on the effort to kill the prey, target-acquisition fixation is indispensable. In a modern nonlethal parallel, athletes express the sensation of being in "the zone," when they are so focused on the game that all movement seems to slow down, they can thread through the defenses, and all of their shots hit the goal. That's target-acquisition fixation.

At times, however, target-acquisition fixation can have deadly results. Aggressive behavior coupled with target-acquisition behavior can lead hunters into dangerous terrain or soldiers into an ambush. This phenomenon has killed many pilots who have crashed while focusing exclusively on the target they are trying to shoot down. Perhaps the most tragic example of target-acquisition fixation was the crash of the entire Thunderbirds aerobatic team in 1982, killing all four pilots and destroying all four high-performance jets. The Thunderbirds fly complicated routines at air shows and other events to promote the U.S. Air Force and aviation. To perform these demonstrations safely, every pilot in the formation must remain in exactly the same position relative to the next plane and often no more than a few feet away. When the leader performs a particular maneuver, such as a loop, the other pilots maintain their relative position so that all the aircraft move in ballet-like unison. Keeping such close spacing in fighter planes requires intense concentration. On this day, the leader's plane suffered a mechanical malfunction and plunged earthward. True to their training, the three other pilots followed, retaining their tight spacing to the very end: so fixated on remaining in formation that they did not recognize that they were hurtling to their deaths.In business, aggressiveness creates a target-acquisition fixation that is equally maladaptive.

This chapter explores the dangers to businesspeople and organizations that stem from hyper-aggression and target fixation. That a competitive instinct may cause trouble could seem counter to common sense, because a push-push-push attitude is so common in business and a focus on priorities so necessary. Many of the best executives are able to bring intense focus to problems and opportunities. However, driven by fear and the emotional brain, target-acquisition fixation can create tunnel vision on business issues just as it can on spatial awareness.

Target-acquisition fixation creates three specific kinds of mental modes that lead to failure. The first maladaptive mode is the Cain-and-Abel conflict, in which people within a company become so fearful that they target other individuals or groups within the company as the "enemy." The second mode is a misguided reliance on problem solving, which is downward looking and backward thinking. The third is hyper-competitiveness, which defines business in terms of the opposition rather than in terms of your own company's vision. Internal conflict is most obviously destructive, but the other two behaviors have equally devastating consequences.

Cain and Abel: The Worst Story Ever Told

Maladaptive, fear-based responses can manifest themselves in any number of other ways within a corporate domain. By far, the most common and most deleterious form of fear is fighting. Sometimes it can occur in petty ways on a personal level. At one company, a usually positive employee occasionally undercut morale with biting gossip about others at work. Observant colleagues soon recognized that her wicked tongue was activated whenever she had had a fight with her husband at home. Fearful for her marriage, she would respond by putting down others at work. (One fear-based quirk of human nature is that we often attempt to elevate ourselves by *putting down* someone else; this is literally the posture that alpha canines assume with subordinate pack mates.) Her friends at work counseled her, and the gossip ceased.

Other times the fighting can be a form of guerrilla warfare. Just about every company has one or two people who whine and complain, who have a negative take on every situation, and who generally serve as "downers" to corporate morale. One executive speaks of being careful not to hire people with "clouds over their heads." Their passive-aggressive behavior comes from not seeing themselves as powerful enough to take on others in a frontal attack. They "leak" fear by their chronic negativity; they "backstab" others (a cogent idiom) when they think they can get away with it.

Most corporate infighting involves, on the surface, a professional issue, but the emotional brain perceives the issue as personal. This might occur when someone attacks a colleague who offers an idea that runs counter to the first person's pet project. The attacker fears embarrassment, a loss of power or prestige, or possibly the loss of position. Such incidents are the seeds for the Cain-and-Abel conflicts that occur far too commonly in many companies. The biblical story of Cain and Abel ends with one brother killing the other in a fit of jealousy and a desire to be "number one" in God's eyes.

A common Cain-and-Abel scenario involves sales and manufacturing. If production under-produces and the sales personnel have too little to sell or cannot deliver product on time to their customers, the future relationship with customers, and the sales team's financial well-being, are jeopardized. If production out-produces the ability of the salespeople to sell, inventory builds up, implying that the sales team cannot do their job and raising the risk of reduced work hours in the production department going forward. If GM makes too many vehicles, the end-of-year sale or the "employee discount sale" not only reduces profits for this year, but also bites into the projected sales for the following year. A disconnect between sales and production that leads to heavy discounting and big ups and downs in production can increase the conflict, as occurred with the southern manufacturer introduced earlier. You can rightly assume that the quarterly rush orders triggered huge fights between the sales team trying to make their numbers and the production team trying to fabricate products on time and budget.

Other times this destructive interaction occurs between individuals within a department or two corporate departments that are peers. At one small company, two founders were highly competitive with each other, criticized and undercut each other, led their cliques in power struggles, and eventually blamed each other when the company went under. One vice president at a major company was a fierce competitor who led a successful yearlong battle with another major company. His product *crushed* the competition. But when no more external foes were left to vanquish, his competitive zeal turned against other groups within his own company. Anyone who had a product or technology related to his department's, he tried to either absorb or discredit. Unfortunately for him, he went to battle one time too often, against another senior leader who had superior technical credentials and equal business success. Forced to make a decision, the company went with the other executive for its long-term strategy, and Mr. Competition departed the scene. Cain-and-Abel conflicts at Disney have involved so many people it is hard to keep the participants straight without a program: Eisner, Katzenberg, Ovitz, and others.

Mergers and acquisitions can create serious Cain-and-Abel conflicts. The dynamic occurred at Enron between the old guard who were schooled in tangible assets and the regulatory environment and the young Turks cultivated by Jeffrey Skilling who took the company into intangible assets and an unregulated environment. When the Hershey Company expanded into nonconfectionary lines and into international markets, a number of existing managers and employees at corporate headquarters could not shake their local and culinary biases. Instead of welcoming new talent and new ideas from other countries, the entrenched employees saw all the changes as a threat. Many people finally lost their jobs, not because of "foreigners," but because of their circle-the-wagons attitudes that excluded outsiders. When Wells Fargo bought First Interstate, the internal conflict led to 40 percent turnover and dismal results for a decade. When First Bank Systems of Minnesota bought U.S. Bank in Oregon, the clash of cultures led to a hemorrhage of talent to local community banks and a loss of 10 percent market share in 5 years.

Historically speaking, the epitome of an adversarial Cain-and-Abel relationship is that of management and labor. Beginning in the late 1800s, workers in many industries developed unions and took part in strikes in response to poor work conditions and low wages. Sporadic violence occurred in a variety of industries. Some of the worst pitted West Virginia coal miners against owners in a series of strikes that lasted a decade and led to violence that killed dozens of people on both sides. The war culminated in a four-day pitched battle in 1921 that did not end until federal troops arrived, siding with the owners.

Fear drove both groups. Labor feared the dangerous work conditions and the near-starvation brought on by meager wages. Management feared that they would be forced out of business by paying higher wages and improving conditions when other owners did not. Similar fears are the root of every labor-management battle. Sometimes the issue is wages. More often today, management's fear is not being able to compete against international competition because of high costs or inflexible work practices, whereas labor's fear is the loss of hard-won benefits and the loss of jobs to nonunion companies or to workers in other countries. Yet labor and management are on the same team. Management alone could not create, produce, and ship products. Without capital, strategic planning, innovative product ideas, marketing, or the other benefits of management, labor would have no merchandise to produce or markets to sell to. Management and labor can work together constructively, if they use their executive brains instead of their emotional brains. Later examples show how management and labor have cooperated to the benefit of both.

The Problem with Problem Solving

Humans pride themselves on problem solving, and rightfully so. When most of the threats to your survival are immediate, problem solving comes in handy. Until recently, most of the issues facing humans were problems; that is, negatives to be neutralized rather than positives to be pursued. In a sense, our emotional brain is programmed to look for and address problems. It was only because our ancestors were able to detect and anticipate dangerous problems that our DNA survived and humanity exists at all. When the world is out to get you, even the paranoid have genuine reasons to be afraid.

The residual of leading from fear has left its mark. As a species, we remain extremely problem-oriented creatures. Think about it. You can drive for days on end and never notice the skillful, courteous drivers who signal their turns and let you merge safely into traffic. But you immediately notice the risky driver who recklessly changes lanes and cuts you off. The risky driver puts you in peril. Having a brain wired to look for peril means that you can be within a heartbeat of succumbing to road rage. The horror, sex, and violence of many popular television shows and movies are enticing because they titillate the emotional brain. "Good news" programs die off quickly for lack of audience. Without conflict or danger, most humans have a hard time paying attention. A show such as *The Sopranos* provides double stimulation to the emotional brain, from the danger this gang poses to outsiders and from the conflict caused by the unstable personalities within the social group. The show offers all kinds of vicarious problems, all of them threatening. In fact, *The Sopranos* offers many lessons on the dangers of problem solving. All of the major characters end up in conflicts because they frantically seek to solve the next, immediate problem brought about by their current behavior. They become quite adept at making their way through the next part of the maze, but they never get out of the maze itself—a maze of their own construction, by the way. None of them ever examines the underlying cause for their biggest issues, the fact that they are in a violent, despicable profession. None of them seeks an "out-of-the-box" solution, such as leaving the profession, although it's a standing joke that any character who disappears has joined the witness protection program.

Strangely enough for those who pride themselves on problem solving, problem solving is another form of aggression that creates a certain kind of target fixation. One CEO used to correct executives who said they would "address" problems. He insisted that they "attack" problems. The psyche quickly begins to view the world strictly through the problem lens, leading to a negative view. That focus quickly shifts the mind into a fear state, and problem solving soon causes more problems than it fixes. A typical meeting focused on problems almost inevitably shifts to blame. With blame being assigned, individuals become defensive. They clam up, they point fingers, they look for scapegoats. Seldom does a "problem" meeting provide constructive results; it tends to reinforce whatever negative behavior already exists in the group.

Despite these shortcomings, problem solving remains the default mode in business. It's what businesses have always done. Within organizations, employees develop reputations tantamount to Michael Jordan or Tiger Woods because of their stellar problem-solving ability. A multi-billion-dollar industry of problem-solving consulting services has arisen to meet the need of fear-based organizations. Yet few companies recognize that problem solving is a negative rather than a positive attribute. It looks for the negative (what is wrong) rather than the positive (what is right). The aggression at its core makes it usually tactical rather than strategic, short term rather than long term, focused on what has happened instead of what is to come—tantamount to racing in the Indianapolis 500 while only looking out the rear-view window—and it invariably degrades into a number of fear-based behaviors. The problem with problem solving is that it diverts a company from opportunities, focuses on the past, promotes conflict, and drains precious energy from the organization (see Table 5-1).

Problem solving has its uses, as we will show. However, one of the most important ways for businesses to achieve greater results is to shift from problem solving to opportunity seeking. Too many people assume that if they fix a wrong they achieve a right. Most often this is not the case. The mindset comes from the medical profession, which for most of our technological age has defined health as the absence of disease. Physicians have only recently begun to understand that absence of disease is just one aspect of health. Real health is having a robust, full life in which you develop your potential. Many people with wasting diseases, serious physical handicaps, or even fatal illnesses take every opportunity that life affords them to grow intellectually, ethically, and socially; whereas many other people who have healthy bodies may live longer and in less physical pain but they live shallow, unfulfilled lives as couch potatoes or misanthropes. Which are the healthier human beings?

Problem solving is alluring because it offers immediate relief from the stress of worry and fear. As a result of instant gratification, problem solving begets more problem solving. When you look for problems, you will inevitably find problems. And when they are found, they are often bigger, "badder," and more numerous than

Problem Solving	Opportunity Seeking
Tactical	Strategic
Near term	Long term
Narrow definition of problem	Broad definition of opportunity
Reactive/negative	Proactive/positive
Easily slides into fear	Moves to higher consciousness
Promotes conflict	Promotes cooperation
Works best with one cause	Works with multiple causes
Looks backward	Looks forward
Tends to find symptoms	Reveals underlying reality

Table 5-1   The Problem with Problem Solving

anyone suspected. But seeing them as problems invariably blinds us to opportunity. Several decades ago, in a wonderful book titled *Life Gain*, Bob Allen tells the story of the poison well. In this story, the village well, the only source of water for miles around, becomes poisoned. Many villagers become ill and die. Recognizing the problem, the villagers become highly skilled in treating the sick; they invest huge sums of money for treatment centers and research to cure the disease. But no one ever thinks of cleaning up the contaminated water or of finding a new source of clean water. In addition to being a telling parable about modern medicine's efforts to cure rather than prevent disease, it is also the parable of a society too focused on solving a problem to see the opportunity for a new way of thinking about the world.

The classic example of misdirected problem solving is the business that spends a fortune improving its customer service without ever asking why its products are so hard to use. Other examples are more subtle but equally misguided. A product company once spent a solid year agonizing over the problem of getting its customers to upgrade to its latest and most expensive product line. The lack of upgrade revenue created tremendous conflict within the company. Technical staff blamed the sales and marketing teams for not knowing how to sell the new product. Sales and marketing blamed the technical staff for not making the upgrade easier. The company made product changes, provided tools to make the transition easier, came up with various marketing programs, and increased sales training, to little avail.

Finally, a new employee scanned through the customer files and realized that most of the company's customers were schools and government agencies. There were no problems inherent with the new product or with the upgrade itself, he realized. However, the new product was twice the price of the old product. The customers didn't have the money. No amount of tinkering with the new product would solve that problem. The fear-driven company had assumed that the dearth of upgrades implied a problem with the capability of the sales team, the difficulty of the upgrade process, or elements of the new product itself. The company had reacted immediately to solve those perceived issues. The company did not see the underlying issue, which had nothing to do with the product but with the nature of the customer. Because they saw and reacted to a symptom, not the cause, the company lost a solid year in which it could have been designing a slimmed-down and less expensive product for its current customers or a new product line for a different customer segment that had the means to pay for it.

Such a scenario is not uncommon. Often, by the time the problem analysis is done and the problem solution is formulated and delivered, the situation has changed so much that the solution is obsolete or irrelevant. In the previous case, the solution was irrelevant from the start, but the problem "solving" created an even bigger issue. The conflict evoked blaming; and blaming evoked counter-blaming. After awhile, the exchange of blame salvos significantly impaired the productivity and social cohesion of the company, to the extent that efforts on future products suffered as well.

In total, problem solving created a huge opportunity cost.

Proponents of corporate reengineering talk about eliminating every part of a business process that does not directly benefit customers. This is consultant-speak for saying, "Find a new vision for how you can reach customers, and spend all of your time on those things." The approach is not about problem solving; it is about finding a new opportunity. This approach causes a good deal of the demoralizing, unproductive work within business to melt away, along with its associated problems. However, the anxiety-creating aspects of business often cause people to reflexively focus on the negative. If you want to learn how to throw or hit a baseball, or shoot a basketball, or hit a golf ball, you study the best players in the world to see what they do right. You do not study struggling minor leaguers to see what they do wrong. Yet businesses focus on the "losers" all the time, part of the problem-solving mentality. One company had a sales team with a huge disparity in results. The highest performer was doing $40 million in sales a year. Another salesperson was doing $20 million a year. The other three members of the team were doing $5 million in sales each. Management worked long and hard to try to "fix" these low performers. No one ever stopped to examine why the top performer could do two to eight times more than everyone else. Even assuming that the top performer had personal talents that could not be replicated, this individual had a number of repeatable, teachable practices that would have easily enabled the low performers to double or triple their sales.

In general, you are better off to study your three big "wins" to see all of the factors that led to success, and then replicate those, rather than to study the seven "losses" to see what you did wrong. You have only so much time to figure out business strategies. Companies that expend huge chunks of valuable time "fixing problems" have little time left over for the processes of constructive, creative, and inspired innovation. They never get to the power of possibilities. Battling the problems can quickly overwhelm you and your company and bring it to a grinding halt.

Bad News, or Good Communication?

You might wonder how to square this proposition with the point of view that many companies suffer because the culture does not allow unpleasant information to reach senior leadership, or senior leadership will not listen to the information when it arrives. Bill Gates has a personal dictum that "bad news must travel fast." Toyota and Wal-Mart make a practice of examining problem areas in great detail. Superficially, they all appear to have a problem-seeking mindset. If, for instance, you tell Gates what accounts you have won, he will ask about the accounts you *didn't* win.

At all three companies, such questions are intended to prime the pump. The underlying desire is to create open communications and instill learning. The primary thrust of the "bad news" dictum is to encourage people to say what they think at all levels in the company. If any employee believes that she can tell Gates anything, no matter how unpleasant, then open and honest lines of communication must prevail everywhere. That employee will not hesitate to tell anyone else, including her direct superiors, things that the company needs to know. Listening is one of the greatest attributes of inspired leadership, and the knowledge that the messenger will not be shot for bringing bad news is a good indicator of a healthy culture. In an individual, the executive brain cannot function correctly without good information from the other parts of the brain. In fact, many improper personal behaviors stem from disruptions of the brain's communication pathways. The same parallel exists with information flow in companies.

Second, a basic tenet of culture at Microsoft, Toyota, and Wal-Mart is the idea of constant improvement. Mistakes are not only accepted at Microsoft, they are expected. "I screwed up. How can I do better?" is a common attitude. After feedback from customers in the early 1990s that its big events were too technical and boring, the company launched a product called Windows for Workgroups with an event, in a New York City theater, structured as a Broadway musical. The song and dance numbers left customers baffled. Very little product information got through, especially to customers watching the event via video links. Complaints poured in. Salespeople felt that they had wasted their customers' time. After backbiting and second guessing within the company about the event and its cost, Gates sent out a broad e-mail that said, in so many words, "Better to have tried to do something interesting and failed than to do the same old event still one more time. It was a fiasco, sure. Now, learn from the mistakes we made and move on."

Microsoft does not focus really on wins or losses but on the learning—the "feedback loop" in company parlance—that every situation provides. Sam Walton instilled in his company the idea that whenever the company made a bad mistake the goal was to fix it and go on. "Work well, then better, then the best" was his attitude. Toyota's problem solving always has a positive flip. Like Microsoft's "bad news must travel fast," Toyota has an "obligatory negative" to find weaknesses in any process. But the goal is not to stop with negativity; rather, the obligatory negative becomes an obligatory opportunity to improve. "How can I do better?" is a question that creates opportunities, not threats. In a similar vein, a good salesperson knows to ask a customer, "What will it take to get your business?" rather than ask, "Why didn't we get your business last time?" One calls upon the listener to positive, expansive thought; the other leads to a negative, constricted view.

But few executives are able to hear negatives and turn them into positives. It is too easy for the fear reaction to be triggered and for everyone in the chain of command, from the CEO down, to begin to react negatively. Soon, the bad-news bearer *does* get shot, at least in the corporate context, and people quit speaking up. Feedback loops shut down. The company ceases to learn. The lesson, then, is that problem solving in itself is not "bad," any more than bad news is bad unless it triggers a negative response. However, problem solving brings with it a tendency to shape reality into a narrow funnel. In contrast, seeking opportunities is an energizing, mind-expanding approach. People are *looking outward*, not *drilling down*.

The Catastrophe of the Competitive Inverse

Hyper-competitiveness closely relates to aggressive problem solving. Everything the competitor does becomes a problem to be solved, immediately. Shifting the focus from the customer to the other company leads to the Catastrophe of the Competitive Inverse. In the dog-eat-dog world of the PC software industry, Borland, Lotus, and Microsoft competed ferociously in several different product categories. They fought each other separately, and as Microsoft's market position grew, the other two companies often joined together to try to stymie Microsoft. The focus on one another instead of the customer meant that if one company introduced a product with three new features, the competitor would counter with five. The press goaded them all on with product reviews featuring the number of new features rather than evaluations of whether the features were needed. In the rush to add new features, bug fixes were sometimes ignored, and customers ended up with 20 new features that they could not figure out how to use along with the same old bugs. The phenomenon was called "feature creep," but in actuality, it was a feature explosion.

A few years later, the same attack-counterattack mentality led Netscape and Microsoft to rush out version after version of Web browsers. "Internet speed" became the cry, with little appreciation for the fact that large customers could not absorb three or four versions of the new browsers in a single year. These classic fear-based reactions and counter-reactions are not surprising given the PC industry was run by young males eager to prove themselves. The business bible for most of these companies was a book titled *Marketing Warfare*, which described a variety of marketing strategies in terms of military maneuvers and conquest. The book was all the more intoxicating to its audience because none of these young bucks would have been caught dead near a military recruiting station.

In retrospect, the fierce competition served none of the companies particularly well. Lotus, which did not want to build products for Microsoft Windows for fear that Windows' success would make Microsoft more formidable, lost its leadership position in spreadsheets because Windows succeeded despite Lotus's foot-dragging. Borland's competitive zeal caused it to bleed itself to death against a better-funded company. Here's where the Catastrophe of the Competitive Inverse applies. Lotus and Borland wasted enormous energy trying to oppose Microsoft. By automatically doing the opposite of what Microsoft was doing, they were assuming that everything Microsoft wanted to do was wrong. Not only is this a poor assumption against a smart company, it also caused them to compete on Microsoft's terms instead of on their own strengths. *Companies that reflexively oppose a strong competitor will almost always lose.*

Microsoft's competitiveness enabled it to win the battle on the desktop and to do well in the server market, but its reputation for the relentless pursuit of victory—some said ruthless pursuit—ultimately led to strong negativity from the press, consumer concerns about its power, a federal antitrust action that was propelled as much by the fear of what it *might* do as by anything it had done, and other lawsuits and regulatory action that damaged its reputation. If these were not Pyrrhic victories, they certainly turned out a great deal different than Microsoft ever expected.

There being no "control," it is impossible to say how the different companies might have fared had they focused more on customers than on competitors, and had they focused more on new markets, an opportunity, than on trying to defend an old market, a variation of problem solving. "Protecting the turf," a reaction of the emotional brain to the sense of territorial imperative, is the most common reason for failure in the computer industry in its first 50 years. You wonder whether any of them would in retrospect do things differently.

One final but telling remark. Lotus likely would have gone out of business except that a group of former Lotus employees, seeking opportunity rather than solving problems, created an entirely new software product, Notes, around the concept of groupware. When Lotus took Notes under its wing, the company had a growth market and a product line for which Microsoft had no answer for several years. The success of Notes ultimately led to Lotus being acquired by IBM, which used it to provide a value-added product line to customers regardless of the system they used. To come full circle, in 2005 Microsoft brought aboard the developer of Notes and his company.

If it seems difficult to believe that fierce competitors might band together for the common good, history is replete with examples far more important than companies jostling for market power. When President Roosevelt instituted a draft before the outbreak of World War II, his election opponent, Wendell Wilkie, could have played upon the unpopularity of the draft to try to sway voters. But Wilkie recognized the danger to the United States of the looming war and the need to have an army in training. He supported Roosevelt, even at the possible cost of the election. Today, nations with different forms of government, with different views on the major issues confronting the world, and with differing economic needs and agendas, are nonetheless cooperating against terrorist activity and working to resolve environmental problems.

In business, the history of the Visa credit card offers similar lessons. Prior to Visa, some number of major banks had their own credit cards. Each bank viewed its card as a proprietary advantage, a way of locking customers into the bank and its services. Each bank perceived a threat if a single card became dominant and it was not theirs. Yet over time, a Seattle bank manager, Dee Hock, was able to convince major banks that the benefits of a single credit card more than outweighed the disadvantages. A single card would exponentially increase the ability of the banks to obtain acceptance by merchants nationally and internationally; a single underlying technical infrastructure would keep costs low. Rather than focus on the problem of potential competition among the members, Visa accepted and encouraged competition as the natural order. Banks cooperated on a narrow set of issues—the technical and legal issues required to create a standard—and competed on everything else. Cooperation grew the market.

After enough banks signed on, the enterprise reached critical mass, not only creating a new business for banks but transforming the world from a cash-and-check society to a credit-and-bank-card society. Ultimately, the executive brain at each major bank (in the form of the CEOs and the brain trust at each institution) overruled the emotional brain. Opportunity won over protectionism.

The Lows Created by Adrenaline Highs

Aggressiveness is often seen as a major positive for business, and problem solving has been the sacred cow of business for 400 years. As a result, many organizations have evolved their entire culture on the basis of adrenaline highs. "Vision" becomes constantly putting out fires, taking on crisis after crisis, knee-jerking to respond to whatever the competitor does. During the heated days of the PC wars, Apple, Ashton-Tate, Borland, Lotus, Microsoft, Novell, WordPerfect, and many others did exactly these things. PC hardware vendors fared little better in similar battles against each other. Focused on each other, they released products that were virtually interchangeable. This commoditization created a price war that Dell Computer won. Only one or possibly two companies will win in a market centered on competition. If it was not Microsoft, it would have been Lotus or Apple. If it was not Wal-Mart, it would have been Sears or Kmart. In contrast, multiple companies can win in an opportunity-centered environment. It makes no sense to fixate on your competition instead of your future. You greatly increase the chance of losing.

For all of Microsoft's competitive fervor, the company had one redeeming trait. While its competitors were largely focused on Microsoft, Microsoft always had its eye on a single long-term objective: to establish a graphical interface on personal computers. However aggressive it may have been, Microsoft never went down the rat hole of making decisions contrary to its strategy, as Borland did when it overpaid for the best-known (but failing) database product in an attempt to buy market share. Microsoft had more than testosterone. It had a vision. For much of this time, Apple struggled because of an inability to deliver practical products around its technology. As it became just a more expensive PC, it lost more and more market share. Upon the return of a greatly matured Steve Jobs as CEO, the company went back to its long-lost vision: make cool products that young people like to use. Apple's iPod and related digital products have created huge new growth *opportunities*.

Somewhere out there today is another company that has another vision that may unseat Microsoft. It could be IBM or Apple, learning from their previous mistakes, or an upstart such as Google using Internet-based services or creating new devices that obsolete PCs. The new company will not defeat the champ by going toe to toe with Microsoft on the company's own turf or by countering them or by incrementally improving what Microsoft offers. That company will win by following their vision and creating a world that Microsoft never saw coming. The new guys will not aggressively compete with the leader. By following opportunity, they will go where the leader ain't.

If it is hard to accept the idea that aggressive behavior and problem solving are inimical to business, if you still have any question about how both mis-channel the mind and the organization, try this exercise. Pull together a multidisciplinary group from your company and tell them that the company is facing a crisis. A competitor is making serious inroads. The company needs to make changes. You need to take aggressive action, *fast*. Tell them that you're aware to some degree of various problems within the company and want to fix them to compete more effectively. You want to demolish the competitor's inroads. (Notice how quickly problems become defined in terms of competitors!) Ask your team to identify the company's major problems and identify a set of solutions; order them to develop aggressive new approaches. Otherwise, serious cutbacks and layoffs will be in store.

Now, pull together another multidisciplinary team from your company and tell them that they have a major opportunity. Tell them the company is looking for new products and services and new markets. Tell them that the company is looking for new ideas, and the people who can come up with the best ideas will be part of the teams that implement them. Do not mention competitors at all. Do not use the word *aggressive*. Simply ask the team to identify the company's greatest opportunities.

You will be amazed at the difference in tone, content, enthusiasm, idea generation, and results between the two teams. Undoubtedly, the "problem" team will identify some important problems and may uncover some issues you want to address. They will certainly identify Cain-and-Abel conflicts! They may find some short-term solutions to specific competitive issues. However, you will invariably find that the discussions *funnel in* toward internal problems. Blame is likely to rear its ugly head. Much of the discussion will be couched in negative terms and phrases. Outward responses will be directed toward competitors and will tend to be reflexive: Whatever the competitor does, let's do the opposite. Or, "Let's do this to them" or "Let's do that to them." It would take a brilliant team (or team leader) to pull away from the black hole of problem-based negativity.

Equally undoubtedly, the "opportunity" team will identify new ways to do business, and possibly some entire new market areas. The discussions will *expand out*. Little time will be spent worrying about competitors, except as a stimulus for ideas. Ideas will leap past today's short-term problems. *The pursuit of opportunity will simply leave behind many of the problems identified by Team One.* Even if the ideas generated by Team Two turn out not to be practicable, the exercise will prove the point that an opportunity focus will create more potential points of success than problem solving will.

If you say that the two tasks are not exactly identical, that problem solving by definition will find a different set of issues than opportunity seeking, the response is: Absolutely! So why is the overwhelming number of your company's meetings, memos, e-mails, plans, and projects focused on problems instead of opportunities? Why do Cain and Abel try to undercut each other instead of working with each other in a way that enables both to succeed? Your culture is driving you toward negativity. Fear-based culture always does. Heisenberg's principle of uncertainty says that observation changes that which is observed. The same is true of inquiry. The questions you ask, positive or negative, shape your perception of the world and *change the reality you are trying to create*.

Therefore, your company culture needs to shape itself toward opportunity. Inquiries need to frame the potential goodness, not the existing badness. Every important business discussion should focus on the way to create new opportunities for your organization. After you have identified the opportunities, *use aggressiveness and problem solving to implement the practical details of the new vision*. In other words, channel the energies toward solutions. As the emotional mind must serve the executive mind, emotional behaviors such as aggression and problem solving need to serve opportunity. A real vision gives plenty of new, enjoyable work for everyone. People no longer have to attack each other to hold their positions.

The Land of Opportunity, Not Problems

"It's not a problem, it's an opportunity." It is easy for all of us to parrot this phrase when we are not the one overwhelmed with problems, and that is why businesspeople often use the comment ironically. "Sales down 10 percent? It's not a problem, it's an opportunity!" But this phrase misdirects us, presuming as it does that the opposite of a problem is an opportunity, that they are the flip sides of the same coin. Sometimes they are. After World War II, Toyota did not have the resources or the potential market to construct a huge American-style vehicle production line. The company developed a small, flexible system that enabled it to build a number of different models quickly. This system became the basis of its future success. Because its first stores were in such rural areas and were so far apart, Wal-Mart could not interest traditional retail distributors in delivering products. Wal-Mart turned the weakness into strength by building its own distribution system, which became the envy of the industry.

By and large, however, eliminating a negative does not create a positive. The opposite of a problem is a zero, not an opportunity. Digging yourself out of a hole does not launch you toward the stars. Fixing a bug does not create a feature. Solving a distribution problem does not create a new product. Improving customer service does not make a product easy to use. Rationalizing product mix does not create a new market. In general, problems and opportunities are unconnected except as our emotional brains seek to twist everything to a problem, because that is how we are wired to perceive the universe. Problem solving is necessary for survival, but it is not sufficient for business prosperity. In fact, it is often a non sequitur in relation to prosperity. The most positive thing about problem solving is that if you solve the most critical short-term problems, you free up time to apply toward opportunities. The danger is that the problem-solving mindset will send you off on more firefighting rather than on generating fresh ideas. To put it another way, business consultant Jim Collins says that managing your problems will make you good, but building on your opportunities is the only way to become great.

Organizations function a good deal like the human brain, with each person in the group functioning as a part. As a human brain repeats behaviors, the behaviors become ingrained. Neurons become connected in ever-tighter bonds that become easier to invoke. So too habits of thought and deed are ingrained in an organization. Culturally, negative thoughts, emotions, and behaviors become easier to repeat over time. They activate the fear centers of the brain of each person. Collectively, the group begins to react in fearful ways. Behaviors become reinforced and habituated. In contrast, positive thoughts, emotions, behaviors, and particularly positive *words* have the opposite effect. Positivism activates the creative centers in the brain. Collectively, the group begins to think and act in creative ways. Positive actions become reinforced and habituated. The best example might be what happens when groups of differing religious views get together. Religion is one of the most emotional topics possible. If the question posed between two religious groups is "How can we solve our differences?" the groups invariably slide into conflict. If the question posed is "What is the best of your belief as it relates to my religion?" then religious groups find common ground and become closer. The same dynamic occurs with negative and positive attitudes on any topic, in any organization.

"Seek and ye shall find" is the motto with problems, but finding and solving problems may have little to do with your company's future, except that a focus on problems may dim that future. Aggressive response focused on a competitor rather than aggressive proactivity to achieve a future can create similar liabilities. As a fear response, aggression creates a tunnel vision of the mind as well as of the eye, often leading to poor decision making. Consider the aggressive but mindless assaults on fixed positions in World War I that led to the highest casualties in individual battles the world has ever seen. Compare this approach with MacArthur's island hopping in the Pacific in World War II. He did not attack every military target. He pored over maps to figure out which islands were the most strategic and attacked only those. He achieved the greatest success with the fewest casualties in that war by ignoring conventional wisdom, looking beyond problems. He established a vision of what he wanted to attain, the islands that would give the United States strategic superiority, and directed all of his energies toward obtaining those objectives.

To quote a Scandinavian proverb, "You cannot make yourself taller by cutting off the other fellow's head." Yet such behavior is so common in business that Cain-and-Abel conflicts become the default in some companies. If you were to pause for a moment, you could probably identify several such situations within your own organization, whether it is a business, a nonprofit, or an academic group. A closer look would show that the conflicts stem from a combination of fear and problem solving, which leads to finger-pointing, blame, and jealousy. Another way to look at it is this: Anyone with the time to undercut, backstab, and poach on others does not have enough constructive work to do. As Grandma would say, idle hands are the devil's workshop. Give people an exciting vision with many growth opportunities, and they will be too busy doing happy work to seek out and destroy others. The rare individuals who cannot personally reset their attitude in a positive environment need to "leave to pursue other opportunities."

Although useful in an emergency, aggression and problem solving over time can impair an organization's ability to perceive its potential and to act on it. Problem solving is at best an antiquated approach to business. Most of the things that companies face are hassles, setbacks, disappointments, and frustrations. They will not take our life, but because we are hardwired for hard times, we frequently respond as if they will. Our emotional brain is quite comfortable with this response, because our emotional self craves instant gratification. Aggression, problem solving and hyper-competitiveness all lead to target acquisition behavior, which is a fear-driven reaction to the world. It takes higher-order consciousness to seek and find opportunity. By biological imperative, creativity and innovation cannot lead the mind at the same time as fear. Staying focused on opportunities is the way to ensure that the executive brain, not the emotional brain, remains in charge of your company's future.

6

The Lesson of the Salmon, or Why Happiness Beats Going Belly Up

As the previous chapters document, maladaptive behaviors create terrible costs for companies. Careers die, jobs go away, companies falter or fail, health and retirement accounts founder, and billions of dollars in investments wash away. These real and palpable harms occur not just in the relatively few organizations in which maladaptive behavior becomes outright criminal behavior. Many, many more companies suffer the same maladaptive behaviors to a lesser extent, and yet the damage to the organization, to its people, and to its public standing can be considerable.

Cultural as well as personality clashes caused serious problems at DaimlerChrysler, especially after German CEO Jürgen Schrempp admitted that he had used the phrase "merger of equals" to lure the Americans into the deal. Unhappiness on both sides of the ocean, particularly after the American division outperformed the organization's flagship Mercedes line, ultimately led to Schrempp's departure. The Cain-and-Abel dispute between CEO Philip Purcell and President John Mack at Morgan Stanley led to alternating waves of departures as first one executive and then the other got the upper hand. In the last go-round, Mack returned as CEO for $25 million a year and Purcell left as CEO with $113 million in severance pay, along with co-president Stephen Crawford, who signed a guaranteed $32 million two-year contract and departed two days later. It is hard to believe that the company's upper management and board spent much time in those two years thinking about such trivial matters as customers or the company's future, which is perhaps why the company's performance and stock price tanked.

During such times of conflict, stress rampages through an organization, creating damage that is often invisible in the short term. Not all stress is negative, of course. "Good" stress, commonly dubbed *eustress*, comes in the form of challenges that invite individuals and organizations to grow, to develop ever-greater potential, and to become smarter, wiser, and more effective in adaptation. Mental calculations of various kinds, for instance, reduce rather than increase stress hormones in the brain. If Morgan Stanley's leadership had been working together on new investment programs for customers instead of fighting for control of the company, they would have experienced eustress. The difference between good and bad stress has to do with whether the *stressee* has a reasonable chance of prevailing in the circumstances.

Such internal conflicts and the allied stress lead to regular breakups of partnership-based companies, where people easily fall into scarcity states and concentrate more on their privileges and prestige than on future opportunities. The ultimate corporate sibling rivalry was Arthur Andersen and what became Accenture. When the newer consulting side began to do more business than the older accounting side, the consultants (who became Accenture) wanted a bigger share of the profits. The accountants (the original Arthur Andersen) felt that the consultants were greedy and failed to appreciate the start that Arthur Andersen had given them in terms of brand, infrastructure, support, and marketing. The groups had legitimate issues to work through, such as the accounting side's move into consulting projects when they naturally fell out of accounting work.

Instead of revealing new ways to think about the future, however, the differences led to a territorial dispute, and negotiations focused on the differences between the groups rather than on what they shared in common. A split may have been inevitable, but it did not have to be acrimonious. The old Arthur Andersen could have treated the situation as an opportunity for a healthy spin-off, providing seed money in exchange for technology that the consultants would develop, referrals for accounting opportunities, and even small consulting gigs that Accenture would otherwise pass on. The group that became Accenture could have been more amenable to finding a solution that worked for both parties, including giving Andersen the right of first refusal on projects Accenture did not want.

The divorce weakened Arthur Andersen not just by removing its fastest-growing segment but by demotivating the leadership and letting fear and anger permeate the organization. It is little wonder that a few years later, feeling compelled to win, Arthur Andersen sold its soul to the devil in its dealings with Enron. The company was afraid that blowing the whistle on Enron would cost them not only that huge business, but other clients who might think that they were too zealous. In a fear state, Arthur Andersen assumed that their honest clients would react with the same kind of fear instead of appreciating an accounting firm that actually did its job.

Imagine the physical and psychic stress that senior partners at Arthur Andersen suffered in the half dozen years in which the company first dealt with its unhappy consultants, then with its unwholesome client Enron, and then with the federal investigation, the flight of employees and clients, and the company's ultimate collapse. Or imagine the stress on the sales manager at the unhappy manufacturing company introduced in Chapter 1 during the days when higher-ups were pressing for more and more "creative" ways to generate sales out of thin air, whether it was giving kickbacks to distributors or keeping the books open for a few more days after the month's close to snare a little more revenue.

In addition to the corporate and social costs, the damage to individual humans from such stress is real and costly. It does not take outright criminality to create unhealthy levels of stress. Far more companies suffer from the "stress flu" of normal fear-based business behavior than ever suffer from the cancer of criminality. Imagine the frustration that built up during the chronic friction at Daimler-Chrysler. Imagine the wasted time and energy during the highs and lows of each clique, the gossip, the rumors, all the negativity that ate away at hundreds of employees at Morgan Stanley during the intrigue and clashes. Before moving on to a description of happy companies, therefore, it is necessary to document the costs to people and to business of running an unhappy business. Such outcomes of unhappy behavior are pervasive but not widely recognized, even though they are the primary reason for the astronomical health costs that businesses face.

Mind, Body Look to Fear First

In all business stress situations—whether it is the extreme example of the boss insisting on creative accounting to cover a financial shortfall, or the more common situations of saddling you with an unrealistic deadline or undermining your authority in some way—your mind and body kick into overdrive to protect you from danger. The sensory input feeds into the amygdala, the almond-shaped area of the brain that functions as the repository of emotional memory. If the amygdala matches the incoming data with anything dangerous that has occurred before, the match triggers an instant fight-or-flight response—unless the data is so overwhelming that it triggers the "freeze" reaction instead. When our ancestors observed the grass moving 100 feet ahead of them on the savannah of Africa tens of thousands of years ago, the amygdala would instantly associate that movement with a lion attack that had occurred before, giving our ancestors a few seconds' notice that could mean the difference between life and death. In a primordial setting, the amygdala was as close to an insurance policy against danger as humans could get.

Our biological early-warning system works exactly the same in a modern office setting as it did with our ancestors on the high plains. In the office, the danger is the risk to your job if you don't comply, the fear of being caught if you do, and the conflict between the request and your own ethical values. The amygdala messages a "danger!" signal to the hypothalamus on the underside of the brain. The hypothalamus, which controls involuntary functions, hits the panic button. It alerts the nearby pituitary gland, the master controller for most of the endocrine system, and the adrenal glands on top of the kidneys. Within milliseconds, hormones surge through the body. The adrenal glands release adrenaline first. If the danger does not immediately pass, cortisol is next.

In all, this cascade of hormones causes roughly 1,440 biochemical changes to occur, all geared to pump oxygen-rich blood to the brain and muscles and otherwise ready you for menace. Adrenaline, for instance, increases heart rate. Norepinephrine increases respiration and raises the blood-sugar level to provide energy for muscles. Breathing becomes rapid and shallow, and muscles become flexed (anaerobic muscle posturing for maximum physical strength).

As the sympathetic part of the autonomic nervous system spools up to address the threat, the parasympathetic part, which regulates all the other life-sustaining functions, spools down. Blood circulation slows to noncritical areas, such as the digestive tract, the immune system, and the reproductive system. Peripheral arteries also constrict. That's why people often experience cold hands before they speak in front of a crowd; nervousness sends the blood to the core of the body. It is a vascular circling of the wagons. The peripheral vessels are the ones most likely to be injured during combat. Smaller vessels mean smaller openings from which to bleed. The combination of increased cardiac output and constriction of the arterial system elevates blood pressure, much as the combination of an open spigot and a restricted nozzle increases the water pressure in a hose. In acute situations, cortisol coats blood platelets, making them sticky and serving as a natural coagulant to help stop bleeding.

We do not need an actual physical threat to have this stress reaction. The body does not question the commands that come from the brain. If the brain tells the body it is under siege, the body cannot know that the perceived danger may be an abstraction, misperception, exaggeration, or downright distortion. The body cannot know that the danger is nonphysical, such as a loss of status or a poor performance review. A dutiful soldier, the body obeys the call to scramble, no questions asked. The worst stressors for businesspeople are the double-bind situations, in which no matter what you do, you're "doomed." For example, if the boss gives you an order that you know other employees will not like, your body will respond as if you are physically cornered, under the knowledge that you face certain conflict with the boss or the others no matter what you do.

Although the example of fraud or other criminal activity is a rare, extreme-stress incident, *any kind* of workplace stress, if part of the usual routine, can create a habituated response. This is especially true

Emotional Assessment: Two Pathways

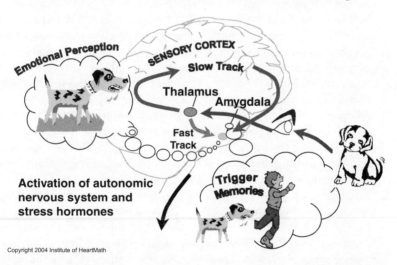

Copyright 2004 Institute of HeartMath

Figure 6-1   Humans have emotional as well as cognitive memories, and the brain is wired to respond faster to emotional than cognitive stimulus. If the amygdala connects a new stimulus to a past threat, the amygdala bypasses the rationale centers in the brain so that the person can respond instantly in threat situations. However, the brain's emotional wiring can lead to illogical, reactive, or over-reactive responses in less dangerous circumstances, whether it perceives a harmless puppy as a dangerous animal or a business situation as an actual life or death matter.

if the trigger is pulled one or more times a day. In a physical situation, the body releases its powerful chemicals through action. Physical release exhausts the buildup of hormones, and the parasympathetic system cycles the body into a natural restorative mode. The need for physical relief is why exercise is a good outlet for stress. The need for physical relief is also why you will often find yourself physically shaking after barely avoiding a dangerous situation such as a high-speed accident. Primed for action that did not occur, the muscles quiver. The need for physical relief to stress is also why, during confrontations, men often yell and women often cry (although the reactions are by no means strictly gender-based).

Without a physical release, the body struggles to "come down." The hormones break down slowly. It takes a while for the unconscious functions such as heart rate and respiration to return to normal. While still agitated, you can easily kick back into total-stress mode and go through the entire sequence again—just as if you had to run for your life again after a brief pause on the plains.

With stress-related hormones pumping constantly, stress at work increases the stress level for a person at home, and stress at home makes things worse at the office. Just as having too much caffeine before going to sleep can cause a restless night that requires more caffeine for proper functioning the next day, elevated levels of stress hormones cause us to sleep fitfully, and the lack of sleep causes us to generate more stress hormones to get through the succeeding day at work and at home. The third battlefront becomes the mind, the individual's worry, depression, or even self-loathing for living an out-of-balance life. In a constant state of siege, keyed up from the unrelieved stress, we tend to play and replay the unhappy events over in our head, causing the body to react again and again. Before long, we are addicted to the adrenaline-cortisol rush. The morning alarm causes our stomachs to knot up or our heartbeat to jump several notches. We function on a powerful and self-reinforcing buzz. Even getting to work or to appointments creates a high-stress state. Stressed-out types habitually leave themselves less time than they need. Cutting things close provides still another excuse to kick into an adrenaline high.

Some people try to flee from the stress through alcohol or other drugs, or through an occasional fling or other risky behaviors. Under stress, they rationalize that they deserve relief, in whatever expedient form it takes. Others keep stress bottled in. A few people "blow" regularly, but venting does not relieve the pressure. The immediate return to the chronic, heightened state of alert overrides any momentary relief.

All of these physiological reactions are intended to save life in the next few minutes, but they are dangerous if the stress of life and work forces them to work overtime. Under constant reinforcement, the body's life-preserving system becomes stuck in the "on" position, as vigilant as a guard in a war zone. As the fear reaction becomes habituated, it becomes easier and easier to kick into react mode and more and more difficult to avoid it or to come down from it. This is a physiological problem as well as a psychological one. For example, when cortisol levels become too high, the hippocampus tells the hypothalamus to cut back cortisol production. However, cortisol itself can damage the hippocampus, the mechanism that keeps its production in check. As a result, the longer you are stressed out, the less functional the hippocampus becomes, and the more likely it is that you will become even more stressed out.

This is not the only problem with adrenaline, cortisol, and other stress hormones. There are documented cases both in the laboratory and in life in which excess adrenaline dissolves the heart muscle. Cortisol's sticky nature helps reduce bleeding in the short term, but the stickiness of blood platelets may play a role in plaque build-up within blood vessels. Adrenaline and cortisol help the brain form fear-related memories, but they prevent the brain from laying down new *nonfear* memories or from retrieving existing ones. This is a great adaptation to the wild but a terrible one for the marketplace, where businesspeople succeed by developing new ideas and concepts.

Although these hormones alter the short-term function of cells and tissues in a usually beneficial way, they also alter the long-term function, including the expression of genes within the cells, in a usually detrimental way. By damaging the hippocampus, excess cortisol can lead to premature aging and Alzheimer's. High concentrations of adrenal steroids increase insulin resistance, producing adult-onset diabetes (Type II). An increase in stress hormones inhibits the number of cytokines, which warn the body of the presence of viruses so that cells can mobilize defenses. This and other long-term dampening effects on the immune system open the body to many illnesses, including cancer. In addition, people who become burned out or depressed suffer from emergency-response systems that have become exhausted from stress. Because these people release too *few* stress hormones, the immune system itself can become hyperactive, increasing the risk of autoimmune and inflammatory disorders. Finally, stress hormones alter the functioning of the blood-brain barrier, enabling toxic chemicals to penetrate the natural protective shield that otherwise would isolate the brain from harmful substances in the bloodstream.

How Do I Kill Thee? Let Me Count the Ways

It is generally understood that stress can kill, but few people realize that stress kills more than Type A executives or workers in high-stress fields such as emergency services. A summary of some of the different studies around the world provides shocking numbers:

- U.S. patients with stress-related ischemia, a lack of blood flow to the heart, were 2.8 times more likely to die than other patients over a 5-year period. More than half of the patients experienced narrowing in at least one major coronary artery or suffered a previous heart attack because of stress.

- Japanese women who reported high levels of mental stress had double the risk for stroke-related and heart-related deaths than those reporting low stress levels.

- Finnish men who were highly reactive to stress had a 72 percent greater risk of strokes and 87 percent greater risk of ischemic strokes than men with less reaction.

- 36 percent of middle-aged U.S. utility workers in high-stress jobs had plaque buildup in their carotid arteries, compared to 21 percent of the men in low-stress jobs.

- French researchers reported that sustained anxiety was associated with an increase in the thickness of blood vessels for both men and women, a prelude to heart disease.

- At one company, a 3-year study indicated that stress was the cause of 60 percent of absenteeism, and stress-related accidents were more serious, requiring four times as long for recovery as those caused by other factors.

- Work-related stress is one of the principal causes of death from heart and lung disease, alcoholism and cirrhosis of the liver, cancer, accidents, and suicides.

- A survey of U.S. federal employees said that 42 percent of all female and 15 percent of all males were bullied within a 2-year period. Another study says that half of all workers report losing time at work as the result of being subjected to rude behavior.

- Stress often spills over into violence. An average of 20 workers are murdered, usually by co-workers, and 18,000 workers are assaulted *per week* in the United States: more than a thousand deaths and nearly a million workplace assaults a year! Violence in the workplace is the second-leading cause of work-related death.

Best documented and best understood of all the impacts of stress is the combination of high blood pressure and constricted arteries that greatly increases the risks of heart attacks or strokes. Sudden cardiac death happens at least 250,000 times per year, many of those deaths occurring at work and many more the result of work-related stress. Heart-related disease causes a total of 500,000 deaths and year, and more than 170,000 fatalities result annually from strokes. Results of all the damage just described vary by survey, and new numbers seem to emerge almost weekly.

Although they may not realize the health implications, people at work are acutely aware of stress. A Northwestern National Life survey says that 40 percent of workers report that their job is very or extremely stressful and that 25 percent of employees view their jobs as the top stressor in their lives. Studies by a variety of organizations including the Families and Work Institute, Yale University, the University of Chicago, and the HeartMath institute put the number of burned-out, stressed-out, or chronically stressed individuals at between one fourth and one third of the work force. Further, Heart-Math and the *New York Times* say more than 50 percent of employees feel overwhelmed by their workloads, and the *Times* said that the workload of 62 percent of employees had increased in the last six months of 2004. A Princeton survey says that three fourths of all employees believe that their jobs are more stressful than a generation ago. Another study by the Conference Board concludes that only half of Americans today say they are satisfied with their jobs, down 10 percent since 1995. Among those who say they are content, only 14 percent say they are very satisfied. St. Paul Fire and Marine Insurance says that problems at work are more strongly associated with health complaints than any other factor in people's lives, even financial or family problems.

The paradox becomes evident. The biological systems that saved us in a primordial world—and that can save us in a life-threatening situation now—can turn against us in the workaday world of the highly stressed business office.

Stressed-Out Organizations, a.k.a. Unhappy Companies

Until recently, to conceptualize any organization as happy or unhappy was outside of mainstream business thought. After all, businesses are legal constructs run for profit. Business decisions and personnel reviews are all supposed to be considered objectively. How does happiness enter into the financial equation? However, as we have seen, humans are physiologically and psychologically incapable of being "objective." Nor should they ever want to be. Although negative emotions hamper business thinking, positive emotion supports cognitive processes and therefore smart business thinking. The assumption that emotion is not central to business interaction, however, means that no one is looking for it. As a result, emotion runs riot. In too many companies, however, it is *negative* emotion. Considerable attention ends up devoted to such topics as bad bosses, poor employees, lousy communication, chronic conflict, high-maintenance customers, and unreliable venders. Business identifies the symptoms but fails to properly name the overall ailment: unhappiness.

Most corporate psychologists would probably call the average company distressed. "Distressed" is more seemly than "unhappy" to most people in the business community.

In gladiator days, the Latin word for *distressed* meant to be physically pulled apart. This sense continues in today's physical definition of stress, which focuses on demand and overload. Essentially, it states that any time a structure is placed in a situation where demand exceeds capacity, a breakdown occurs. Place a load of 100 tons on a bridge designed for 10 tons, and the bridge collapses. The same result can occur with organisms when placed under physical or mental stress. Physical stress is overt, but mental stress is often covert, breaking down the biological systems inside while remaining invisible until the organism itself fails.

A common form of mental stress occurs when reality differs from expectations. Falling below a certain sales quota for the quarter creates stress for everyone in sales. The stress is more or less linear. If the reality of sales is off expectations by 2 percent, the stress is minimal. If the reality is off by 40 percent, the sales department will be drowning in cortisol. Stress happens when we fail to meet deadlines (especially unrealistic ones) or budgets or other deliverables; or when we have ambiguous job responsibilities or a lack of control over tasks or a sudden upsurge in tasks; or when we have conflicts with other individuals or teams working on common projects.

Stress is also related to social hierarchy within an organization. In his new book, *The Status Syndrome*, Michael Marmot, a professor of epidemiology and public health at the University College, London, says that social hierarchy signifies how much control you feel over your life and that this sense of control is directly related to disease. Even after correcting for other factors, Marmot found that lower levels of control at work consistently led to more disease. Factory workers are more likely to have heart disease and a shorter life expectancy than a university professor, not because the factory job might be physically more difficult or more dangerous, but because of stress related to social position. This fact may explain why companies that go out of their way to reduce hierarchy have noticeable reductions in stress.

Many common work problems create gaps between expectation and reality. (For the employee low on the social hierarchy, that gap is the social and financial difference with others in the organization.) These gaps create a threat to our well-being by the implied lack of performance on our part. We know someone will come looking at the poor results. Thus, the final definition of stress and the one most aligned with the theme of this book is that stress is the cognitive, emotional, biophysical, and behavioral reaction to threat, real or perceived. We say real or perceived because the response is the same. Physical stress can tear the body to pieces. Mental stress in the business world makes you *feel* that you are being pulled into pieces. In either circumstance, the biological systems scream just as loudly in protest.

Stress reactions are costly. Very costly. Not all events are worth the same price, but many executives often respond as if they are. Stressed executives can exhibit the same heart rate increase, elevated blood pressure, and hormonal release when running late for a meeting as if confronted by a thug with a knife. The human toll is the equivalent of paying $1,500 for a $50 sweater. Do that too frequently and your resources will be spent. Take similar exhaustion across the organization and the tally becomes astronomical. Many distressed companies not only fail to realize how distressed they are, but also how much that distress costs them in productivity and profit. Here are some staggering numbers.

- A Canadian consulting firm, Chrysalis, says that stress is responsible for 19 percent of absenteeism, 40 percent of turnover, 30 percent of disability costs, and 60 percent of workplace accidents.

- Healthcare costs for stressed workers are 46 percent higher than those of other workers, roughly $600 more per person.

- The Medstat Group, a health information company, reports that out-of-control stress is the single most expensive lifestyle risk, accounting for 8 percent of total healthcare costs.

- Between 1981 and 2001, medically related personal bankruptcies increased 2,200 percent so that today roughly half of all personal bankruptcies are caused by medical costs. A goodly portion of those medical costs are related to workplace stress.

- 82 percent of people bullied in the workplace leave their jobs, 38 percent because of their health.

- 31 percent of women and 21 percent of men bullied in the workplace are diagnosed with post-traumatic stress syndrome.

- Workplace violence among government workers costs the U.S. federal government alone $180 million annually.

Current health-care costs are high, at more than $7,000 per person, representing more than 14 percent of the gross domestic product in the United States. These expenses are projected to increase between 11 and 13 percent in coming years. If the increases average 10 percent a year, the per capita cost of health care will be more than $11,000 annually by 2010, and family coverage will cost nearly $18,000. Even though 80 percent of Fortune 500 companies believe they have a responsibility to promote the health and wellness of their employees, health care is by far also the cost of greatest concern to those same CEOs. Starbucks, which prides itself in its employee programs, says that it now spends more on health care than it spends buying coffee. The largest single private U.S. provider of health care, GM, projected that its U.S. health-care costs for more than one million current and retired workers and their families would be $5.6 billion in 2005. GM has estimated that health and pension costs add $1,500 to the price of an automobile, making it difficult for the company to compete and make a profit. (One reason is that national health programs in Japan and Germany and other nations mean that competitors to U.S. industry have health costs that are inherently much lower.) Its employees and retirees complain that GM has the issue backward, that its mediocre auto designs force it to constantly discount the price of its vehicles, making pension costs appear disproportionately high. Even the agreement in 2005 between GM and its unions to reduce benefits $1 billion a year may not be enough to get GM's cost structure in line with the industry.

How Not to End Belly Up

Americans' working hours increased 3 percent from 1979 to 1999. Collectively, Americans are working about two weeks more per year than are their closest business rivals, the Japanese. Americans have more material possessions to show for the effort, but studies also show a diminishing level of happiness. Chasing after the proverbial pot of gold at the end of the rainbow has not brought much emotional satisfaction. We as a society are sleeping approximately two hours less a night than people living 50 years ago, a sign of overwork and stress. Far too many people whose jobs should help sustain life find their jobs become a source of stress and fear, killing them spiritually, emotionally, mentally, and physically. They are unhappy people working for unhappy companies.

To say a company is unhappy is to imply that the business concerns itself with feelings that are inappropriate in the workplace. Yet the very lack of awareness that work is an emotionally based and often emotionally charged environment is what causes the negative emotions to go unchecked and positive emotions to go unused. Companies already stressed by downsizing have no qualms about asking their employees to increase their workload beyond capacity. Out of fear of losing their jobs or a desire to turn the company around, employees often display amazing abilities to work under pressure. However, as this chapter demonstrates, "above-and-beyond" performance for too long a time comes at a fearsome cost. Asking someone to sustain too great a load for too long a time undeniably leads to detrimental outcomes. Athletes understand the ongoing impact of physical and mental strain and pace themselves not only to avoid burnout and injury, but also to peak at the right time, coming into major events physically rested and mentally enthused. The military uses its understanding of stress to schedule troop deployments into battle (see Figure 6-2).

The exhausting perils of stress exact as huge a toll on organizations as on the individual. Total cost to business of stress-related causes— disability and death, insurance and medical expenses, accidents, loss of employees, sick leave, and reduced or lost productivity—totals between $250 billion and $300 billion annually in the United States. This amount greatly exceeds the total profits of the Fortune 500. Companies and employees alike must develop well-thought-out strategies to identify, defuse, and overcome stress. Otherwise, employees must learn the hard way the message of the salmon, the title of this chapter and the moral of this lesson.

Have you ever wondered why salmon die after spawning? For salmon to make their way back up the rivers from the ocean to their spawning grounds, hurdling rocks and fish ladders, fighting currents and dams, their adrenal glands become hyperactive. The constant "on" cycle causes the control mechanisms to fail and the adrenals to keep pumping. After spawning, salmon do not die from the exhaustion of swimming upstream hundreds of miles or from the sweet collapse of reproduction. The fish die from an excess of stimulation. If you remove the adrenal glands immediately after salmon spawn, the

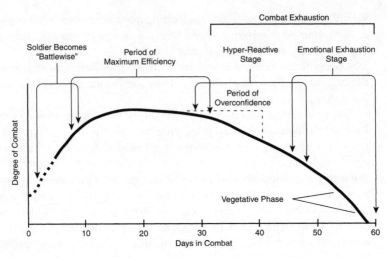

Figure 6-2   Studies have shown that soldiers exposed to combat—the most stressful situation imaginable—cycle through a predictable psychological and physical response. In the first few days, soldiers are trying to stay alive and learning to function while in mortal danger. For roughly another three weeks, soldiers can perform well in battle. Eventually, however, the stress begins to exhaust their physical and psychological systems. First they become overconfident, then hyper-reactive, and finally collapse in complete physical and emotional exhaustion. Understanding this phenomenon, the military attempts to rotate troops out of battle zones on a regular basis. The same exhaustion cycle happens to people in a high-stress business environment, though the curve is extended over many months or years instead of weeks. Eventually, however, a culture of unrelieved pressure will break employees down. (The original research was performed by Swank and Marchland in 1946; data updated by Watkins, 1997.)

fish live on, quite happy to take retirement ease in their natal streams. Nature does not care that the adult salmon die from adrenal overload, because by now the salmon have procreated. But you may not care to go belly up from work-related stress. Strategies identified in the next chapter can help ensure that you do not flail yourself to death on the boulders of business.

7

What's a Body to Do? Personal and Corporate Strategies for Health

Ask not for whom the stress tolls, it tolls for thee. Each and every person in business runs the risk of a stress-induced collapse. As some people might give out after hiking 10 miles and other people might give out after 20 miles, some individuals may react to stress faster or fall to the ravages of stress sooner than others. Some people may go a good deal longer. But, if your business life is the equivalent of hiking 25 miles a day—or doing a series of exhausting sprints all day long, day in and day out, year in and year out—eventually you and your body will wear out.

This chapter discusses personal and corporate strategies for maintaining and improving the physical and mental capacities and the resilience of employees in face of the stress that everyone faces in the workplace. Exploring the newest discoveries in the area of heart-brain interconnectivity, we also reveal the surprising and positive role that appreciation plays in the psychic and physical health of individuals and business teams. The focusing of positive emotions not only helps us minimize stress, but also enables us to take our mental energies as individuals and as teams far beyond what a typical frazzled workgroup is able to achieve.

Just as an individual has a responsibility to prepare properly for an arduous hike, each individual in a company has a responsibility to train—quite literally—for the rigors of work. Just as a group leader must plan a hiking route that takes into consideration the abilities and skills of each individual, an organization must have a work philosophy that takes into account human capabilities and the danger of overextension. The issue is both a humane consideration and a business practicality. An organization that creates an expectation of chronic super-human effort, expecting its people to just "tough it out," soon finds itself exhausting its strongest members, who have to carry the loads of the weaker, and paying excessive costs to salvage the fallen.

Failure of either the individual or the organization to take responsibility can quickly destroy a team. One individual at a high-growth company went on disability leave at the peak of every major project. He claimed excessive workload, yet his team managed to complete the projects without him, one person short. After a while, of course, nobody wanted to be on his team, and his career faded. On the organizational side, a newspaper publisher once cut costs by filling all job openings with entry-level employees. Over time, their collective inexperience shifted more and more work to senior employees, who under the mounting workload first began to max out their sick leave and then began to leave. In little more than 18 months, the publisher lost almost the entire staff that had turned around his newspaper, and he had to repeat the rebuilding process. Whatever money he saved in salary was more than offset by costs related to health care and the constant hiring and training.

Avoiding such collapses is the responsibility of the organization not to require more than what is reasonable, and of the individual, who must be able to respond to stress, a reasonable amount of which occurs in the best of organizations. Businesspeople obtain as much satisfaction from professional accomplishment as athletes do from reaching a personal best. Almost by definition, a happy project is one that calls for the maximum effort a human being can give. The good stress, eustress, of such projects strengthens our mental and physic abilities rather than breaks them down, but even eustress requires reasonable mental conditioning. Also, happy companies can go through down periods in which tension and workload increase, and employees must be able to sustain effort during difficult times to help the company recover.

Just as individuals have a responsibility to be physically and psychically fit for duty, an organization must provide an environment that is physically and psychically healthy. Personal and corporate responsibility are involved in four distinct but closely related steps. Two steps involve the individual, and two involve the organization. The first step centers on the individual's personal mastery of and responsibility for his or her own high-performing psychological and physiological health. The second step consists of the organization's specific policies and programs to bolster the health and well-being of individuals. The third step involves tools and techniques that can be made available to the individual to improve the person's psychological and physiological resilience. The fourth step consists of the ways that a company reduces stress through changes in its corporate culture. Corporate culture is covered extensively in Chapter 8, "Humility, the Most Courageous Form of Leadership," and following chapters, because it is the primary component of a happy and health company. This chapter covers the first three steps, all related either to the individual's health or to the individual's actions, in order.

Step One: Personal Mastery of Stress

Personal mastery of stress and the work environment begins with a recognition that stress is a palpable force in the workplace and that individuals must proactively prepare for its dangers. First is understanding that in most business situations, stress is normal rather than abnormal. Related to this is awareness of stress symptoms. Recognizing the physical manifestation of stress is often the first step in reducing or controlling a stress reaction. One manager recognized that his first responsibility in a constant-change environment was to convince new employees that chaos was normal and that it *was not their fault*. Rather than experiencing change and uncertainty as a series of calamities, he taught his team that disorder was an exhilarating experience that provided opportunities. Like a river-rafting experience, the environment could not be controlled but with the right skills could be navigated, enjoyed rather than feared. When he moved to a new position, he sent his team this message to reiterate the need for them to embrace uncertainty as a given:

> *Our strength was in staying focused and doing good and sometimes great work despite the confusion and uncertainty that marks the creation of a new business—not to mention staying calm in the general panic of the other teams around us. It seemed like the first task in every project was to slap the hysteria out of the other groups and then get down to work. ... If there's anything I hope each of you learned from that time, it was how to structure and organize a project—any project—when you're starting from scratch or there is otherwise no structure defined from the outside. That lack of definition was the nature of our work. ... People talk about working outside the box, but that assumes a box exists. The real thinking work is knowing how to make a box from nothing, and how big to make it, and when to push it out or draw it in. People who can do these things become the company's stars.*

Step Two: Programs to Bolster Health and Well-Being

An obvious area in which organizations can help employees with stress is through good health-care programs. A comprehensive program for health promotion includes six major factors: primary disease prevention; secondary prevention through intervention and assessment; disease management through behavior and pharmaceuticals; illness absence management; management of demand for health services; and disability management. Most organizations have major gaps in one or more of the six factors. Few companies have good statistics on absences caused by illness, for example. Often, companies have no data at all on white-collar workers, who being on salary rather than on hourly wages seldom report sick time even if they are supposed to. Also, 48 percent of all patients in doctors' offices and 60-plus percent of all patients in emergency rooms do not need to be there. Skilled nurses on the phone or online could treat most of these people at dramatically reduced costs, but most companies do not have programs that support such approaches.

Too many companies have traditionally purchased whatever health plans they can afford and hope the costs will stay in line, without realizing that corporate culture and individual responsibility have dramatic impact on overall employee health and on health-care costs. Some CEOs take the attitude that employee health is none of their business, whereas other CEOs see health as something intrinsic to corporate values. Roughly 25 years ago, the CEO at Kimberly-Clark, a health and hygiene company, decreed that the company would have the healthiest workforce in the country. The company implemented a program of preventive medicine that included complete physicals and stress tests, medical clinics at major plants and mobile clinics at smaller ones, fitness facilities, and so on. The result was substantial improvement in employee health.

Today, many employers are investing heavily in employee health management. Because health-care costs are rising so rapidly, it is difficult for any program to promise a reduction in costs, so thoughtful corporations weigh their program costs against national or industry trends. One multinational corporation, spending nearly half a billion dollars a year for health costs, agreed to establish a model program. During the planning sessions, the chief financial officer said that he would not look at the costs for three years, but after that he expected that his company's costs, on a percentage basis, would be three percent below the national average.

Achieving such reductions without employee buy-in is difficult because many health issues are lifestyle issues. Obesity, smoking, a lack of exercise, poor nutrition, an inability to manage stress, and similar lifestyle issues are associated with 50 to 70 percent of all illness and medical problems. Between 70 to 80 percent of the aging process involves factors under the individual's control, according to Dr. Mehmet Oz, co-author of *YOU: The User Guide* and one of the surgeons who repaired President Clinton's heart. A Rand study shows that physical activity can reduce health costs by 8 percent—the same percentage that stress increases health costs, according to the study by the Medstat Group. Other studies show that regular exercise in middle age reduces elderly dementia by 50 percent and Alzheimer's by 65 percent. If you take care of yourself and get regular screenings, you are far more likely to live long and prosper than if you let yourself go and then turn yourself over to the medical establishment to make repairs.

Wellness programs, which provide structured efforts to improve employee lifestyles and screening before the onset of disease, also improve health and reduce costs. Every $1,000 spent to help people quit smoking yields $10,000 in savings over later treatment. A $100 mini-exam that finds a person on the verge of having a heart attack can save $10,000 in post-attack care. Yet health insurance companies that demand a formal ROI justification for a $50 wellness program will pay $1,300 annually, year after year, without blinking an eye *after* a disease has struck. The same pattern holds at the national level. Less than 5 percent of the $1.8 trillion that Americans spend on health care goes toward prevention rather than cure. Even progressive companies spend 80 times more for cure than for prevention.

It is not surprising, therefore, that in most companies wellness programs are voluntary. Some wellness programs consist of little more than posters and a snappy article or two in the company newsletter. Even good voluntary programs have the intrinsic problem of self-selection. The people who participate tend to be healthy already, whereas those who do not participate are the ones who need the programs the most. For employees collectively to see improvements in health and for companies to see a reduction or flattening of costs, health-care and wellness programs must be integrated so that all employees participate. A 10 percent savings in costs for the 10 percent who volunteer would be dwarfed by a 5 percent savings if 100 percent of the employees participate.

R. William Whitmer, CEO of Health Enhancement Research Organization (HERO), which is dedicated to improving corporate health management, learned this lesson 20 years ago, as part of a $3 million government grant to improve health care for the city of Birmingham, Alabama. Employees were given a choice between participating in an annual, confidential, no-cost medical screen that was a prerequisite for employer-provided insurance, and providing for their own health insurance. About 97 percent of the employees chose the city coverage. Like today, those years, 1985 to 1990, were a period of rapid escalation in health costs. National costs increased 16.5 percent a year, and other large regional employers had similar increases, but Birmingham's costs increased only 2 percent a year. No other changes were made in the health plans except for the screening. *The overall return on investment was $10 for every $1 spent on the health management program.*

Whitmer thought that the concept of making a medical screen a prerequisite would lead other major employers to adopt it. Although the results have been positive, very few have. Later studies have shown that hundreds of prevention and wellness programs have either enhanced health or lowered costs, with ROI consistently ranging from $3 to $8 for every dollar spent, and indirect savings adding another dollar or two. BP, for instance, created a program that helped employees seek medical treatment for various conditions at one of its oil refineries; the company saved about $5 million as the result of reduced absenteeism. Overall, however, the fear of confrontation with employees or unions has been too strong.

As health-care costs rise, however, and as more and more employees have to pay larger and larger amounts out of their own pockets for health care, pressure may well develop from the employees themselves. By and large, health-care premiums at any one company in the United States are the same for everyone regardless of individual health or lifestyle. The idea is to spread costs evenly among the employee base. However, employees are beginning to understand that unhealthy lifestyle choices of fellow employees are the primary reasons that their own costs are rocketing upward. Isolated conflicts have occurred in some companies between "healthy" and "unhealthy" employees. Already, roughly 6,000 U.S. companies refuse to hire smokers. At least one company, a medical benefits organization in Michigan, fired four employees who refused to submit to a breath test.

One of the major debates in health care will be about whether the system should shift to a more "capitalistic" scheme in which, as bad drivers now pay extra for auto insurance, people who manage their health badly will pay higher premiums for health care. For example, a company might offer an individual any and all smoking-cessation programs that the person wants for three years, after which the person's health premium increases if the person still smokes. Conversely, people may pay less if they take positive steps. The Boeing Company sought to tie the amount of employee health premiums to wellness or health-management programs in its most recent pact with its mechanics. The provision did not survive the final round of negotiation, but it represents a major shift in attitudes. The debate will involve personal, political, and economic issues. Those who live healthier lives may tire of subsidizing the habits of those who do not; and those who smoke, who eat poorly, or who drink in excess may feel under assault by society. Everyone will worry about whether such a system might be extended to people with genetic dispositions to disease as opposed to a lifestyle that leads to disease. IBM was the first major corporation to promise not to use genetic information in any matter involving hiring or benefits. Congress is considering legislation to make such pledges mandatory after at least one company attempted to deny health coverage based on genetic tests it had done on blood samples without employees' knowledge.

As this difficult situation indicates, health care and health programs directly intersect the axes of corporate responsibility, corporate support, and personal responsibility. Organizations have a responsibility to reduce stress—the subject of most of the rest of the book—stress making it harder for people to avoid risky behavior such as smoking, alcohol abuse, and eating disorders. Corporations genuinely want to provide health packages to reduce and manage stress for employees as part of an overall compensation package. For health packages to be affordable, however, employees must take responsibility for themselves in managing their own lives and bodies.

Step Three: Tools to Improve Resilience

Improving employees' functioning under stress involves new ways to use the capabilities within the body, mind, and emotions; and many of these new ways involve the heart. Just as scientists once described the brain in far too simplistic terms, so too have scientists traditionally classified the heart as nothing more than a mechanical pump responding to the brain's electrical signals. However, nature is always more complex than human categories. Just as scientists have learned that the brain's functionality is quite distributed, interrelated, and complex, they have also begun to learn that the heart's role in human physiology and psychology is more than that of circulating blood and oxygen through the body.

Far from being a mere pump actuated by the brain, the heart has its own complex mini-nervous system that generates its own electrical impulses. Unlike most other muscle cells, heart cells can contract on their own. Specialized cells in the upper-right atrium, the sinoatrial node, initiate the heartbeat and synchronize with other heart tissues, which contract at different intervals to create the familiar two-stroke *lub-dub* pattern in humans. Without input from the primary nervous system, the heart would beat approximately 100 times a minute. Electrical signals from the brain and hormones in the bloodstream from the sympathetic system accelerate the heart's base rate; nerve signals and hormones from the parasympathetic system decelerate this base rate. At any nonstressed moment, the parasympathetic system is telling the heart to slow down, resulting in the 70 beats or so a minute typical of most adults.

In addition, the heart, not the brain, generates the most powerful electromagnetic field in the body. The field generated by the heart as measured by an electrocardiogram (ECG) is about 60 times greater in amplitude than brain waves recorded by an electroencephalogram (EEG), and the overall magnetic field of the heart is 5,000 times stronger than that produced by the brain. According to the Institute of HeartMath in Boulder Creek, California, the heart's field is powerful enough to be picked up several feet away with a Super-conducting Quantum Interference Device (SQUID) magnetometer, an instrument used in a number of scientific disciplines to measure minute magnetic fields. Interestingly, HeartMath's research also shows that the human energetic system is capable of detecting another person's heart field at a distance. We can "feel" each other, even without touching.

Research also indicates that the heart sends more signals to the brain than the brain sends to the heart, implying that the heart has tremendous potential to affect the brain's functioning. The heart sends nerve impulses via the spinal cord and the vagus nerve, the large nerve running from the brain to the body's core and affecting breathing, circulation, and digestion. The heart is also an endocrine gland, secreting its own hormones, which change the heart rate, increase blood flow in the kidneys, regulate the body's balance of salt and water, relax vascular smooth muscle, and even regulate the creation of vascular smooth muscle.

In fact, research by HeartMath and others indicates that the heart communicates with the brain in multiple ways: through nerve impulses, hormones and neurotransmitters, pressure waves, and its magnetic field. The conclusion is that the heart's activities influence emotional perception, motor activity, and higher mental functioning. Rollin McCraty, director of research at HeartMath, postulates that these conduits of information, coupled with the heart's rhythms, create patterns of information that significantly affect the body's biological systems, including thought processes. His studies show that heart rhythms cause brain waves, particularly the alpha wave, which is associated with relaxation and introspection, to become synchronized, or *entrained*. Another intriguing area of HeartMath's research strongly implies that the heart responds to emotional stimulus *before* the brain, so that the heart is partly an organ of intelligence whose input becomes folded into the brain's overall response. In other words, emotions result from the interaction of the heart and brain, with the heart providing primary input and the brain sorting out patterns and relationships from all the inputs it receives, including those from the heart.

Heart-rate variability, it turns out, provides the most direct indicator of how the autonomic nervous system functions. Specifically, McCraty and his colleagues have found that negative emotions, such as anger, frustration, or anxiety, cause heart rhythms to become more

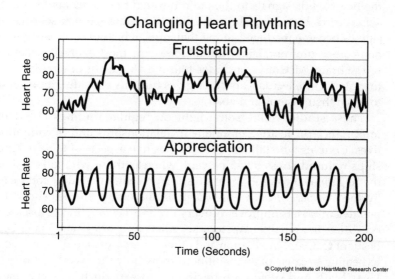

© Copyright Institute of HeartMath Research Center

Figure 7-1 A frustrated state leads to heart rhythms that are erratic and disordered, indicating reduced synchronization of basic biological systems and more disordered signals being sent to the brain. A state of appreciation leads to heart rhythms that are smooth and steady, which cause brain rhythms and other biological systems to become more coherent. Coherent heart rhythms improve cognitive performance in a range of tasks, including short- and long-term memory, auditory discrimination, and spatial working memory. (Source: www.heartmath.com)

erratic and disordered, indicating less synchronization between the sympathetic and parasympathetic branches and more disordered signals being sent to the brain. On the other hand, positive emotions, particularly appreciation, cause heart rhythms to become more coherent. Coherent heart rhythms cause respiratory, digestive, brain rhythms, and even electrical potentials measured across the skin to become more coherent. This improved synchronization across the body's physiological systems, McCraty posits, improves fluid exchange, filtration, nutrient absorption, and other cell-level activities. These changes help to explain the link between positive emotions and improved health and longevity documented in many studies. Equally important, HeartMath studies consistently show that coherent heart rhythm improves cognitive performance measured across a range of tasks. Short- and long-term memory, auditory discrimination, and spatial working memory are all examples of cognitive functions that have been demonstrated scientifically to improve when people achieve greater coherence in their heart rhythms.

To explain this further: When a person is in a state of appreciation, the heart sends signals to the brain through the vagus nerve and the spinal cord. Bypassing the amygdala (the mind's threat sensor), the signals become mediated in the thalamus, which in turn engages the neo-cortex, prefrontal, and frontal lobes, the most evolved structures of the brain. McCraty concludes that the alignment of emotion with the mind's intellectual capacities gives humans a greater opportunity to reach their visions and goals.

These studies shine some light on regular findings about the importance of positive emotions in relationships and in individual lives. Couples who talked about the positive aspects of their relationships reduced stress by 15 percent, whereas those who talked about the negatives increased their stress 48 percent, in a study conducted by the *Journal of Family Psychology*. Innumerable studies show that positive mindsets improve recovery in almost every kind of disease or condition imaginable. Western scientists and physicians have been hesitant to accept meditation and other "energy-centered" approaches to healing because of an inability to show how they work. Studies by HeartMath and others are beginning to explain the mechanisms. Researchers at the University of Wisconsin, for instance, have demonstrated that Tibetan monks skilled in meditation produce more powerful gamma waves in the brain than untrained individuals—more powerful than any previously recorded in healthy people, in fact. Gamma waves are associated with the knitting together of different brain circuits to create higher mental activity and awareness.

Wisconsin's study also showed that monks, who meditated on unconditional compassion while hooked up to electronic sensors, had more activation of the left prefrontal cortex, which is associated with positive thoughts and emotions and which corresponds to Heart-Math's findings that coherent heart rhythms activated the left hemisphere of the brain as a whole. Another study by Wisconsin shows that people whose prefrontal cortex is more active on the left side also have a stronger immune response against disease. Relaxation techniques can help somewhat to improve coherence, but HeartMath has found that the greatest and longest-lasting changes occur when people achieve sincere feelings of appreciation, love, and compassion. Meditation *without* the focus of a positive emotion such as compassion does not appear to have the same global effects on physiology as those meditative practices that do.

In related studies, psychologist Barbara L. Frederickson calls this outcome the broaden-and-build model. Whereas negative emotions such as fear and anger narrow an individual's immediate repertoire to specific survival functions, positive emotions such as joy and contentment broaden an individual's habitual modes of thinking and build the individual's resources—physical, emotional, intellectual, and social—for coping with difficult situations in the future. Empirical studies by Frederickson and Levenson show that contentment and joy speed recovery from the cardiovascular aftereffects of negative emotions. Frederickson's clinical experience indicates that cultivated positive emotions last long after the initial positive experience has ended. Results from Wisconsin and HeartMath concur that the brain can be trained to produce long-term structural changes that reinforce both positive emotions and higher mental functioning. The patterns become the brain's new default frame of reference, which the body then seeks to maintain.

This deep heart-mind connection creates the potential for individuals to reduce stress and induce a positive mental state. One approach is to learn techniques that will positively refocus the mind just before or during stressful situations. The idea is to intercede before a person succumbs to stress, thereby relieving the time and energy needed to reestablish a calm, thoughtful state. The simplest example is teaching a parent to count to 10 before responding to a misbehaving child. Stopping to count helps the adult break the frustration-anger cycle. The other approach is to train the heart and mind to develop a person's capacity to sustain positive emotions and physiological coherence for longer periods. HeartMath, for instance, has developed tools that use both of these approaches for adults, young adults, and children. One such tool is the award-winning Freeze-Framer software program. This consumer biofeedback program includes a finger sensor that plugs into your PC computer to give you real-time feedback on your physiological coherence.

Studies have shown that these appreciation-generating techniques reduce cortisol production, reduce blood pressure, reduce the amount of medication required by patients suffering from many physical ailments, improve hormonal balance, and increase the body's production of antibodies against pathogens. In addition, mental-health professionals report that positive-emotion and emotional-restructuring techniques have achieved great clinical success in patients suffering a variety of emotional disorders. In one study, positive-emotion techniques were used to reduce test-taking anxiety among students, resulting in test scores that show one to two years' improvement in grade level, much higher than that achieved by traditional test preparation. In another study, 32 at-risk middle school students exhibited significant improvement in psychological functioning. In yet another set of studies, several hospitals demonstrated significant improvements in staff retention and patient satisfaction after hospital nurses and administrators had learned the HeartMath self-management techniques. Resulting cost savings exceeded $1 million per year at each of the hospitals.

Even more intriguing than bioelectric connections between the heart and mind within a single person is evidence that similar kinds of interactions are possible *between* people. Dana Redington of the University of California at San Francisco discovered that the heart rhythms of therapists who strongly empathized with patients often fell into cycle with those of their patients. Levenson and Gottman of the University of California at Berkeley found that during periods of empathy, the heart rate of one spouse mimicked the rate of the other. Similar entrainment has been demonstrated multiple times during sleep by couples who have healthy relationships.

In addition to the psychological empathy in such situations, the HeartMath group has determined that the shared empathy may have a direct physical cause. In carefully controlled experiments, HeartMath has found that the heart rhythms of one person can affect the brain patterns of another person who is in physical contact or close proximity (6 to 18 inches). Such entrainment occurs only when the two people are each in a strong state of internal emotional coherence. Coherence is so important to the process that it is highly unlikely that a negative person with incoherent internal heart-mind rhythms could adversely affect another person. This cardioeletromagnetic communication appears to be an innate human ability that heightens awareness, increases sensitivity to others, and results in a deeper level of understanding between people.

Connections That Are Physical, Psychological

The implication of this and similar research is that the emotional interconnections between people may be physiological as well as psychological. The studies strongly imply that people who want to communicate well with others need to be in a highly coherent emotional-mental state themselves, thereby heightening their sensitivity to what others feel and say. The research also provides insight into how and why people either connect emotionally or struggle to get along in personal interactions, why some meetings are highly productive and others are not, and why some teams are effective and others clash constantly. The idea that people should develop techniques to improve their internal heart-mind coherence is not so much about personal tranquility or self-awareness as it is about ways to improve social bonds with other people in a variety of organizational settings.

We see this result regularly, particularly with family businesses. Dealing with all the decisions that businesses face, compounded by the long-term intimacies and strong emotions that are part of family ties, interactions in family businesses can quickly turn stressful or even hostile. Our practice is to have family business meetings begin with each member sharing something he or she appreciates about all the others. This approach is not always easy for certain participants, but we have seen repeated evidence that the exercise shifts the brain into higher gear for all parties and most often leads to constructive meetings.

This effect is by no means limited to family organizations, of course. Several years ago, we worked with a company that had employed a Catholic priest as an ethicist. A tactical meeting involving a group of department heads quickly degenerated into issues of silos and turf. After some amount of time wasted in bickering and contrariness, the priest asked whether he might have the floor. He stood behind one of the participants, putting his hands on the person's shoulders. "What do you appreciate about him?" the priest asked, insisting that everyone else in the room reply. The priest went from person to person around the table, asking for appreciative comments for each. When he was finished with the nine people in the room, he sat down and thanked them for the opportunity to explore the things they appreciated about one another. He said nothing else. Finally, one of the participants asked him whether there was anything more he wanted to do, and he said no. As the meeting resumed, the whole demeanor was different. In the end, they found ways to give and take and worked out compromises that met all their needs. The priest understood intuitively that appreciative feelings alter people into a more cooperative frame of mind.

In like manner, Talent+ (pronounced "talent plus"), a nationwide executive-evaluation and selection firm, has a "morning formation" in which employees start off the day by recognizing their peers for positive work-related behavior. As with most companies, Talent+ has several core values to guide it. The difference is that this company takes the time to review and rehearse those values daily. The formation begins with an employee reading the selected value of the week out loud. After the reading, several employees cite specific recent behaviors they have observed in others that exemplify this value. Each week focuses on one particular value. Lasting between five and eight minutes, the brief morning formation not only sets the tone for the way the company begins its daily operations, but also reinforces a corporate cultural consciousness as to why every employee came to work that morning.

Benefits of Managing Health, Stress

Being a happy company is a lot more than self-managing stress or providing stress relief for hard-working employees. At the same time, the changes needed in terms of personal responsibility and corporate culture are the stepping stones to many of the other positive steps that individuals and companies need to make to become happy. And happy companies undergo stress like any others. They have to respond to down economic cycles and other typical business issues. Happiness does not come from coasting. Happiness comes from hard, joyful work. *Happiness comes from exertion that challenges but does not break us, in the service of a goal that excites us.* As a result, companies and employees alike must develop well-thought-out strategies to identify, defuse, and overcome stress. Taking personal responsibility for recognizing and adapting to stress is a start, but health-optimizing programs are needed to help people develop physical and psychological resilience; and tools and techniques are needed to help reshape the individual's interior functioning to achieve a coherent emotional and psychological state. These techniques include relaxation therapies, cognitive therapies aimed at teaching optimism, and strategies to find positive meaning in fundamental aspects of work. The HeartMath programs are examples of ways to cultivate positive emotions and are proving themselves in major corporations, public agencies, and health-care systems that expect to save hundreds of thousands of dollars a year as the result of stress reduction.

Many other programs also exist that help employees develop positive behavioral models. BP believes that its comprehensive health-management and stress-reduction program for its 110,000 employees could save the company as much as $1 billion annually. All of the programs described here and elsewhere in the book are designed to call on positive emotions that induce the body's physiological systems into a natural state of coherence, and induce the person into a higher state of mental and emotional functioning. When consistently in that state, the body and mind tend to return there by default. The overall impact is superior mental and physical health. As one of many examples, a Duke University study of 800 heart patients found that those who reported positive emotions and joy were 20 percent more likely to be alive after 11 years than those who reported negative emotions.

People have long spoken of the heart as being the center of emotion, and today when people "speak from the heart," they speak from an emotional rather than logical perspective. At the same time, people who want teams to communicate well speak in terms of being on the same wavelength. The latest in science indicates that both of these ideas are literally true. Synchronizing the heart and mind turns out to be not only the best way to eliminate stress but also the best way to enable people to be their most creative and cooperative in business. When a person consciously makes the choice to practice appreciation (even in difficult times), to focus on what is right, to lead from strengths, and to look for possibilities that can be transformed into reality, the change in signals along the heart-brain circuitry leads to optimal performance and creativity. Appreciation does not simply give someone a warm feeling in the stomach. Appreciation enables human beings to bring their best to the table. It is critically important to grasp the idea that in bad times or good, the most adaptive response is to operate from the highest brain function possible. This higher-level functioning also leads to optimal personal interactions. "Optimal personal interactions" is an impersonal way of saying "happy interactions." It is the happy interactions within a working group that cause people to awaken each morning looking forward to work with passion and joy.

8

Humility, the Most Courageous Form of Leadership

Beyond managing stress and working to improve the health of employees, companies need to intentionally create a positive atmosphere. They need to introduce *happiness* into their corporate culture. Early in this project, we spoke to an entrepreneur whose specialty was investing in a business, building the management team, selling the company when it became a going concern, and repeating the process with another company. At any one time, he had interests in a half a dozen companies or more and was directly engaged with their management. Because he had not specialized in a particular industry, he served as a good representative of small to medium business. We asked him, "What makes for a happy company?"

He was nonplussed. He had never before thought of a company in terms of being "happy." Until we explained what we meant, he was not even sure that it was appropriate to think of a company in terms of happiness. When the light went on, however, he responded by saying it "begins and ends with the number one guy every time"—the leader. He rattled off the necessary positive traits of a great leader: one who has integrity, who is smart and has great intuition, who has both an honest mission and a missionary zeal about it, and who has employees who will follow him or her in good times and bad. About a week later, the businessman called back. Intrigued by our question, he had brought up the concept of a happy company at a meeting of the CEOs of his various enterprises. The individuals became so engaged with the topic that they created their own eight attributes of the positive enterprise. Here they are:

- Good leadership and the company's—the people's—belief in the leader.
- A culture built around a team, a winning team. People who like or at least respect one another and take pride in the organization.
- A belief system that seeks achievement and does what it says it will do, seeking the best product, the best value proposition, and the best service. Pride in the enterprise. Pride in seeking the most talented people in the sector.
- Fairness in treatment of all employees, in terms of compensation and promotion, with rewards going to those who achieve.
- Accountability and autonomy. People at all levels know what they need to do and are allowed to do it without micromanagement. With that freedom comes accountability. The company is not a social club, and nonperformance has consequences, but Big Brother is not looking over your shoulder, and personnel reviews are fair.
- As flat an organization as possible. Little to no hierarchy. People feel free to act regardless of where they are in the organization.
- Employees are treated with respect as opposed to being treated like indentured servants, peons, or slaves. The company listens to employees and values their knowledge and the information they bring about company issues.
- The organization is disciplined, working together toward its goals.

This off-the-cuff brainstorming is fascinating in several ways. First was the eagerness with which these seasoned CEOs jumped at the idea to define the happy company. The energy unleashed by such a positive question shows the latent desire of people to be part of a good organization, as well as the power of positivism itself. Second was that their concepts and wording were in some instances almost word for word the same as our independently developed ideas. (Their list also paralleled the work of other scholars and consultants in the field.) Third, having heard their definition, we all wanted to go work for such an enterprise!

Superficially, the most striking thing is the self-evident nature of the list. It seems like nothing more than common sense to say that good companies have honest, positive leadership, a team approach, fair treatment for empowered employees, great discipline, and a balance of authority, responsibility, and accountability. But if the principles are so apparent, why are so few companies happy? At the highest level, the reason is that the list is no more specific than the stock market advice to "buy low, sell high." It tells you the destination, but not how to get there. To buy low and sell high requires tremendous knowledge and patience and an almost superhuman ability to avoid market fads and the herd instinct—all these things or an ability to see the future. Further, you must not only do a good job, you must do *better* than everyone else. After a review with his broker of his portfolio performance over the past 10 years, one person was disappointed to find that his results were almost exactly the market average. A friend pointed out that the fluid nature of stocks—good ones attract the same investors, and bad ones repel them—and the thousands of analysts and many millions of investors all seeking riches made it almost impossible for an individual to do appreciably better than the whole over any period of time.

The problem in rising above average performance in business, as opposed to stock-picking, is not the huge sample size or its self-averaging nature. Instead, the problem is that humans in a social setting tend to default to the same set of social behaviors. Thus most organizations are self-averaging only because, like everyone else, they lock into feeling and acting from the survival brain rather than the executive brain. An overwhelming number of companies are lackluster because they culturally replicate fear-based behaviors that lead to short-term thinking or other self-defeating behavior, plodding along and reacting to events rather than driving toward a vision inspired by the executive brain. They are not doomed to mediocrity. But by failing to unleash human potential, they behave in ways that lead to mediocre outcomes. The essence of creating and maintaining a happy company is to find those actionable, repeatable behaviors that create a culture that enables whole-brain functioning by all employees. Find such an atmosphere and you find happiness flourishing like orchids in a hothouse.

Bully-Bosses Make You Laugh Until You Cry

The boss at a nonprofit group refused to let an employee leave work to go to the bedside of a grandmother whose death was imminent. The boss explained that bereavement leave did not begin until *after* the family member died. Another boss created a screensaver proclaiming himself to be "greater than God." A boss at a hotel went around to the rooms of departing guests to steal the tips intended for housekeepers. Some male bosses have felt compelled to comment on the figures of overweight female employees, and one said that a woman needed to learn how to walk like a lady instead of charging around like an elephant. A business owner—little man, big gut, gold-nugget jewelry out of a bad Hollywood movie—told a female employee that she was wearing "intoxicating" stockings. This gentleman also inserted vulgar commentary on government forms and viewed porn on his office PC in view of young female employees.

It is sociopath bosses such as these who provide the fodder for Scott Adams' workplace satire, the Dilbert cartoon. The run-ins with bad bosses are all too common. It is estimated that 90 percent of all employees have had to deal with a "psycho-boss" at one time or another. The Business Research Lab (www.busreslab.com) keeps a running tally of such encounters online, and National Public Radio and other media have done shows on the topic.

Some of these stories are so wild that they are funny, until they happen to you or someone you know. One friend of ours had a demoralizing encounter at her first important job after college. The company made medical devices, so quality was paramount. The company president gave her a mandate to scrub the organization to improve the quality processes. She found a problem with one system right at the close of the quarter, and she was going to shut down the process. Her vice president barred her from the production floor to keep the line running, the manufacturing equivalent of cooking the books so that his department could make its numbers. Young, in her 20s, and not knowing how to deal with the situation, she obeyed her boss and let the line stay open. A week later, the CEO came down and asked her, in front of the vice president, why she had not shut down the process. Rather than come to her defense, her vice president betrayed her. "I'm embarrassed for you," he said to her in front of the CEO, as if she had acted on her own rather than at his insistence.

Criminal psychologist Robert Hare, whose psychological checklist is used worldwide to diagnose psychopathic criminals and to keep people with psychopathic tendencies out of sensitive fields such as firefighting and nuclear power plant operation, is so concerned about the danger of psychopaths in business—people with hypnotic charm that masks their lies, cons, and thrill-seeking manipulations—that he wants to screen senior business leaders, too. "We screen police officers, teachers," Hare says. "Why not people who are going to handle billions of dollars?"

In stark contrast to the behavior of game-playing egoists is the behavior of Tommy Franks's commander in Vietnam. Then a young artilleryman, Franks was on the verge of being made a scapegoat for artillery damage in a town that had been caught in a raging battle between U.S. and Viet Cong forces. Franks's commander, Lt. Col. Eric Antila, interposed himself and told the investigators that he had personally signed off on every single shell that Franks had fired. If they wanted to blame someone for combat damage, they needed to go after him, a well-known senior officer, not some expendable junior officer. The investigation was quickly dropped. Antila's personal accountability was a major inspiration to Franks and one reason he made the Army his career. Franks ultimately became commander of U.S. forces in Afghanistan and Iraq.

Human behaviors are notoriously difficult to change, but changes in attitude and culture—rather than in organizational structure or business practices per se—are the only way to differentiate yourself long term. To have any meaningful effect, changes in organization or execution must spring from the attitudinal change in leaders, the social change in the organization, and the biological change that results in the minds of employees as they shift from stress behavior to positive behavior. Structural changes in an organization by themselves cannot create business change. Done for the wrong reasons, the shuffling of people and responsibilities may do no more than further mask existing problems. To paraphrase a well-known spiritual saying, organizational change must be an outward sign of an inward change. As companies consider organizational structure, they cannot think only in terms of, "Where do I need more bodies?" Rather, they need to think, "What behaviors do I want to change on my team, unit, division, or company?"

This concept of changing behavior in specific ways is both maddeningly simple in concept and maddeningly difficult in actuality. It takes focus and tenacity, the organizational equivalent of saying, "To buy low, you must identify a specific company with intrinsically good fundamentals, good management, and good growth prospects whose price is low today only because an open market sometimes makes mistakes." To build a happy company, you must find the few actionable principles that really make a difference, that can revolutionize culture. You must then take specific steps to drive those principles deep into the company, into every level and into every one of its behaviors. *The principles must become so intrinsically part of the culture that they not only become ingrained in each employee but eventually become manifest in the actual physiology of each individual person, in the wiring of the person's brain and in the balanced interplay of heart and mind.*

This tall order begins with a short acronym: HAPIE. A happy company consists of the following elements:

H	Humble, inclusive, inspirational, innovative, and heartfelt leadership
A	Adaptive, enthusiastic, emotionally intelligent employees
P	Profit for all who contribute to the company's success, with the focus being ROP (return on people) in addition to usual metric of ROI (return on investment)
I	Invigorated stakeholders, vendors, and clientele who serve as first-line marketers for the company
E	Engaged, constructive community citizenship

Some of these attributes are obvious counters to the negative examples described elsewhere in this book, which are representative of too much of daily business life. Other attributes may be less obvious at first glance, especially the first word of the acronym, *humble*. Bear with us. Our definition of the happy company, HAPIE, coalesces years of our own research and personal experience. For example, one of us compiled 10 years of psychological profiles of leaders. The very best leaders of those hundreds of profiles match the leadership profile above. The definition is also supported by the observations and studies of other consultants and scholars. As one example, Talent+, the executive-selection firm, has accumulated a database of more than 30,000 executives for 50-plus years and does constant research into leadership and management skills. Talent+ says that the difference between an average executive and a high-talent executive is that 80 percent or more of the high-talent executives map to the characteristics we describe. Other authors and research organizations have similarly developed extensive profiles of winning leaders, described most notably by Noel Tichy in *Ethical Challenge* and Warren Bennis in *Organizing Genius*. Although their methodology and terminology vary, the traits that they ultimately identify as necessary for success are consonant with ours.

Another trait of successful executives is that they have a mental model of excellence based on their own life experiences. The archetype for that model is invariably an individual who they admired when they were starting out or who helped them at a crucial juncture in their career. Not only do these models influence their own behavior, they also serve to help them develop their own employees. Thus, good leaders perpetuate good leaders. Indeed, the definition of a great company is one that culturally produces generation after generation of good leaders. More than excellent products, for instance, GE has been producing great managers since the 1950s.

Because of the importance of such early models, we also reconciled our data and the studies of others with our own personal reactions to the world. Who were the people who inspired us? Who were the people who made us want to be better people ourselves? For one, it was the mother who taught us how to read people and the father who taught us how to communicate. For another, it was a teacher who saw enough potential to help turn a flunk-out into a scholarship winner. For the third, it was the person who saw enough potential to hire for our first real job and who has served as a role model for 40 years. These people were not the only positive models, of course. There were other family members, teachers aplenty, and spiritual guides. Years on, there were positive bosses and mentors. In 110 years of combined professional experience, we have worked with and learned from many, many fine individuals. To a person, every one of the people we most wanted to emulate had the traits we now associate with the happy boss: humble, inclusive, inspirational, and demonstrating innovative-visionary leadership. Unless you are a sociopath or other type of psychopathic boss, your most inspirational models are too.

What it Takes to Be HAPIE: First, Humility

Some executives shy from the word *humility* like a horse from a snake. A few may find the word offensive. They relate it to the notion of forced submission (humiliation) rather than voluntary modesty. Or they assume that humility means that they must wear sackcloth and ashes rather than enjoy the perquisites of their success. In fact, humility of character is not an embarrassment but a gift. Far from implying a lack of ability, confidence, ego, or will, humility is a manner of expressing those capacities in a way that engages others. Humble leaders operate from conviction, either from moral values that cause them to act beyond themselves or from a deep belief in the company's mission. In fact, some such leaders may be cold, anemic, or arrogant until they connect to their mission, and then their entire behavior becomes energized and their focus intense. Humble leaders know they have gifts. They just keep them in perspective, as they also do their lifestyle. Humble leaders enjoy the pleasures of life; in fact, they appreciate them rather than take them for granted. Humble leaders have powerful egos, meaning appropriate self-esteem as opposed to an overinflated self-opinion. They are demanding, but driving their demands is a capacity for caring and a desire to help others excel, rather than a desire for personal domination.

History comes alive with such examples. Jesus challenged religious orthodoxy by associating with the rabble and teaching universal love. Muhammad rejected ethnic and class distinctions and sought better treatment for slaves, orphans, women, and the poor. Martin Luther challenged the excesses and indulgences of the religious establishment. Gandhi used civil disobedience to oust the British from India. Mother Teresa scolded world leaders face to face to do more for the deprived. These were people with a profound sense of self-worth, and their actions changed the lives of hundreds of millions of people.

World War II provides a more macho example of humbling your way to victory. America's finest general in the European campaign was George Patton, who manifested superior battle strategy, unyielding resolve, and ineptitude in matters personal and political that resulted in his sitting out D-Day as a decoy. Later unleashed, he led the Allies across Europe, including the rescue of the trapped American army at the Battle of the Bulge. Nonetheless, in the largest and bloodiest war in human history, Omar Bradley and Dwight Eisenhower, the relationship guys, won out over the classic alpha male. Roosevelt knew that they were the only men who had the trust to keep the unwieldy and often cranky alliance together. A similar point about hubris could be made regarding Douglas MacArthur, who won the war in the Pacific with limited means, oversaw the reconstruction of Japan, and led U.N. forces to early and brilliant victories in Korea until his ego overran his considerable abilities. It is telling that in Eisenhower's presidential campaigns the tagline was not "I fear the general" (as it would have been for Patton or MacArthur), but "I like Ike."

These various leaders demonstrate that true humility is a form of courage. It requires people to subsume their personal needs and pretensions into causes beyond themselves. *Humble leaders are those leaders willing to give away power.* They recognize that more overall good occurs if they spread power through the organization or community than if they hoard power for themselves. Charlie Horn, founder and chairman of ScriptSave, which offers programs that reduce the cost of prescriptions for companies and individuals, puts it best when he says he has a "deep-seated belief that ScriptSave not be limited by the limitations of Charlie Horn." This belief carries over to current company CEO, Lori Bryant, and all members of the executive leadership team.

That is why "humble" includes most of the people at the top of *Fortune's* list of wealthiest Americans. Warren Buffett, the investment guru, and the Walton clan of Wal-Mart carry the best of America's heartland virtues. Sam Walton lived well, but not ostentatiously, because he saw more value in using corporate wealth to build stores or give customers better prices than by living a big showy lifestyle. He had nothing but contempt for "overpaid CEOs who are really just looting from the top and aren't watching out for anybody but themselves," because "every dollar spent foolishly comes right out of our customers' pockets."

Bill Gates lives a bigger and showier lifestyle than Walton did, but like Walton, he achieved his wealth by focusing on the company, tying his future to Microsoft's stock performance. He once wrote a memo telling employees not to spend money just because the company had it, and he flew coach until the volume of Microsoft employee travel caused the travel agency to automatically upgrade him. When his schedule necessitated a private jet, he paid personally rather than out of company funds. No stranger to magazine covers, he is astute enough to parlay his fame into meeting people he admires, such as South Africa's Nelson Mandela. Far from being threatened by talent, Gates has spent many years wooing the industry's best and brightest to join his firm. Warm and fuzzy Microsoft is not, but no one can accuse the leadership of not being open to new people and to new ideas that stretch the firm and its abilities.

Finally, a practical reason exists for CEOs to be more humble. Research by leadership consultant Marshall Goldsmith shows that business leaders have a high and largely unjustified regard for their abilities. His studies show that 85 percent of all business leaders rate themselves as being in the top 20 percent—even the leaders of failing companies! Goldsmith's explanation is that, as they move up through an organization, leaders superstitiously associate *all* their traits with their success, when in fact they are successful *despite* some of those traits. They become "delusional," unable to hear any feedback that is not consistent with their own self-image.

Perhaps this inflated sense of self helps explain the salary inflation of CEOs. In 1980, the CEOs earned 42 times the salary of the average production worker. In 1990, the ratio increased to 100 to 1. Now, the ratio at 367 top U.S. corporations is 431 times, and the spread continues to grow, according to the Institute for Policy Studies. Many studies show no relationship between CEO pay and company performance. Financial writer Michael Brush compiled a list of the five most egregious examples. The CEOs at Ciena, Sanmina-SCI, Sun Microsystems, Bristol-Myers Squibb, and Albertson's received compensation of tens of millions of dollars per year for four years while company stock values declined calamitously—93, 78, 76, 48, and 39 percent over four years, respectively.

With some of these companies, the delusional shell is so thick that the board of directors evidently cannot see through it, never mind the CEO. Humility—an openness to the way others perceive us—is a major step in cracking the delusional shell and pointing corporate leaders and boards toward the shareholders the company is supposed to be in business for.

Ego Satisfaction Through Results

In business, the natural desire to serve others becomes a proper aspiration for leadership. This concept, formulated by Robert Greenleaf, who coined the term *servant-leader* in 1970, has led to an entire school of thought on the proper approach to leadership, which differs sharply from the person who leads because of the need to acquire power or material possessions. Humble leaders express their ego through serving customers and helping employees to grow. Their ego reward comes through results and the *company's* success. Their tendency is to accept blame for failure and to praise others for success. Having a strong work ethic and a quiet confidence in their own abilities, they also recognize the hard work and contributions of other people who have helped get them where they are.

Arrogant leaders express their ego through their status in the company and society. They ascribe their success to their own remarkable abilities and photogenic qualities. They are also the first ones to point fingers at others when things go wrong or to claim ignorance when corporate problems emerge. The media are treating us to the weird spectacle of all these CEOs who ruled as corporate potentates now claiming a pitiful, woe-is-me ignorance about all the horrible wrongdoing that occurred on their watch. It's an Alice-in-Wonderland world in which gross incompetence becomes the preferred legal defense to charges of felony misconduct.

With arrogant leaders, the focus is always on *them* and their needs. (The root word of *arrogance* means to claim for oneself.) With humble leaders, the focus is not on them but on what they are trying to achieve. Sam Walton, who parlayed small-town merchant wisdom into the world's largest retail chain, once said, "Submerge your own ambitions and help whoever you can in the company."

Arrogance does not equate to criminality, but its limitations hurt companies in other ways. Like the tortoise over the hare, humility wins over hubris when it comes to sustained company performance. Jim Collins, in his book *Good to Great*, found in an extensive survey that humble leadership was one of the major reasons for the long-term success of many remarkable companies. Collins's goal was to find average companies that turned into great companies and then figure out how the companies did it. His methodology was to identify companies whose stock performance had been average for at least 15 years, then outperformed the market substantially for at least another 15 years. The company also had to outperform its own industry, to ensure that the industry itself had not become the darling of the stock market, as high tech did during the 1990s. Of the 11 companies that met his criteria, 10 of the 11 had homegrown leaders, and all of the leaders were humble. They were anything but weak, timid, ineffectual, or any other negative that some might associate with the word *humble*. They were typified instead by "personal humility and professional will." Their mindset was of the plow horse, not the racehorse, and it often took many years for them to build an organization before it broke out. When it occurred, however, success endured. "Rock star" CEOs, on the other hand, were six times as likely to show poor results against the same standards. In fact, there seemed to be an inverse relationship between the number of personal headlines a CEO received and the performance of the company over anything but the shortest term. (A tongue-in-check news article during the Enron-WorldCom era claimed that a CEO who received personal headlines was 25 percent more likely to go to jail than an anonymous CEO.)

Another aspect of humility is an executive's willingness to be hands on. Too many American executives have the notion that to do actual work is beneath them, that execution as opposed to grand strategy is demeaning for someone in their position. In contrast, Toyota's management philosophy is expressed in the phrase *genchi genbutsu*, or "go look, go see the actual situation." *Gemba* is the Japanese word for the actual place, and leaders also talk of "going gemba." The idea is simple. Leaders can lead only if they know what is actually going on! Intense observation by leaders combines with hands-on involvement. The first president of Toyota's Georgetown, Kentucky, plant was known to go into trances observing manufacturing processes, then fire off memos on things he had seen that could be improved. The next president of the plant moved his office from the "white-collar" building to a spot directly over the main manufacturing area to be more actively engaged. Young engineers in Japan have been asked to stand for hours inside a circle marked on the floor of a manufacturing facility to practice the art of deep observation. They learn not to rely on spreadsheet data but to observe the process first hand. The approach is the same as that used by anthropologists to understand cultures (participant-observation) as well as by forensic scientists investigating a crime scene. This approach continues as Toyota employees climb the corporate ladder.

As described in the book *The Toyota Way*, by Jeffrey K. Liker, this attitude of engagement begins at the top. At Toyota, getting your hands dirty is not a metaphor. Kiichiro Toyoda, who made Toyota a world-class automobile manufacturer, once came across an engineer puzzling over why a machine was not operating properly. Wearing business attire, Toyoda rolled up his sleeves and thrust his hands elbow-deep into grimy oil to pull out sludge that was clogging the filter. You have to get your hands dirty to solve problems, Toyoda told the engineer.

That action captures Toyota's approach to leadership. Managers must go and see for themselves—and do themselves, if necessary—so that they have more than a superficial understanding of a situation. Wawa, a 500-unit, fresh-food convenience chain in the mid-Atlantic states, requires executives to spend one week a year in their stores to learn first hand about issues they might not otherwise uncover. The manager of a water-conditioning company in Las Vegas takes over the routes of his employees for a day when they reach a safety goal, a nifty combination of keeping your hand in and showing appreciation. Sam Walton took pride in having done every job related to retail from sweeping floors to buying product to arranging merchandise to handling the bookkeeping. It was easy for him to assimilate new ideas and to be able to teach others how to incorporate them into practical store operations. A great storehouse of knowledge within a company, and the ability of leadership to teach that knowledge, is a hallmark of great companies.

This hands-on approach applies to any conceivable project. Brian Muirhead, the manager for the Pathfinder project that successfully landed the Sojourner rover on Mars in 1997, found that the most effective managers under NASA's faster-better-cheaper mandate were those whose natural inclination was to be hands on. Jim Goodnight, the CEO of SAS Institute, still writes code for the software company. In addition to supervising the work of others, other SAS managers do "real work" for which they are personally accountable. Senior leaders keep their hands in because they enjoy the work and because they want to set an example to other team leaders and employees to be involved at a deep level. Business strategist Keith McFarland describes a CEO who each quarter commits to five specific, measurable goals for himself and challenges everyone else in his company to create similar goals for themselves within 48 hours. People work harder and become more inspired when they see their managers working side by side with them rather than issuing orders from the safety of the rear.

To avoid being drawn into every little project or detail, leaders should think of themselves as a *strategic reserve*. They should make themselves available on a select number of the most crucial or time-critical matters. These are where their own experience is most invaluable, and where they should be paying close attention anyway. Muirhead personally handled a serious problem with a faulty sun sensor, the failure of which would have made navigation to Mars impossible. A manager at a high-tech company regularly signed himself up for at least one task critical to each of his employees' success (and to their personnel reviews). On that project, *he* would report to *them*. Some employees found the situation awkward until he actually delivered on the assignments. Their working relationship improved immeasurably when they saw that he was willing to hold himself to the same performance standards as he held them. The exercise was more than team building. By providing extra, experienced help on his staff's most crucial assignments, he improved the likelihood of a breakthrough and multiplied the team's (and his own) overall results.

Seen in this perspective, humility is at the heart of organizational development. Humility enables an honest appraisal of the leader's strengths and weaknesses. Acknowledging what they lack, humble leaders are able to bring in other people who have complementary strengths. L. Ben Lytle, then CEO of Anthem, Inc., one of the largest health-benefits companies in the United States (since merged with Wellpoint, Inc.), did not hesitate to hire people with complementary strengths in operations and finance. One of those individuals, Larry Glasscock, succeeded him as CEO. Being self-aware enough to hire people with complementary skill sets is a business strength, because a new CEO with dissimilar strengths will do different things rather than be locked into the "same old, same old." Jack Stupp, who pioneered the discount store concept in Canada, sent his senior staff to an offsite with a consultant every year for 20 years. At that meeting, the senior executives talked confidentially about all of their issues and concerns with the company, including feedback on Stupp's performance. Afterward, the consultant wrote up a summary of the points raised. The comments led to changes in both operational practices and Stupp's management style. The fact that Stupp solicited honest feedback and consistently made changes based on that feedback created a culture of trust in the company.

In contrast, arrogant leaders do not want to hear from good people. In fact, they are likely to run off good people, whom they perceive as threats. One boss invited a woman to take a difficult job running a department that was in trouble. Initially, he was very supportive, but as soon as she succeeded in turning the department around, he began to constantly berate her and to encourage her employees to complain about her. She understood why the department had struggled so much beforehand: The leader would not brook success in a subordinate. She left, and co-workers tell her that he has continued the pattern of verbal assault against anyone else who does a good job. The boss is "safe" for now because he makes his numbers, but his behavior has left him stranded at this level in the organization. When he ultimately leaves, the several departments under his thumb are likely to collapse from the lack of a qualified successor.

Management by Mobile Empathy

From humility comes empathy, and empathy is a mindset that enables appreciation and listening. Not to be run over by others, as the meek might allow, but to get the best of everyone by hearing and synthesizing multiple viewpoints without defensiveness. Tom Kelley, of IDEO, which has developed a range of innovative products—among them, personal digital devices, sports goggles, defibrillators, and kidney transport systems—says that demographics and other traditional marketing data assume that you already understand everything about your customers and therefore already know what questions to ask about them. If you know everything, then all you have to do is tell employees what to do. Product development becomes mechanical rather than creative, often resulting in feature glut rather than innovation. On the other hand, empathy that comes from working closely with other people (employees, clients, and customers) enables you to rediscover why you are actually in business. Empathy opens you up to asking why about all aspects of a product and business. The "why" then causes you to engage with others, taking "you" out of the equation.

Empathy leads to appreciation, which can be demonstrated by a simple gesture or by a large financial reward and company-wide laudation. At a time when professional women were uncommon and were sometimes asked to get coffee for their male counterparts, one woman's boss made a point of getting her the first cup of coffee every morning. After that, they alternated. Over time, the boss helped her learn the company's operations and politics through regular lunches and other mentoring.

Empathy and appreciation create great *listeners*, who are able to hear and synthesize the best ideas of everyone. IDEO speaks of "active and empathic listening" to customer needs. Among the great companies Jim Collins identified, Walgreens has prospered through group dialogue and collaborative insights. Circuit City's CEO uses board meetings to solicit answers from the directors rather than merely summarizing company facts and figures. Listening need not be quiet and diplomatic. At management meetings, Pitney-Bowes executives have to field blistering questions from the sales staff who are dealing directly with customers. Intel, Microsoft, Nucor, and Wells Fargo have cultures in which people—equals by merit rather than by title—engage in ferocious arguments in search of the best ideas. Toyota's Georgetown, Kentucky, assembly plant uses the old-fashioned suggestion box. In a recent year, employees made more than 80,000 suggestions to improve operations. Toyota implemented 99 percent of them.

Sam Walton was the doyen of "the listening leader." For more than 40 years, Walton toured his stores, constantly gathering the best of what each store was doing, quizzing associates for their best ideas, and talking directly to customers about their needs and wants. He was the virus that spread the best practices across the chain. He pushed his senior managers out to the field to listen to the people in the stores about process and merchandising, and buyers had to work in the departments they bought for. He insisted that every manager return with at least one new idea that paid for the trip—and managers went out weekly. Realizing that truckers saw even more of his company than he did, he would show up at the truckers' break room at 3 a.m. with a box of doughnuts to glean the truckers' knowledge of stores and operations. When they asked him for more showers in the dressing room and he delivered, he solidified their confidence in him and ensured an open conduit of informal but valuable information.

Empathy is also at the heart of Peter Drucker's notion of managers walking around and learning from direct interaction with employees and with company operations. Given the popularity of Drucker's books, you would assume that all businesses today feature CEOs and managers strolling about, but in fact most have retained their insularity. When an appreciative inquiry process created interaction among various departments, one manager realized that he had not stepped foot in the manufacturing facility in more than a decade. Done properly, "walkabouts" work. Muirhead used them to see first hand the work of different teams on the Mars project. By gathering a comprehensive sense of the Pathfinder mission's actual as opposed to formal status, he could determine where the "grease" needed to be applied. Sam Walton said he practiced "walk and fly around management" because of his penchant for hopscotching around a region in his plane, showing up unexpectedly to see what was happening in different stores.

Empathy can also help ensure that these walkabouts unearth the deeper issues, not surface issues or quick-fix problems, as important as those may be. Walk-around management enabled one manufacturer to eliminate the theft of hundreds of thousands of dollars in parts and equipment annually, but the deeper issue was the bitter divide between management and labor that made labor's wholesale thieving so blatant. Without resolving the cultural issues, the alienated workforce was going to continue to undermine the company in dozens of other ways.

Then there was the CEO on a walkabout who discovered through employee complaints that the company was inhibiting innovation by requiring more than 275 separate signoffs for any new idea. The CEO appointed a task force that removed more than 200 of the checks, speeding innovation. Success! Not exactly. Chris Argyris, a Harvard professor and business consultant, points out that the company never examined the underlying issues: How had the company accumulated so many brain-stifling processes to begin with? How long had employees been hampered by them? What was it about company culture that had prevented employees from questioning or correcting these issues before? Why did the CEO need to intervene? The goal is not to hand out solutions to one-off problems like a king tossing out candy on a public holiday. The goal is to uncover the root issues, the patterns beneath the surface that, combined with other data, may provide profound insight into company operations as a whole. If the first time you walk around you are deluged with complaints, the response would not be to catalog and work down the list but to examine a culture that would generate so many.

Empathy Enables Merger of Cultures

Empathy's automatic environment of inclusiveness is an effective trait outside of the company as well as inside. Lytle, a newly minted CEO for Blue Cross and Blue Shield of Indiana in 1989, recognized that unless the company could combine with other small- to medium-sized insurance providers to get economies of scale and diversify revenue, all the companies would be at risk in the rapidly changing world of health care. Up to 1996, when investor-owned companies were allowed to hold a franchise, Blue Cross and Blue Shield franchises were held either by mutual insurance companies or not-for-profit organizations. Until 1996, no cash could change hands in the merger of two Blue Cross mutual insurance companies, nor could management benefit. There was no incentive for companies to merge except a willingness to act in concert on behalf of their mutual customers. Six Blue Cross and Blue Shield organizations were located within a four-hour drive of Blue Cross and Blue Shield of Indiana, and all jealously guarded their individuality and territories. In four years of seemingly fruitless talks, Lytle heard a litany of reasons why the other companies needed to remain independent. Fear of change and loss of control seemed to leave the companies paralyzed.

But Lytle listened and learned. Mixed with the uncertainty were genuine concerns. While he focused on the opportunity—better leverage for contracting with health providers, increased ability to borrow, consolidated management and information technology costs, and better service to customers—he also empathized with the other companies' desire to maintain their unique fingerprint in their own communities. Finally, he said, "Okay, if your concern is to not lose employment, we'll guarantee employment for x number of years. If it's community support, we'll guarantee the same level of charitable giving for x number of years. We won't move all the management positions to Indianapolis. We'll maintain what is good about your organization."

One CEO admitted that a major barrier was that he did not want to lose his own CEO position in the merger. Lytle said, "Fine, you be CEO, and I'll be number two." When the CEO realized that Lytle would concede his own position on behalf of the greater good, he rescinded his demand to have the top job. Lytle engineered the merger of four mutual insurance Blue Cross and Blue Shield companies and later bought four not-for-profit Blue Cross and Blue Shield companies that were in trouble. (Of the roughly 120 Blue Cross and Blue Shield companies when Lytle began his efforts, consolidation reduced the number to about 40 within a dozen years.)

At the same time, because of concerns of massive government intrusion into health-care financing, Lytle was seeking revenue diversification in an area close to Anthem's core business, preferably with higher margins, a high growth rate, and a low capital requirement. The solution was to form Acordia, which became the seventh-largest health-insurance broker in the country before it was ultimately sold. Lytle's leadership style with both companies was the same. Whatever the formal organizational structure, he treated the team as partners, with him acting as general partner, rather than acting as CEO toward subordinates. From the first merger in 1993, neither new company, Anthem or Acordia, had a single blowup in customer service, management, or technical systems. The companies never had an outflow of seasoned talent. Anthem never took the attitude of "we acquired you," but rather "we're making a new company, and you're equal owners." Lytle's formula was to go into each company and work with respect. Empathy was the glue that bound the new organization together.

Why Humility, Empathy, and Inclusion Work

Humble leaders succeed sociologically and biologically because they seek to build connections. They draw people together and create cohesion. They do not tout or flout themselves or their abilities, they just go about their business successfully. They create an inviting environment where people want to come and work. This behavior makes us feel safe. As humans, we recognize these qualities as being profound. The attitude creates positive emotion, gets us inspired, and stimulates the creative centers of brain. With the fear centers quiet, the left prefrontal lobe becomes active. Creativity and innovation flow. Talk naturally moves to the future and to possibilities. Humility is also an appreciative state of mind, one in which leaders recognize their good fortune in having had their opportunities and being rewarded for their hard work. Gracious about their own success, humble leaders can put themselves in the position of their associates and ask how they would perceive good leadership and how they would want to be treated. Appreciation leads to optimal autonomic functioning; coherence of the heart, mind, and endocrine system; and activation of the creative centers in the mind. Feeling appreciation *for* others and receiving appreciation *from* others results in the same positive biological response.

If humility can be the source of so many positive corporate attributes, the question arises for the board of directors who have an arrogant CEO; or for the CEO who sees arrogance among the senior staff; or for the CEO who recognizes arrogance in himself or herself. What can you do to shift arrogance to humility? The problem is not trying to change a leopard's spots or to turn a scorpion into a teddy bear. Arrogance is the signature of a mind trapped by fear at the survival level, so the person sees the world as a place of scarcity and shifts into hoarding mode. Humility is the signature of a mind operating from the higher capacities of the executive brain, so the person sees the world as a place of plenty and, however tight things may be in actuality, shifts into sharing mode. Operating from the executive brain rather than the survival brain does not require anyone to have a personality transplant. You simply have to learn to use all of your capacities, not merely the ones left over from the hunt. The chapter covering the *A* in HAPIE—adaptive, enthusiastic, emotionally intelligent employees—describes in detail how this transformation can occur for leaders and employees alike.

In conclusion, humble leaders are tough-as-nails leaders who are effective at everything but self-aggrandizement. By not putting the company focus on themselves, by spreading power, they are able to motivate and energize an entire organization. By taking the "hits" when things go wrong, they free their people to take risks. They are able to seed leaders and grow them. They develop a cadre of like-minded (but not necessarily like-skilled) executives who develop other leaders below them. Everybody wants to be like Mike—because

Mike is a great leader. With leadership constantly growing and talent constantly blooming, the company becomes more than the sum of its parts. By giving away power, humble leaders become the ultimate practitioners of enlightened self-interest. They humbly lead their companies to the top.

Being Grounded in Order to Reach for the Stars

Humility's root is *humus*—"the earth." It connotes being grounded in common sense and decency (to temper the ego), being rooted in reality (to recognize fallibility as well as strengths), and being gritty enough to get things done. Humble leaders need not be the salt of the earth, but they apply a model of good leadership—from earlier mentors, from life experiences, from moral values—in ways that engage those around them. The means are as simple in theory as they are difficult in actuality:

- Understand the strengths of yourself and your high command in a way that is as hard-nosed as understanding the company's underlying financial model.

- Welcome rather than fear individuals with complementary strengths or contrary ideas. By operating from what is best in you and empathically engaging with others, you will find a way to synthesize differing viewpoints to create a unifying vision. With a common vision, diversity is a strength. Without one, diversity is a civil war.

- Go see, go do. Do not become trapped in the big office. Few CEOs need to be told to engage with customers, but many do need to be reminded to engage with employees. Directly understand the most intricate issues and operations that engage the company. Sam Walton took an IBM course for retailers in 1966 because he had heard that these things called "computers" were the coming thing. The early exposure resulted in his company's main competitive advantage becoming its sophisticated IT system.

- Grow with your business and keep getting your hands dirty with every aspect of business. The most successful companies are run by such people: Gates, Jobs, Walton, Schultz at Starbucks, the Toyoda family at Toyota, and so on. These are all leaders who could, at any moment, pitch in on any of their company's most complex operations.

- When you change the organizational structure, do so with the fundamental idea of changing behavior and culture around future possibilities, not simply redeploying bodies around new functional areas, or trying to achieve "efficiency," or otherwise trying to solve an organizational problem. New leaders especially make the mistake of shaking up the organization to give the appearance of doing something. This rule means you need to know the future you are chasing and the behavior you want to improve or redirect.

■ Grow your own leadership. Very few companies succeed by bringing in a Jedi knight or a Darth Vader from the outside. Hewitt Associates has found that 85 percent of the most successful companies promote from within. On the rare occasion that the perfect fit is from outside the company, that person still needs inside talent that knows the operation. Companies succeed by having leadership that is broad, deep, consistent, and versed in company culture—none of these words means "stagnant" or "blinkered."

■ Develop a coaching and teaching mindset to develop the skills of people at all levels. Reward senior employees for growing and nurturing the newer ones. At The Phelps Group, a marketing communications company, each client team bears the final decision and responsibility, but all teams have access to coaches in the various disciplines. These coaches are experienced individuals who regularly offer guidance and feedback. At Accenture, part of the review for each partner is based on their mentorship and the success of those people under them. Partners who fail to mentor properly, or who burn out their employees through demands for excessive billing—a practice known by the gruesome term of *killing your babies*—discover a downside in their end-of-year split of the earnings. At Dell, pay is partly based how managers nurture others. Johnson & Johnson evaluates executives on how well managers export their talented employees to other groups. Other companies rate managers on how well their former reports do in new jobs.

9

From Gut to Sight to Heart, the Role of Visionaries

HAPIE companies are those with *humble*, inclusive, visionary, inspirational, and heartfelt leadership that strives for a culture of innovation; *adaptive*, enthusiastic, and emotionally intelligent employees who make the company's vision their own; *profit* for all for all who contribute to a company's success, with the focus being return on people in addition to usual metric of return on investment; *invigorated* stakeholders, vendors, and clientele who serve as first-line marketers for the company; and enjoy *engaged*, constructive community citizenship that stimulates and reinforces the most positive attributes of the organization. The preceding chapter described humble, inclusive leadership. This one delves into visionary, inspirational, and heartfelt leadership. All of these leadership attributes help create the culture needed to succeed.

CEOs are probably tired of hearing that they need to have vision, as if it were a commodity that can be picked up on a commercial exchange. Vision can also be presumed where it does not exist. Some leaders create images of themselves as visionaries when they may have been lucky, ruthless, one-trick wonders, or simply solid performers who happened to operate in a rising market. A few leaders have held the "visionary" mantle up as a shield to prevent scrutiny of their actions. If you question them, you do not "get" the vision. Conversely, sometimes vision is described as if it is a 300-page guidebook with the future neatly described and organized, and all that the company has to do is execute on the grand plan.

Vision can be developed, but it is pretty much something that leaders either have or do not. Either it emerges out of a person or it does not. Smart CEOs know whether they really have the knowledge, passion, and experience that will drive vision, or whether to partner with someone who has such sight. Meaning nothing more—or less—than the ability to anticipate and to imagine (to see in images), vision often begins not with sight but with a gut sensation. In folk tradition such as the Sioux, Kansa, and the Blackfeet of the American Plains, the vision quest is a time of personal seclusion and physical ordeal in which adolescent boys came to an understanding of their role in the tribe and universe. You do not have to go off in the wilderness for 40 days, but you do have to wander inside your head for some length of time. Visionaries do not stare blissfully into a contemplated future. They do not begin with a mental model of what lies ahead. They do not sit in rooms and strategize or act with strategic intent. Visionaries are people undergoing an often painful birthing response. Steve Burke, who helped lead Comcast into the top position in the cable industry, speaks of visceral reactions toward future possibilities.

Visionaries become engaged emotionally, psychologically, and physically, which explains why personalities as diverse as Thomas Edison, Sam Walton, Bill Gates, Steve Jobs, and so many others have pulled all-nighters as they rushed forward toward something strongly but vaguely sensed. They churn through all their knowledge, they feel their environment, they react spiritually to an emerging potential. Walton was described by colleagues as operating on a "crazy intuition that not another man in the world's got." He played what-if games and analysis, constantly evaluated competitors, and regularly inspected stores, but he relied on his "gut" to sort through the mass of data and experience to make decisions. He and other visionaries are over stimulated by their own imagination—and boom, something happens.

That something combines knowledge, experience, and a constant scouring of information to create intuition. The root of the word

H	Humble, inclusive, inspirational, innovative, and heartfelt leadership
A	Adaptive, enthusiastic, emotionally intelligent employees
P	Profit for all who contribute to the company's success
I	Invigorated stakeholders, vendors, and clientele who serve as first-line marketers
E	Engaged, constructive community citizenship

Figure 9-1   Elements of a happy company.

intuition means both to look on and to consider, to understand something without having to consciously think about it. It is a kind of tacit knowledge that emerges from the interplay of the conscious and unconscious mind. Intuition is what enabled Edison to solve a problem with his original phonograph, which could not reproduce the "sh" sound, as in sugar, even though he could not explain how he did it. Eventually, instinctual impressions do emerge in the mind as images. According to legend, the chemist Friedrich von Stradonitz's dream of a snake eating its own tail led him to deduce the ring-like structure of benzene. Einstein imagined the universe in three-dimensional terms, and then developed the mathematics to describe what he saw. All world religions speak of seeing a higher reality that guides our behavior in the here and now. Poets see images in their minds and put words to them. Novelists play out scenes in their heads and hasten to write them out before they fade. Michelangelo famously spoke of seeing the image within the marble and carving away everything else.

Entrepreneurs similarly can imagine the future. Not in the sense of literally predicting an event, but of being able to see in their mind's eye a plausible if nonobvious new way of doing something. As Walton pursued his innate sense of what the ultimate retail experience would be, other visionaries have seen beyond the here-and-now to create a mental state akin to memory but about an experience that might happen, rather than one that has. Entrepreneurs and inventors do not necessarily grasp the magnitude of this potential change, but they do grasp the importance. Walton confessed that he had no sense of the scope of what he was starting but simply knew that his approach to retailing was right. He overshot the mark because real imagination comes only in the super-size. Walton set out to reinvent retailing. Henry Ford set out to reinvent transportation. Gates and Jobs set out to democratize computers. Edison set out to create the electric light, the phonograph, the movie camera, and a national electrical grid to support these and other gadgets. Edison said, "When I am trying to make a thing, I always play my blue chips first. I try to think of the biggest thing that could be done, and then do it." Compare this comprehensive view of the future universe with legacy airlines or some automobile manufacturers, who reel from event to event and react to one competitor's move after another, while trying to protect old habits, old processes, old pricing models—a vision that has not been revisited since 1950.

As visionaries address the emerging patterns, the future comes more into focus, but it may be years before the full picture can emerge. Microsoft's initial mission, "a computer on every desk," came many years after Gates and his co-founder, Paul Allen, began punching in zeros and ones on the first primitive PC. When the vision comes into focus, however, the visionary can often see the likely direction of sectors in surprisingly concrete terms, as Edison did in predicting the helicopter, computers (machinery that would rival the brain for performance), and robots (machines that would put other machines together).

Such a combination of knowledge and intuition is so powerful that the U.S. military has used it for "remote viewing," in which highly intuitive and specially trained individuals, given as much information as possible, imagine the most plausible threat scenarios that U.S. forces might encounter—war games taken to a higher plane of consciousness. Even the TV show *Numb3rs* is based on the idea of combining data, intellect, and intuition to predict future scenarios (in this case, the likely behavior of criminals). Businesspeople can use scenarios to sharpen their own "look-ahead" skills and help develop an embryonic vision. Consultants from the Center for Applied Research (CFAR), a management consulting firm specializing in strategy and organizational development, once worked with a small family-owned business that was about to pass from the second generation to the third. CFAR was hired to help prepare the two young family members for their future role in running the company, along with an older nonfamily member who was then the COO.

At the beginning of the first meeting, the consultants handed the group a packet of material. One was a press release purporting to name the current CEO (the father) to a presidential commission, which would remove him immediately from the business. The other materials were letters, one from the company's chief supplier and the other from the company's bank. Both stated concerns about the changed business relationship because of the father's imminent departure. All three clients were speechless; the nonfamily COO turned white; one of the family asked for an aspirin. Although they quickly discerned that the documents were bogus, the subterfuge served its purpose. The two family members and the one nonfamily member recognized how ill prepared they were to assume the mantle of leadership. The scenario continued with the three new leaders meeting with the fictive supplier and banker. The hard questions raised by those interactions underscored the lack of definition in the team's respective roles and the lack of knowledge of the two family members in important aspects of the company's business.

Although more dramatic than most, CFAR's intervention ensured that a potentially abstract review of strategy and succession became one that engaged everyone on a deeply personal level. This day led to more scenario planning, but now the plans were based on the three people talking honestly about their personal desires and the way they hoped to work together. The additional scenarios helped uncover each of the participant's assumptions, mental models, and their view of the company's future.

CFAR guides such players through simulations to force a deeper view of the needs, plans, and intentions of all the parties and give everyone the potential to see second- and third-order consequences of decisions. Reflecting on these consequences leads people to insights that then remake the mental model. Handling ever-more-complex situations gave the people greater confidence, eventually leading from fear and reactivity to choice. In this case, the COO realized that he wanted to remain with the family firm, when before his future and his desires were uncertain. The two young family members realized that although they too wanted to play a major role, the COO's greater experience was invaluable. The vision that emerged was not so much about the company's future as about the role that each person wanted to play in that future.

After the consulting engagement, life imitated fiction. The father was offered a role in an industry organization that required him to leave as CEO. (He remained as chairman.) The nonfamily COO stepped up to CEO, and the two family members took more senior roles that gave them broader experience. Succession was secured on the basis of the combined vision of the new generation of leaders.

Seeing and Acting on the Patterns

Whereas less-experienced or less-insightful individuals often need structured scenario planning to help uncover their interests, competencies, and leadership potential, classic visionaries are able to instinctively find patterns in the murk. They constantly construct scenarios themselves and test the company's behavior against them.

The way in which an intuitive leader works can be seen in the style of Steve Burke, who joined the Comcast Corporation in 1998 after a successful career at the Walt Disney Company, where he developed the Disney Stores, restructured the company's European organization, and became president of ABC Broadcasting. Comcast's acquisition of AT&T's cable properties under the guidance of Burke and CEO Brian L. Roberts created the nation's largest cable system but was only the first step in the transformation of Comcast into a $70 billion world-class communications company. Traditionally, cable companies have viewed innovation as a scourge introduced by satellite companies and other competitors, and the proper response is to get Congress to block those competitors from moving into their territories. In contrast, Burke has led efforts to provide customers with faster performance, video on demand, voice over the Internet, and other ease-of-use technologies that can make broadband a "one-stop" solution for any communication-related service.

Burke has been able to make substantial changes in an organization of 55,000 people because he does not require all the facts and figures that another leader might require before making decisions. By being in touch with his "reactions to information" as well as the information itself, he has the ability to apply intuitive analysis where hard data is insufficient or contradictory. Being able to act quickly on partial knowledge was instrumental in 2001 when Comcast bought AT&T's broadband business, which had begun to bleed customers. Burke created an integrated and diverse core team of 150 action-oriented individuals. Meeting with them weekly—often on-the-fly, rather than in formal session—he worked through various scenarios, exploring possible outcomes and comparing those with previous successful and unsuccessful ventures. His mindset was more pattern recognition, much as a human recognizes a face from the past, than numeric pro and con, much as a human evaluates cost versus benefit.

When Burke begins to see a pattern in the information he is gathering, he does not seek exhaustive analysis or try to create a set of testable scenarios. Instead, he validates the pattern by talking with his team, the leaders of functional groups in the organization. In this way, he can move quickly. He does not ignore quantitative data, but he uses it to support what he learns first hand. He constantly recalibrates his view. If his direction creates a positive resonance, he keeps moving forward. If the pattern changes or detours, Burke does not hesitate to change either. This intuitive process enabled Burke and Roberts to align the new Comcast/AT&T organization with Comcast's vision. The company not only stanched the loss of customers within a few months, but also increased margins and paid down Comcast's debt by more than $7 billion, all within two years.

Rod Eddington, the CEO who led British Airways through one of the most sweeping restructurings in aviation history, is a scientist by training and therefore wants to see the data, to get all the appropriate issues on the table before making a decision. Yet Eddington, who in 2003 was named by his peers as the airline industry's leading executive, also relies on his intuition, especially when he has to act quickly. When he first joined British Air, he gave himself 90 days to come up with a plan for the struggling airline. He talked to staff, shareholders, managers"—anyone who would give me 15 minutes"—and asked what they liked and did not like, what was broken and what was being done well, and how to improve the airline. From those dialogues, he quickly developed a picture of the organization's strengths and how to build on them and just as quickly began to act. Data gives you information, he says, but intuition tells you when to listen and when to act. His early intuitive steps, followed eventually by detailed formal plan, turned British Air around.

Eddington also adds that the question really is, "Whose instincts do you trust?" In the first hours after the Air France Concorde crashed in Paris in 2000, senior British Air officials were wrestling over whether to ground their own Concordes. Seldom are all of an aircraft type grounded because one in the fleet goes down, but the supersonic Concorde was the flagship for both British Air and Air France, had never been involved in a major accident before, and only a few of the type existed. After hearing all sides, Eddington turned to British Air's senior pilot, who had been flying the Concorde for 25 years, and said, "You know this plane better than anyone else. It's your call." The captain recommended grounding the British planes for 12 hours until Paris could provide more information, and this is what British Air did. This situation demonstrated not only the value of trusting the instincts of the most knowledgeable person present, but also the value of having a humble CEO willing to do just that.

Trusting that a pattern will emerge is part of an intuitivist's mindset. Steve Jobs says that the dots in your life do not usually connect going forward, but you need to have faith that they will connect later when you look backward. Jobs took a calligraphy course in college for no other reason than his appreciation of the art. He could never have predicted that this course would provide the inspiration for providing beautiful typefaces with the Macintosh a decade later. The dots connected because calligraphy was one element in Jobs's emerging sense of design, which has always been a strong suit for Apple against the square gray boxes of other computer companies. Call it guts, destiny, karma, or life—Jobs's own life experience has convinced him to trust intuition, even if it leads you down wandering paths to begin with.

A visionary must be intuitive, but intuitivists are not necessarily visionaries. Intuitivists execute on what they understand, which makes them great problem solvers or great administrators, but visionaries/entrepreneurs use what they understand to create a new way of doing things. The difference is seen in the creation of Endo Pharmaceuticals, a company that specializes in pain management.

In 1997, DuPont Merck wanted to offload drugs whose patents had expired, on the assumption that generic equivalents would render the lines unprofitable. But Carol Ammon, president of the U. S. Pharmaceuticals Division of DuPont Merck, felt in her heart that patients did not necessarily need new medications but rather more flexible and effective ways to take existing medication. Timed-release formulations for opiates, for example, would create fewer initial side effects and last longer. Powerful drugs that could be absorbed via skin patches rather than ingested via pills could be better tolerated. If she had been only an intuitivist, Ammon would have remained with DuPont Merck, applying her skills toward the next generation of drugs. As a visionary, she created Endo to pursue her dream. A leveraged buyout led by Ammon and Mariann MacDonald not only created a company with $600 million in sales, but the reformulation of existing branded and generic drugs also keeps Endo's R&D costs relatively low, and the outsourcing of manufacturing keeps its organizational structure simple and its focus tight. *The right vision creates its own kind of streamlining.* Ammon and MacDonald received the Greater Philadelphia Ernst & Young Entrepreneur of the Year Award in health sciences in 2003, and Ammon was named CEO of the Year by the Eastern (U.S.) Technology Council in 2004.

Jim Collins has shown that CEOs of great companies are equally successful leading on behalf of their own vision or someone else's vision. If a CEO lacks the personality profile just described, the leader needs to ally with someone who has it. Vision is not, however, the strategic plan, which should be the guidebook for achieving the vision, or the business model, which provides sustainable revenue to achieve the vision, or any of the steps needed to execute on the vision. So visionaries may need to pair themselves with world-class, operationally oriented executives. Walt Disney was the artistic visionary, and brother Roy was the financial genius. Sam Walton was Wal-Mart's visionary, and brother Bud was an operationally driven executive. Intel's most profitable years occurred with visionary Andy Grove at the helm and operationally excellent Craig Barrett in the position of COO. At the design firm IDEO, David Kelley is the visionary, and brother Tom, an MBA, is the general manager. At Waggener Edstrom Worldwide, one of the largest independent public relations companies in the world, CEO Melissa Waggener Zorkin and executive vice president Pam Edstrom both fit the "dreamer" category. The two have thoughtfully surrounded themselves with a cadre of highly talented, highly experienced senior executives who know how to get things done.

Inspiration Completes the Picture

Coupled with a big vision is the need to have an inspirational one. Of the three broad personality profiles to be discussed in the chapter on employees, affiliators naturally respond to inspiration, and power-motivated individuals need inspiration to avoid going over to the "dark side" of personal power trips and greed. The last group, achievers, can work without an inspirational vision—the work itself inspires them—but inspiration helps convert them from problem solving to opportunity seeking. Without inspiration, a company soon fills with people who work strictly to make money. Such employees seldom have the motivation to persevere through the hard work needed to succeed, they seldom make good team players, being in it only for themselves, and they are the first to whine and sow dissension when times are tough.

To perform at their best, humans need to believe that they are involved in something bigger than themselves. This need springs directly from the emotional brain, which seeks personal and social connections, and from the executive brain, the seat of altruistic behavior, which recognizes the long-term strength that comes from cooperation. There is a hot debate as to whether humans are really altruistic. The deterministic view has been that humans will selflessly aid or sacrifice themselves only for people who are related to us, as part of a genetic survival mechanism. However, both formal testing and life experience show that our entire species will act for the benefit of others, not just for our own offspring and the survival of our own genetic pool. In one test, the "Prisoner's Dilemma," subjects received a greater individual reward if they turned against the other party than if they cooperated. The results showed that if the people believed they were working with a human rather than with a computer, they were much more likely to cooperate than to double-cross the other. Further, altruistic behavior activated the reward areas of the brain in the neocortex and frontal lobes, whereas selfish behavior did not. *When working with other humans, people naturally chose the win-win option, and the win-win option gives humans a chemical rush!* (In a real-world counter-parallel, police actively engage the fear of crime suspects to induce them to choose the "me first" option and turn in the other party in exchange for a lighter sentence.)

Scientific tests strongly imply that altruism is neither a cultural trait nor an occasional individual trait but one deeply embedded in the wiring of all people. Altruism—and voluntary cooperation—must therefore have played a major role in our surviving and thriving as a species. When some scientists say that altruism is ultimately enlightened self-interest because a good deed is usually repaid, they forget that each individual must believe that the generosity will be reciprocated and thus altruism must already be ingrained in human behavior.

Enlightened self-interest is highly indirect and subtle indeed for such examples as poor people sharing food with a hungry stranger; teachers dedicating their lives to teaching the neediest; medical personnel and relief workers providing aid in regions wracked by war and disaster; firefighters rushing into burning buildings to save people; strangers rescuing other strangers from all kinds of harm; soldiers risking life and limb to drag injured buddies to safety. Countless other daily examples do not draw notice because altruism is so common that it is not newsworthy. Selfish behavior makes the news because it is often scary and also because it is rare. *The desire to work with others and help others is a fundamental part of what it means to be human.* Altruism may be the defining signature of our race, more so than our other "civilized" traits, none of which—speech, tool making, culture—would amount to much unless mutual support and cooperation are a given. Organizations that tap into this altruistic drive have much more motivated employees—and ones working from a much more creative level of consciousness—than companies that have no higher mission or that fail to express the one they have.

Some organizations have missions that are intrinsically inspirational. Medical care is one. Yet many organizations in medicine are anything but inspirational. Whether hospitals, insurance providers, or health maintenance organizations, they seem peopled by bureaucrats and bean counters who drag themselves to work each day to perform with graceless mediocrity. The complexities of regulations and paperwork that dog this field have caused companies to lose heart, or they are run by people who saw a trillion-dollar industry and rushed in to make a buck. A failure to believe in the core mission quickly devolves into running patients through like cattle, creating fraudulent bills as some doctors and hospitals have done, or cooking the books as HealthSouth did.

Even if the field of endeavor is itself inspiring, the leadership must personally identify with and act from that mission for that inspiration to carry over into the organization. One organization found such a way to define its mission: "It's for Mom." When Mary Brown Stephenson developed cancer in the late 1970s, her son, Richard J. Stephenson, could not find a medical facility to treat the patient as well as the disease. After her death, he founded Cancer Treatment

Centers of America (CTCA) with the goal of turning medicine from being centered on hospitals, doctors, and reimbursement to being rigorously and totally centered on patients. CTCA takes a multidisciplinary approach to health that combines world-class medical skill; state-of-the-art medical, surgical, and radiological technology; and supplementary therapies that include nutrition, mind-body medicine, and spirituality.

Rather than having a technical standard of care, CTCA uses the "Mother Standard of Care," a reflection of how each employee would want his or her own mother cared for. (Continuing the family motif, a young patient said that the doctors "treated me as though I was their own daughter.") CTCA plants a tree for every patient who survives for five years, and the organization has planted hundreds, even though many patients come from other physicians who have given up on care. One such survivor honked her horn every time she drove past the office of her previous physician, who had told her to "go home and get her affairs in order"—doctor parlance for "go away and die." (CTCA persuaded her to discontinue the "hello, remember me?" to the other doctor.)

CTCA's unique approach has made it the most highly esteemed patient-care organization in the United States, with the highest "net promoter" scores yet recorded. Net promoter, a concept developed by Fred Reichheld, measures customer loyalty on the basis of the number of customers who actively recommend your company versus the number of customers who disparage your company. The net promoter number has been shown to directly correlate to short-term customer purchasing habits and long-term corporate profitability. A typical company has a rating of 10 percent, meaning it has 10 percent more boosters than detractors. An excellent company could have a rating of 80 percent. CTCA outscored *everybody*, including such major service enterprises as the Ritz-Carlton Hotel Company and Four Seasons Hotels and Resorts and product companies such as Microsoft and Dell.

A company's area of expertise may not be awe inspiring on its face, but the right leader will imbue the mission with heart. Providing accessories for dogs may not sound like inspirational work until you learn of the love Ruff Wear employees have for dogs and of the company's constant efforts to provide better equipment not only for regular dogs living active lifestyles but also for guide dogs, dogs involved in search and rescue, or the latest, "combat boots" for canines sniffing out bombs in Iraq. An auto dealership may be about volume and margins or it may be about providing affordable, reliable transportation to the public. A home builder may be about the cost of land, materials, labor, and markup, or it may be about providing families with a warm and secure nest. A restaurant may be about rapid turnover during the peak hours or about giving people a pleasant respite from a harried day. Starbucks could be about the price of coffee beans and retail space, but the company's desire to improve the spirit of people's lives translates into a special kind of customer service. CTCA could be in the business of medical treatment, but prefers to be in the business of patient-centered hope.

Microsoft's original mission—a computer on every desk and in every home—led the company to drive toward volume and market penetration, which is one reason the company often seemed cold and calculating. Finally, the company looked deeper and asked: Besides the sales opportunity for us, *why* do we want a computer on every desk and every home? The answer is the company's deep belief in the empowering nature of technology that people can use directly. Today, Microsoft's mission is to help people and businesses throughout the world realize their full potential, and the company has grown noticeably warmer in its behavior toward consumers and partners. The company's motivations have shifted from *inward* to *outward*, from "what we are trying to achieve for ourselves" to "what we are trying to achieve for others." As the company takes the mission to heart, helping others achieve their potential will mean that a good deal less time will be spent worrying about the features in a competitor's product or a competitor's moves in the market, and a good deal more time will be spent brainstorming about how computers can transform the future. Instead of beating about in old markets, the company can create new markets, as Apple did when it introduced the iPod.

At The Phelps Group's annual holiday party, the associates called Joe and Sylvia Phelps to the front of the room to give them a gift. The entire company then proceeded to say the company mission, "We're here at The Phelps Group to do great work for deserving clients in a healthy working environment to realize our clients' goals and our potentials." The wood-frame house reverberated with the voices speaking in unison. Phelps was emotionally moved then, as well as the next morning when he had an epiphany. For all of his adult life, he had been a goal-oriented person on a mission to do something worthwhile. Hearing the group recite the company's mission, he realized the potential of a group with a common goal. The emotional power of that moment has driven Phelps and his group ever since. Not simply because they had a common set of operational goals, but because they all believed in the same thing, and that thing was bigger than business as dollars-and-cents. The organization had discovered the mission behind the mission and was ennobled by it.

Even if altruism is not a company's goal, the mental shift takes individuals out of themselves, reducing the chance of reactive, fear-based behaviors. All of the previous examples characterize a similar transformation, and such change is all that is often necessary to create an inspirational calling.

Seeing Is Making Others Believe

Vision is seeing. Jack Welch, the former CEO of GE, says that the leader's unending responsibility must be to remove every detour, every barrier to ensure that vision is first clear, then real. How that vision manifests itself affects how you personally approach your business, how you act day to day in business, and how you teach your employees to think and act every day in business. Vision must be big enough to reshape a market segment and inspirational enough to direct and unify the motivations of you and your employees. A lot of people like to talk about the value of diversity, but diversity without a common goal is chaos. A vision will pull you together, as well as pull you to above-and-beyond efforts, not because it is required but because you cannot help yourself. Vision and inspiration are not just great personal motivators. That motivation translates into solid company performance. All of the positive example companies mentioned here are also highly profitable. In an age of struggling medical providers, CTCA's inspiration-based, comprehensive, seamless, holistic, and patient-first approach generates more sustained growth than that experienced by comparable medical centers.

A meaningful mission also helps you remember why you as a person were born and why your company was born. This means the vision must *move* you. At IDEO, the first person on a project to design a new car seat for children was a father who had already tried out 10 seats for his own kids. No motivation needed. Marco and Sandra Johnson began what became a multimillion-dollar medical-training business in California when Marco, a firefighter and paramedic, came home from work agonizing over the death of accident victims because bystanders did not know first aid and his wife became upset at the idea of children dying unnecessarily. Vision is not limited to the CEO, of course. The board of directors should share in the company vision and regularly review the CEO in terms of progress toward that vision as well as progress toward the numbers or toward specific actions in the business plan. Vision is a quality that should be an aspect of people throughout the organization. Every manager of a group should have a vision of that group's function. Every individual should have a vision of his or her individual role.

At any level, checking in on your vision over and over is one core trait of a happy company. ScriptSave ends all employee meetings with customer testimonials from holders of their prescription cards describing how much money the cards have saved customers or about how company employees treated someone. This standing agenda item, called "Leave a Legacy," is based on Stephen Covey's seven habits of highly effective people. Each of CTCA's centers of excellence begins its monthly board meetings with a "patient impact statement" by a patient who is in the hospital that day and is willing to speak to the board. The patient is asked questions about how services at each hospital can be improved. This part of the meeting does not end until the board is able to grasp a comment that would lead to an improvement of services from the patient's perspective. "It's a powerful motivator when you have someone with stage-four cancer still alive five years later, thanking you for giving them the chance to see their child graduate from high school or to see the birth of their first grandchild," says Robert Mayo, vice chairman of CTCA. Both companies constantly remind themselves that the organizations have a social value in the outside world and that employees should serve others as they would like to be served.

Leaders who believe in a vision and mission beyond the financials are themselves more believable, more credible. People said that if you visited with Sam Walton a little bit, you simply felt better. His belief in the potential of his company and his employees to make life better for poor people gave him a mystical ability to arouse confidence and trust. He could inspire people, breathe life into others. All such leaders fill their employees with the enthusiasm of their dreams, making them believe and come to life with it. When Joe Phelps and Melissa Waggener Zorkin talk about marketing communications or Ben Lytle speaks of one of the health benefits companies he has led, the excitement in their voices is palpable. They are energized about their mission, about their customers, about their employees. Not about themselves. Not about profits, except as they prove the value of the mission.

Vice Admiral Richard Carmona, the U.S. surgeon general, illustrates the command of a leader motivated by mission and emotional connection to others. A high school dropout from the streets of Brooklyn, Carmona went on to become a decorated combat veteran and the top graduate of the University of California Medical School. He served in U.S. special forces and rose to be the highest-ranking physician in the U.S. government. Even now, Carmona also works as an emergency room physician, a sheriff's deputy, and a SWAT team commander in his hometown. *His mission is saving lives.* His service in special operations and his duties on the street bring him face to face with real life. When he begins every speech with a heartfelt comment to his subordinates that he could not carry out his mission without their help and support, his voice and his body language make it clear that these words are anything but perfunctory. He has chosen to operate from the executive brain so that his experiences of the horrors of war, the rough world of the street, and the desperation of the emergency room have taught him compassion rather than having left him traumatized. This rich personal context—intellect, values, and empathy—gives him a powerful, heartfelt capacity to motivate almost anyone.

Many leaders are inspired by the work itself, by their product or service and their ability to improve people's lives, however modestly. For other people, inspiration is built on a spiritual foundation. An example of spirituality in business is Leland Kaiser, a health-care businessman, psychologist, and futurist who believes that capitalism will ultimately succeed only if it is based on what he calls spiritual economics, "a humanistic capitalism, a nurturing capitalism, a caring capitalism" guided by conscience instead of greed—a system that works for everybody, not just for the privileged few. He challenges business leaders to have the courage to work from their moral centers and from a perspective of abundance rather than the scarcity mindset that leads to greed. He lectures CEOs on the concept that you do not pick your job, your job picks you. In other words, special skills, knowledge, and experience have put you in a unique position of leadership. Do something more with that position than just grind along a strictly economic path. Have the courage to change some small part of the world for the better.

This notion of spiritual economics is embodied in the experience of John McNeil, who became president and CEO of North Hawaii Community Hospital on the Big Island in 1997 after studying under Leland Kaiser at the University of Colorado. One year into start-up, the hospital was losing more than $100,000 a week and had used most of its line of credit to meet payroll. Within three months of McNeil's arrival, the hospital achieved a positive cash flow; within a year, it achieved a positive bottom line. The hospital continued to grow through acquisition of land and the creation of new services, including a new imaging center.

Located on a sparsely populated island and lacking the heavy state subsidies that other island hospitals received, the hospital succeeded despite expert opinion that it could not support itself. The transformation occurred along the same lines as CTCA's efforts, by putting the patient first, treating the patient as well as the disease, and calling upon patients' spiritual reserves as well as the staff's own medical expertise. Crediting Kaiser's teachings as contributing greatly to the hospital's mission, vision, and values as well as to team building, McNeil also deflects praise for the turnaround to the hospital team, the board, and the community of the island. McNeil has since become CEO of the Philadelphia center of CTCA.

Many people associated with CTCA are inspired by specific beliefs, but spirituality is not limited to a particular tradition. Rather, it is a recognition that human beings are part of a universe and a moral context much greater than themselves. To paraphrase William Channing, spirituality is that within us that is "open to light," regardless of the source. And even the most hardcore free-market maven speaks of "enlightened" self-interest. In their book *Spiritual Capital: Wealth We Can Live By*, Danah Zohar and Ian Marshall define spiritual capital as the "wealth we gain through drawing upon our deepest meanings, deepest values, most fundamental purposes, and highest motivations, and by finding a way to embed these in our lives and work." They take emotional intelligence one level deeper by defining spiritual intelligence as the ability to access those deepest purposes and highest motivations. Zohar and Marshall encourage business executives and leaders to become knights of this philosophy to spread higher values. The knightly principles are that there is something sacred unfolding in the universe, that life and all its enterprises, including business, are interconnected in a richer fabric of existence, that a healthy individual has a responsibility to engage with the world, and that service conveys a deep sense of humility and gratitude. In addition to their actual work duties, knights serve to uplift the culture within their organizations.

Kaiser also uses the concept of the knight, the English root of which is *cniht*, or "servant." Kaiser has taken health-care CEOs on pilgrimages to castles in England, where he puts their social obligations in the context of the selfless Knights of the Round Table. The Holy Grail today, he tells the CEOs, is to protect the wellness of humankind. Top-down, authoritative leaders who have gone through the program have emerged as servant leaders; lukewarm leaders have emerged as powerful advocates for a spiritual dimension to their organizations. Finding the spiritual core inside every business—what makes it meaningful as well as productive—is the final aspect of being a visionary.

You do not become an accidental visionary. Birthing the idea is difficult enough, and achieving a business vision requires as much discipline as any other creative endeavor, whether it is painting the Sistine

Chapel or writing *Anna Karenina*. To build an organization that can achieve a vision, CEOs must create an *intentional culture*. All of the leaders at ScriptSave came from other organizations, some with thousands of employees. Founder Charlie Horn, CEO Lori Bryant, and their executive leadership team took what was best about those organizations and incorporated those things into ScriptSave, while designing out the things that they did not like. When the company was small, they put in place the HR and organizational development programs they would need to grow, and they have disciplined themselves to continue those programs even in hectic times and rapid growth. Although crises are the times when leaders can easily excuse themselves for not following through on training or intense employee communication, these are also the times when employees are most looking at you to come through with your promises. Creating an intentional culture to execute on the vision is as important as the vision itself, as the next chapter shows with regard to creating a culture of innovation.

A Quick Peek at Vision

If it does not pick you up and throw you down, it's not a vision, it's a plan.

If you do not have a vision, somebody close to you better have. Otherwise, it is a matter of time before creditors arrive to repossess the furniture.

Few visions materialize fully formed. Look for emerging patterns in the clouds of business chaos. What scenarios might these patterns portend? How do they relate to other experiences?

Trust your instincts, but only after you have stuffed yourself full of quantitative data and customer feedback.

Use scenario-based training to hone your "remote-viewing" skills. Equally important, use scenarios to train the next generation of leaders.

Find the mission behind the mission, that which will make you and your employees jump out of bed in the morning and race to work.

Create an intentional culture. Hire, train, and organize around the mission, keep the mission in front of people daily, and ensure that all employees *act* the mission daily.

You do not have to be charismatic, but you have to personally believe in the mission. If you do not believe in the mission, neither will your employees, and an exciting career in the fast-food industry awaits you all.

Have fun. The future is so exciting you have to wear shades.

10

Organizing for Innovation

An intentional culture is the spine on which a positive organization builds. A mediocre company may have a strong but rigid culture transmitted by a fear-based boss or a wishy-washy culture promulgated by a leader with no firm business or moral vision. An excellent organization is one in which the founders build on a strong vision to take active steps to create an atmosphere in which innovation can prosper. Building such a culture is the last major role of senior leadership, the final aspect of the H in HAPIE.

Innovation is so important that a search of an online bookseller turns up no less than 7,256 books indexed to that topic. Of the top 50 entries, a dozen are books that have graced the best-seller list. Most have one of two underlying premises:

- Innovation requires a separate space outside the normal business processes in order to bloom, the fabled skunk works. Or,

- Innovation can be inserted into an organization through various practices and procedures.

Both cases assume that, cultivated like a rare flower or injected like collagen, innovation is a rare and precious thing added *to* an organization. But this presumption is wrong. Innovation in an organization is like consciousness in a living being. It is not something separate, but something that rises organically from the being itself. Innovative companies have evolved a common set of practices that eliminate the make-work and corporate friction that stymie innovation. The positive practices do not *create* innovation so much as letting air into the organization so that innovation can grow on its own. The practices do not provide specific solutions to innovation so much as they reflect a common underlying mindset that distinguishes the innovative company from the noninnovative company. Innovative practices become ingrained in a company when and only when employees believe that the *leaders* believe in the value of creativity.

Leaders of innovative companies, in addition to hiring great people, purposefully set out to achieve innovation. They do not leave innovation to happenstance or to the occasionally brilliant individual. They do not design their organizations first and then wonder how to insert innovation. They design their organizations to encourage creativity. Teresa Amabile, head of the Entrepreneurial Management Unit at Harvard, who has studied creativity for nearly 30 years, tracked 238 people working on creative projects in 7 different companies in different fields. Using the subjects' own notes about what they accomplished each day, her research countered several prevailing myths, among them the myth that creativity comes from "creative" people. She found instead that you either work in a company that encourages creativity or you work in a company that discourages creativity. Simple as that. The most important aspect in the promotion of innovation may simply be the message that management *cares about* innovation more than it does about such matters as status, social conformity, internal processes and rules, or preordained results. The difference can be seen in comments by Utz-Hellmuth Felcht, chairman of Degussa, the world's largest specialty chemicals company. Felcht says that every organization has a bureaucrat who, faced with change, will say, "Hey, we don't have a rule for that—we have to create a rule." Felcht says that instead of creating rules he encourages employees to do things their way, to seek the opportunity while accepting the risk and responsibility.

H	Humble, inclusive, visionary, inspirational, and heartfelt leadership
A	Adaptive, enthusiastic, emotionally intelligent employees
P	Profit for all who contribute to the company's success
I	Invigorated stakeholders, vendors, and clientele who serve as first-line marketers
E	Engaged, constructive community citizenship

Table 10-1   Elements of a happy company. This chapter concludes the leadership topic, the *H* in the acronym, with a discussion about the way to inculcate innovation into the organization.

In some ways, the original skunk works—a separate operation used to concentrate efforts on innovation—has had an insidious effect on subsequent thinking. The concept goes back to Lockheed's development of super-secret reconnaissance aircraft in the 1950s, and the name goes back to an ill-smelling plastics plant upwind of Lockheed's clandestine facility. Undoubtedly, pulling together some of Lockheed's top engineers under Kelly Johnson led to innovation, but the main reason for separate facilities was the need for military secrecy. We will never know whether interaction with other aircraft design teams could have led to more elegant solutions than the ones the team developed for high-speed, high-altitude flight, whether such interactions may have led to still other technical breakthroughs, or whether such interaction and shared efforts may have dramatically reduced costs. Or, of course, whether such interaction may have gummed up the skunk works with bureaucracy. The power of collaboration can remake the world as well as companies. America's Manhattan Project, the effort to build an atomic bomb in World War II, was kept secret and physically isolated from everyone on the outside. But within the project, physicists, metallurgists, chemists, and others worked directly together to solve the technical problems related to a fission bomb. Germany's research into the bomb was hampered by the separation of the three or four teams that were involved. Germany never got close, and the United States used the atomic bomb to bring an end to the war in the Pacific.

A subtle distinction exists between creating a talented team to carry out a particular project and separating a team from the general organization because the general organization is dysfunctional. Many companies have successfully used skunk works to create new products and services, but never addressed the organizational gunk that led them to resort to skunk works in the first place. IBM's leadership did not "get" the notion of a personal computer, but did allow a few IBM managers to go off in a skunk works to develop the IBM PC. When the PC business took off, IBM brought it "in house" so that it could be properly "managed" along with its mainframe business; which is to say, constrained so as not to compete with IBM's more costly machines. Within 10 years, IBM's market share for PCs had plunged from 55 percent to 5 percent. Within 20 years, IBM was out of the PC business entirely. The company's mainframe business survived just fine, but IBM's Cain-and-Abel reaction caused the company to miss most of the industry growth, which was on the low end.

It is understandable how a company that had dominated the landscape for 20 years with room-sized equipment could miss the switch to smaller hardware. But Digital Equipment Corporation (DEC), whose minicomputers had undercut mainframes, sat idly by while PCs undercut its minicomputers. Rather than recognize that the correct trend was to ever-smaller computers, DEC dismissed PCs as engineers' toys and missed the move to PCs entirely. (Far too late, three different DEC skunk works produced three different, *incompatible* PCs that never sold worth a lick.) DEC disappeared, absorbed by Compaq, which was absorbed by HP.

As happened with IBM, DEC, and many other companies struggling with change, skunk works can become a way of sidestepping the cultural and human issues in an organization that keep it from adapting. The PC did not represent a radically new approach that required new manufacturing processes or software design. The IBM PC used largely off-the-shelf parts, and the software came from third parties, including a little company called Microsoft. *The only reason to resort to a skunk works for the PC was to enable management to ignore it.* At best, IBM and DEC management might have hoped that the PC would become a nice little adjunct to the main business. At worst, it was a way of dealing with a fad until it faded. The issue was not technical. Overwhelmed by existing business issues, corporate leaders did not want to take on a challenge that by definition would force them to rethink their company fundamentals.

A like mindset has plagued the major airlines in their efforts to counter the low-cost competitors such as Southwest, JetBlue, or easyJet that pioneered new approaches to routing, booking, seat assignments, frills, and pricing. The legacy airlines have spun off their own discount airlines, none of which have succeeded, but have not made structural changes in their own operations until forced into bankruptcy. They continue to try to preserve their ancient and revered pricing concept of ripping off the business flier whenever possible. A cartoon by David Horsey sums up consumer frustration nicely. In the cartoon, a flight attendant on an overcrowded plane asks a passenger how the trip could be made more pleasant. The passenger says, "Don't cram us in like sardines. … Don't charge 50 different fares. … Don't make us fly into hub cities. Don't feed us inedible meals." To which the attendant replies, "Sorry, what I really meant was, do you want more peanuts?"

Rather than fear the discount airlines or try to run them out of town, British Air looked to learn from them, seeing what they do well that could be applied to its own operations. For example, British Air has eliminated many unprofitable short-haul flights, concentrating on the long-haul routes where its strength, terrific customer service, comes into play. Among internal changes, it consolidated 20 health-care programs for different employee groups. Similarly, IBM began its rebound when IBM began to ask what it did best. This was not building the biggest and baddest machines on the planet, but helping customers build business solutions and providing the service and support, the systems integration, consulting, and (yes) hardware necessary for those solutions. Bingo. Suddenly different classes of machines are not competing for the same customer's business. Instead, they are networked together in the most sensible way for the customer. Had IBM had this vision when PC technology was introduced, the PC would have been welcomed joyfully into the ever-growing family of solutions, instead of being treated as an unwanted orphan who threatened to take food off the plates of the real children. *A worthy vision always evaporates internal competition.*

A skunk works is fine for a real R&D project—for example, if IBM develops a chip that uses atomic structures rather than silicon surfaces to store data and so is applying science in ways that are radically different from existing processes. A separate operation also serves for well-defined, short-term projects. Anthem, the health-benefits company, created cross-functional teams to manage the integration for its mergers and to quickly combine shared services such as human resources, information technology, and finance. Anthem believed that the more people it involved in integration, the greater the buy-in all employees would have to the new combined company.

This approach served as a test bed for desired corporate behavior among all groups. Care should be taken that skunk works are not created because normal corporate culture and normal business processes stifle innovation. The very fact that skunk works are separate entities creates disunity. It is too easy for management to treat the skunk works as a sop to some temperamental talent in the hopes that they will get their wild ideas out of their system and come back to their "real" jobs; or for skunk works employees to "act out" as prima donnas or elitists. Rather than take innovation out to the skunk works, bring the skunk works into the company. Use skunk works to pioneer new approaches with business or technical models that are then incorporated into the mainstream organization. The goal of separation is to limit complexity long enough to create a functioning solution, nothing more.

For example, in the mid-1990s, a Philadelphia electric company, PECO, was struggling to shift from the old utility model, with its lackadaisical attention to customers, to a new customer-service model needed to compete in the age of deregulation. The company pulled together people from all parts of the organization and established them on a separate floor to develop new business processes. This skunk works created teams that consisted of customer service representatives, engineers, and field personnel to develop best practices; redesigned the inside of electrical trucks to make them more functional; streamlined the flow of work orders to improve productivity; and came up with more ergonomic desks for customer service. Before, if a customer needed new or different service, the customer was given a fixed date, however inconvenient, and had to potentially wait all day for the service person to arrive. After the changes, the customer was asked for a preferred date, given a choice of morning or afternoon, and asked whether the beginning or the end of that period was preferable. When all the kinks were worked out, the new working model was brought forward into the entire the organization. The purpose of the skunk works was not to be a self-contained entity but to give life to an idea, and then to integrate it into the organization.

Another company used the same approach to create e-commerce solutions for customers, which required cooperation from separate organizations that had their own physical areas, their own operating rules, and their own reward systems and career paths. The skunk works approach integrated the different groups in a way that created a new service model and a new organizational model for the rest of the company that is being rolled out now. This tack worked because the entire company bought into a process in which the vision, mission and mandate, and decision-making rules of the skunk works were clearly delineated in a formal charter.

As usually conceived, skunk works help somewhat by attempting to instill the notion of innovation into some part of the company, but the things that mark a successful skunk works are things that every organizational team should have: a lack of distractions and internal overhead; a bold, well-conceived goal; specific deadlines; and barely enough money to achieve that goal. Whereas a noninnovative leader might have skunk works for R&D or a few pet projects, the innovative leader designs every team, from accounting to sales to manufacturing to customer service, along the same highly focused, fast-moving lines. In most cases, those teams are multifunctional. Meaning, there may not be separate accounting, sales, manufacturing, and customer-service departments. Form follows function.

The Team That Sits Together Invents Together

Other common elements among innovative companies are decidedly low tech or low concept, but they work by fostering cooperation and human interaction. The first of these is nothing more than seating assignments.

Physical equality, physical proximity, and physical openness lead to cross-pollination. Cross-pollination is a word you hear again and again in innovative organizations, regardless of field. Cross-pollination begins with the simplest of all actions: not distinguishing people by rank, and putting everyone physically together. Nothing stifles an organization's creativity faster than the notion that rank is more important than action or merit. The trappings of office can become a major distraction as well as a divisive issue. People quickly slide into acquisition mode without being aware of the negative effects it causes. IDEO's Tom Kelley's first job as an MBA was to measure the square footage of the offices at a consulting firm because one partner thought his new office was smaller than the offices of other partners. A small manufacturer wondered why he was having labor discontent when he and the other managers worked in climate-controlled offices while his employees labored in a plant with a faulty heating and cooling system. One CEO had an upper-story office separating him from the rest of the company. Employees had to be buzzed in and to have an escort. If a visitor needed to use the restroom while waiting, the person had to walk the long way around so as not to pass in the CEO's view (apparently, so as not to unsettle him with thoughts of the destination). The CEO could not understand why employees were not buying in to his idea for a more open, egalitarian culture.

Innovative companies use physical layout to show a decided preference for individual performance over hierarchy. The first act of Paul O'Neill as CEO of Alcoa was to tear down the executive suites and create offices the same size as everyone else. Ken Iverson, CEO of Nucor Steel, reduced the number of management layers to 4, reduced the central management team to 22 for a multibillion-dollar corporation, left most marketing and production decisions to each mill, and did away with reserved parking spaces and special health benefits for executives. Class distinctions were also eliminated on the floor. All employee hard hats were the same color—previously, foremen and managers had different colors from everyone else. The only special colors allowed were for safety inspectors and visitors. JPL brought all 200 engineers from a variety of disciplines into one large building specifically to generate creative heat from the mix of talents working on the Mars Pathfinder project. Before the Prius hybrid vehicle, each chief engineer at Toyota moved around to meet with the different teams involved in design and development of a new vehicle. The chief engineer for the Prius, who was less experienced than other chief engineers, brought the entire team into one large room to have all the expertise close by his side. The results were so successful that the *obeya* approach ("large room") is now a Toyota standard.

Concerned with the sheer scale of Wal-Mart stores today, many consumers are unaware of the company's long history of innovation. In 1962, Wal-Mart's low-price strategy was a major innovation in retail, and the first Wal-Mart store was only the third self-service store in the entire country. Many of the company's best ideas came when Wal-Mart senior executives were jammed together, no farther apart than a paper clip toss, into ratty floor space described as "early bus station." Later, when he was chairman and a new CEO was allowing cliques to form in the executive offices, Sam Walton immediately relieved the CEO of command. As GE's Jack Welch says, "Collocation is the ultimate boundaryless behavior and is as unsophisticated as can be. ... One room, one coffeepot, one team, one shared mission."

Close proximity spurs informality and interaction, which spurs innovation, particularly among people in different fields or areas of expertise. At IDEO, a beach umbrella that follows the sun was built on a swivel tilt device originally developed for computer monitors, and a hinge for a computer laptop originated as a bicycle spoke—the result of cross-pollination. On the Mars mission, an engineer struggling to create software to time an event availed himself of a hardware engineer next to him, resulting in a hardware trigger that took only 15 minutes to design. At the time, the idea of putting hardware and software engineers together was considered radical. During its mergers, Anthem made certain to shift executives through a variety of positions to achieve a well-rounded view of the new organization. Toyota rotates employees to different teams to create greater understanding of all the issues related to manufacturing the entire car.

When possible, Waggener Edstrom Worldwide assigns employees to multiple teams. A new employee might serve a junior role on a large team, a mid-level role on a medium-sized team, and a front-line role on a small team. The employee has the opportunity to absorb culture and operating knowledge on the large team, develop teamwork skills on the medium-sized team, and demonstrate leadership skills on the small team. The overall experience provides a wide-angle view of the company and its client business. A Waggener Edstrom career path sometimes constitutes a physical as well as professional journey. On the road to a senior management post, a West Coast-based employee could serve stints on the East Coast and Europe specifically to learn technical, public relations, and management skills and to develop cultural awareness that might be used in a final posting in Asia. Such employees are expected to educate colleagues on how to make connections around the world. This cross-pollination effort is not a random process by which different people happen to apply for positions in different locales. This is a program by leadership to grow talent and generate the knowledge and breadth of experience that leads to context, creativity, and intuition.

IDEO employees also work on multiple teams on the premise that variety energizes. Sam Walton took cross-pollination so far as to swap Wal-Mart's company president/COO with the CFO/vice chairman. Both men had been doing good jobs before. Both did better jobs by coming into their new roles with different but related perspectives. A generation later, history pretty much repeated itself when Wal-Mart swapped the heads of its U.S. and international operations.

See It. Understand It. Do It. Fix It.

Real-world focus and a bias to action. Toyota's mandate to actively listen and go out and observe the real world has fueled a lot of innovation. The chief engineer for Toyota's 2004 redesign of the Sienna minivan insisted on driving an existing minivan with his family throughout the United States, Mexico, and Canada. Forget marketing surveys, he wanted to know how such vehicles were used in actual life. His trip led to five major safety and convenience changes in the 2004 Sienna. To validate their intuition, Ammon and MacDonald at Endo Pharmaceuticals analyzed the prescribing patterns of physicians, providing the necessary insight to develop modified dosages of Percocet and Endocet, a Lidoderm patch used to treat localized pain, and an extended-release morphine sulfate, which is a generic form of MS-Contin. Kevin Plank, then a football player at Maryland, tired of having cotton undershirts that became soaked with sweat when he played. He tested a variety of fabrics until he found one that would keep its fit while wicking sweat away, paid a tailor to develop prototypes, tried them out on himself and his teammates, and refined them further. His real-world experimenting turned into Under Armour, a $200 million sports clothing business.

ABC's *Nightline* television show highlighted IDEO's real-world approach to innovation, which is to precisely determine the customers' "journey," break it into component parts, and then prototype like crazy. With a TV-imposed deadline of one week, IDEO came up with a new design for a shopping cart by directly observing how customers were using existing carts and the problems they were having at every step of the shopping experience. Among other innovations, the new IDEO cart had individual baskets that neatly stacked into the cart so that multiple people could go different directions simultaneously to gather food. In an analogous project, UPS brought its hand-truck vendors together with its truck drivers to rapidly determine ways to build a better hand truck, based on the drivers' real-world experiences. The results included an apparatus with redesigned tires, multiple hand grips, and a new fold-down support. In a local soap-box derby charity race, which the company has repeatedly won, IDEO has learned repeatedly that creating a quick prototype and then test-ing, testing, testing always won over vehicles that were elaborately designed and little tested. "Fail often to succeed sooner" is a company mantra.

For the radical new airbag landing system on Mars, the most advanced supercomputers could not design and refine the bags quickly enough to meet the timetable. Taking a "hammer to fit" approach, the Pathfinder team outlined an initial design, dropped things off buildings, saw what broke, and refined the system until things quit breaking. The process was nothing more elaborate than "sketch, build, test, evaluate, modify." NASA's "faster, better, cheaper" approach prevented the use of redundant systems that typi-fied earlier spacecraft, so exhaustive tests of "single-string" (nonre-dundant) systems were mandatory. UPS uses a "try it and test" approach in its labs to quickly determine ever-better ways to apply or read bar codes on boxes as they whiz by on conveyor belts.

A company as unusual as its well-punctuated name, the U.K. firm ?What If! once took over a pharmacy after observation and filming of the habits of consumers in the pharmacy chain led to the conclusion that the packaging of medicines and a "sea of sameness" among prod-ucts had confused and demotivated customers, so that they bought less and sometimes bought the wrong product. The ?What If! team ran a live trial for three days, experimenting with new merchandising setups that included redesigned category titles, clearer labeling and clearer shelf communications, and new point-of-sale solutions. The results of the live trial and subsequent implementation led to a pro-jected 5 percent uplift in health-care sales.

Microsoft's technical and business model is to quickly develop a prototype, test it hard and fast, and refine it until the solution works, or fails and is discarded. For the projects that pass the test, the com-pany applies the money needed to make the project succeed. "Test and invest," as the approach is known, is also used by successful media companies to constantly evaluate the effectiveness of cam-paigns, shifting the money to the media showing the best returns. Sam Walton confessed to a strong bias toward action. "Nothing in the world is cheaper than a good idea without any action behind it," he said. His motto: Do it. Try it. Fix it. Iverson of Nucor Steel said, "Don't study the idea to death with experts and committees. Get on with it and see if it works."

All of these approaches are radically at odds with the traditional approach of using focus groups to test ideas. A focus group consists of a group of consumers gathered to discuss some product, service, or marketing-related issue. Often dominated by one or two individuals, either positive or negative, a focus group may not reflect overall consumer opinions. Also, what customers say they like or dislike about a product or service is often at odds with their actual behavior. Seldom if ever does a focus group help create a new idea. People don't know what they don't know until they see a new approach already well on its way.

Real-world testing is not built on the goal of pushing ahead with sloppy projects that have been given little or no thought. Rather, it is to recognize that most learning about any product or service does not come from the abstraction of marketing surveys, product specifications, computer designs or formulas, or an engineer's deep thoughts. *Most learning occurs when real people begin to use something.* No amount of "preplanning" can possibly create a world as complex or unpredictable as the world of human beings, with their penchant for using and breaking products in unexpected ways. In addition, whether internal or external, the customer for a product or service often does not know what he or she really wants until the person has something real to engage with and respond to. IDEO clients often like the best aspects of several different approaches, all the more reason for many quick prototypes. The sooner your product is being handled, the sooner your insight will grow as to the best way to improve it— the sooner you will be able to eliminate killer flaws or see an unanticipated use that might become the primary reason for the product to exist.

Brainstorm More Than Once in a Blue Moon

Real brainstorming involves everyone. IDEO has a regular brainstorming process, if the word *process* can be applied to their well-considered but decidedly informal efforts to generate "spontaneous team combustion." IDEO's David Kelley devotes a chapter to brainstorming in *The Art of Innovation*, but almost every topic in the book is a variation or expansion on the basic idea of regular, intense interaction among a variety of lively people. IDEO's modus operandi is to have lots of brainstorming sessions with as wide a variety of people as possible, not just experts or senior executives, and not just once every few months. Brainstorming is part of business as usual, happening *all the time*. The regularity of such sessions helps explain the highly energized atmosphere of IDEO's offices, which has the feeling of any company that loves what they are about more than they fear failure. We would love to see an experiment in which a participant in a highly engaging brainstorm session was hooked up to an electroencephalograph. We predict that the brainwave state would be similar to that of the monks in their highly meditative state.

Additionally, IDEO has a twice-monthly lunch with no agenda, just "play time" during which individuals can do a little show-and-tell with their latest gadgets and toss around their latest ideas; and "clubhouses," in which people with common interests get together to talk, as writers often get together to read and critique one another's work. Anything to give people a way to share and expand their ideas. For 12 years, The Phelps Group has had Thursday lunches where teams at a critical point present their media work-in-process to the company at large and take comments, a process that Phelps calls a "full-feedback environment" for developing creative concepts. The audience sometimes offers specific feedback and sometimes tosses out more ideas.

To constantly seek the best ideas for public relations counsel, Waggener Edstrom pulls brainstorming teams together from multiple locations and from multiple areas of interest such as software, hardware, biotech, and consumer groups to concentrate on the issues of a particular client. Many a visiting executive—even vendors and clients—have been pulled into brainstorming sessions when they call at a Waggener office. Another, more far-reaching form of brainstorming involves the "Dreaming Teams," a cross-section of employees pulled together to expound on, among other topics, what their dream clients would be, and why, and brainstorm about how to get them. From the many sessions, the company has captured several of the most intriguing ideas, including interest in the emerging digital music industry, and is pursuing those areas as new business opportunities. The people who came up with the ideas are the ones leading the charge.

Usually the brainstorms involve strategic public relations issues, but the many practical ideas that emerge demonstrate how brainstorming can repurpose a good idea for multiple uses. For one software client, a Waggener Edstrom team came up with a tongue-in-cheek coffee cup to hand out as a promotional item at a convention. A later brainstorm for another client in a different field morphed the idea into street carts where the client's potential customers could tank up on free espressos and lattes before going inside to a convention.

Innovative companies also use innovative technologies to advance their cause. Waggener Edstrom, which has about 600 employees in more than 20 locations worldwide, uses teleconferences, e-mail topic lists to which employees subscribe, Web log (blog) discussions on various topics, intranet postings of best practices, and so on to "integrate brain cells across geography." During The Phelps Group's "Brain-Bangers' Ball," as the Thursday lunches are known, a scribe takes notes, which are displayed electronically on a large screen to ensure that the ideas are properly captured, and the summary is e-mailed to each team.

The U.K. firm ?What If! adopts freshness as a core competency in helping other companies become more creative. On the assumption that using the same stimulus leads to the same responses, ?What If! believes in constantly seeking new stimulus to generate new and different ideas and creative connections. Freshness is considered a creative behavior as well as a company value. To stimulate fresh thought, associates regularly participate in activities, such as planting trees, learning exotic dances, and taking trapeze lessons. The company is not afraid to take chances when working with stimulus. Working for a client on an oral hygiene project, ?What If! brought in both a veterinarian dentist and a "lady of the evening" as "naïve experts"—experts in their fields who are naïve to the particular issue and are used purely as stimulus. (Creating interesting environments to release stress and stimulate creativity is not a new idea. Daniel Burnham and John Root, the architects who oversaw the 1893 Chicago world's fair, installed a gym in their office. Burnham gave fencing lessons to employees, and Root played the piano for their entertainment.)

?What If!, which routinely ranks as one of the United Kingdom's best companies to work for by the *Financial Times*, also puts its money where its mouth is. In addition to consulting with other companies on innovation, ?What If! invests some of its own funds to launch ventures it finds particularly innovative. Among the ventures they have taken to market are a new lighting concept store, a frozen organic food company, fast-food concept stores, and a range of natural-remedy medications for children.

Organizations run into trouble when they do not recognize the difference in personality traits or what they mean regarding progress toward a goal. At every level of brainstorming and refining, leaders need to know which step they are on and whether the discussion is moving outward (brainstorming) or inward (solution refinement), and which they want to achieve at that moment. Leaders need to make sure that the industrious do not foreclose ideas before they are fully developed and the imaginative do not derail the organization during its dash to project completion. To recognize and appreciate both, managers need to have a measure of both the dreamer and the deadline driven, knowing when to let an idea percolate and when to drive the team to closure. Good managers are "dreamers who ship" (our phrase).

Raise Visibility for Innovation

Visible innovation, visible recognition. Innovative companies also raise visibility for innovation, in two senses of the word. The first is the use of visual signs to keep new ideas directly in front of people. Many companies put visual reminders of their best work and their awards where customers and employees can see them, but this is only the first step. Walt Disney, the man, used to put his cartoons on the wall for comments from others. At The Phelps Group, client teams put projects on the wall for comments. IDEO draws a big visual map of all the ideas in a brainstorm. The constant reminders keep the creative juices flowing in background mode even if the mind is focused on something else at the moment. In Anthem's mission room for integration of shared services, all project plans were posted on the walls. Anyone could go in to see where integration was at any one time. The visibility of the project kept the team centered on the critical path, and the system also enabled people to track and obtain resources (for example, a data architect for an HR project). For all of its sophisticated technologies, Toyota's world-class lean-production system ultimately rests on large, visible signs indicating the status of inventory throughout its plants.

The second sense of visibility is recognition, often in a playful form. The IDEO engineer who stayed up four nights running to develop a new shopping cart received an award that shows Superman about to hurl an old-style shopping cart into outer space. Hunter Douglas Window Fashions celebrates various milestones and successes with zany presentations that feature faux Oscars and employees dressed as aliens. ScriptSave puts a lot of energy into making meetings fun as well as informational, sometimes having dancing or showing brief movies and providing popcorn, all to highlight the company's progress and achievements. The parade of employees at Wal-Mart management meetings is to recognize innovation, and the goofy cheers that Wal-Mart CEOs lead are designed to lighten the mood so that nobody, including the boss, gets taken too seriously.

Recognition can also be serious. At ?What If!, each quarter an employee is awarded £250 for demonstrating, beyond the call of duty, one of the company values: freshness, bravery, action, passion, or love. These values, and the names of the award winners, are inscribed on the wall for all to see. Microsoft product teams earn Ship-It awards with every release. Quasi-team members—for example, public relations or advertising personnel—receive an award only if the core team believes that their contributions are substantial. Years after leaving the company, one marketing executive still proudly displays the eight Ship-It awards he was voted by product teams.

Waggener Edstrom gives "WExcellence" awards internally for the most innovative work within the agency. Every employee and team is eligible. The awards, affectionately known as "Wexxies," are set up in a "playoff system" over a period of months to engage as many employees and to keep the anticipation going for as long as possible. Plaques are given out at agency business meetings to teams that have won. Winners are again celebrated at an annual dinner with the CEO, an event that culminates a weeklong celebration of innovation. Small offices and small teams have won as well as bigger and better-staffed teams. The technology services group has won for its smooth integration of Internet services into company business. A Wexxie award does not directly lead to financial reward, although having one listed on a performance review is not likely to *hurt* an individual's rating. The spotlight is on recognition, role modeling, and setting of expectations that innovation is not only encouraged but expected. At ?What If!, people nominate other employees on a quarterly basis for having fresh ideas, showing passion, or taking some innovative action. The stories are written up to make heroes of the nominees.

Do Not "Ghetto-ize" Creativity, and Make Your Employees Smile

The many examples in this chapter show that similar patterns of behavior exist in innovative companies across all industries, from manufacturing to retail to space exploration to information industries such as health benefits and public relations. The examples are varied, but varied does not mean random. In every case, leaders have created specific programs with the intent of encouraging innovation. Waggener Edstrom has a defined process to develop creative ideas and take them from brainstorm to actuality. The company considers the process the crown jewels of its intellectual property. IDEO *is* its creative process, one so valuable that many companies now come to study the culture rather than to have a product developed.

Similar practices will work for your company if you genuinely desire to have innovation bloom. The structure depends on your overall needs and individual talents. One simple technique is to make the organizational structure a function of the work to be done rather than a static entity into which projects have to be shoehorned. Dismantle silos. Create a modular company by using the "studio" approach, named for the way talented cross-functional teams with many diverse skills come together to produce a movie, then split up when the movie wraps. Studio teams reduce bureaucracy and enable fast response to challenges. Involve everyone, not just the talented few. Team leaders come from all parts of the company, not just from the executive suite, when new projects arise.

If you keep a traditional structure, move people around regularly and give them different levels of responsibility. Think in terms of SWAT teams rather than armies, anything to generate speed and flexibility. Toyota's manufacturing facilities are designed for short lead times and speed because simpler, faster systems provide the flexibility to design and build in quality. Whatever tack you chose, the underlying message is to develop an energetic, idea-seeking culture. Do not try to add it on with separate structures. Do not "ghetto-ize" innovation by placing innovation in a skunk works, thereby telling the other 95 percent of the organization not to bother thinking. Recognize that well-led collaborative teams substantially improve results (see Table 10-2).

Topic	Well-Led Teams	Poorly Led Teams
Innovative ideas adopted	61%	23%
Deadlines met	83%	33%
Marginal employees re-motivated	48%	9%
Projects staffed effectively	72%	54%
Conflicts resolved	87%	22%

Table 10-2 Teams that operate with a culture of collaboration, invoked by excellent leadership, show substantial improvements in performance. In addition to the improvements shown in the table, well-led teams can reach 55 percent more milestones or tasks accomplished, spend 35 percent less time in unproductive meetings, make 38 percent fewer errors, and stress or burn out 63 percent fewer people. (The numbers are extrapolated by George West, based on his knowledge of motivation and psychology, from research by Carl E. Larson for the book *Teamwork: What Must Go Right/What Can Go Wrong*.)

Like consciousness, innovation has much to do with connected-
ness. Whatever structure you choose must encourage and reward collaboration. Harvard's Amabile found that collaboration rather than
competition leads to more creativity because collaborators share and
debate ideas (whereas competitors hoard information). Brainstorming, the most intense form of collaboration, is a way to create group
intuition. When you engage team members, stimulate them, and provide them feedback, the answers naturally rise to the surface. Brainstorming is also a way to move fast without sacrificing quality. In
1976, NASA's missions were high-weight, high-cost, complex missions planned and executed over many years. Now NASA's "go-go-
go" mandate means that complex decisions have to be made in a third
the time and executed with fewer backups and higher potential risk.
In 1976, it took two weeks to physically prepare the materials for a
color advertisement or other marketing materials. That was 20 trips
down the freeway, 14 showers, and other moments of think-time during which an advertising executive could tweak the layout or improve
the text. Now, the mechanical processes can be done in a day. Achieving the same quality of thought and reconsideration means that
instead of 1 brilliant person mulling a topic for 20 days, you need 20
brilliant people cogitating hard for 1 day. Technology has pushed
every field into fast-forward. Each year, every organization in every
field is expected to perform faster, better, cheaper. By engaging the
brains of the entire organization, you create the positive atmosphere
and the sheer number of ideas needed to find the one or two great
ones that lead to success.

Evan I. Schwartz, in his book *Juice: The Creative Fuel That Drives
Today's World-Class Inventors*, describes creativity in terms of characteristics such as crossing knowledge boundaries, visualizing results,
applying analogies, and embracing failure. These traits come from the
engagement of all of a person's mental capacities moderated by the
executive brain, or what we call whole-brain function. Jim Collins has
three principles for success: 1) Do what you are best in the world at; 2)
do what drives the economic engine; and 3) do what you care pas-
sionately about, to ensure that you strive always for excellence. None
of these principles reference competitors or marketing warfare. They
are positive attributes springing directly from the person and organization. The first and third principles engage the human spirit, and the
second requires cool logic. Again, whole-brain function moderated by
the executive brain.

Establishing an intentional culture that values interaction,
freedom, and choice leads to the characteristics of innovative companies mentioned in the literature. If you peruse any of the books on

creativity and innovation—the 7,256 will take a while—you find that authors either identify various capabilities that come from higher human consciousness or identify practices that support higher human consciousness. It is not the particular personal attribute or business practice that matters so much as the company's ability to create an atmosphere that enables latent creative abilities to emerge, particularly among groups. Innovation occurs not by accident but by construction. Successful leaders consider the art of encouraging innovation to be one of their major job requirements. They evaluate ways to change the organization to achieve more innovation with as much rigor and regularity as they evaluate financial results. More often than not, the changes that work involve ways that humans relate to one another or to the mission rather than ways related to the economics of the business model.

One final point. Positive leaders and positive group dynamics produce more innovation than fear-mongering taskmasters. Amabile found in her 238 test subjects that creativity was positively associated with joy and love and negatively associated with anger, fear, and anxiety. Still more interesting, she found that people are likely to have a creative breakthrough today if they were happy yesterday. She concludes that a positive mental state enables people to make cognitive associations overnight that express themselves as a creative idea the next day. It is pleasing indeed to report that creative breakthroughs are the result of a happiness hangover.

Innovation Stimulation

Management must want innovation or any check box will be a way of pretending to do something but not committing to it. The leaders of the culture must want to set their people free, in which case best practices can stimulate the creativity that is naturally present. Among the ways that leaders can consciously and practically encourage innovation are these:

- Direct attention to what is best about your organization to determine how to apply the "skunk" mentality to it as a whole. Rather than create a skunk works to eliminate distractions and create intense communication, for example, develop an organizational structure and culture that provides these benefits to everyone. Think in terms of cross-functional teams that come and go with projects.

- Use skunk works as pilot projects to pioneer new approaches applicable to the entire organization. Charter any skunk works with a specific mission, process, deliverable, and due date. The deliverable should include ways to export the best of the project to the company at large.

- Put your best people on opportunities, not problems. Toyota assigned its best engineers to the Prius. Waggener Edstrom assigned Claire Lematta, one of its most experienced and versatile vice presidents, to develop the company's European business. She increased European revenue three-fold in 3 years, growing the London office from 8 to 45 people and expanding to Munich, Paris, and Brussels.

- Reverse the cost spiral. Instead of beginning with a big project and lots of money, which causes people to pile on features as well as mechanisms to lower risk, start with a bold objective and limited funds and say, "How can we do this?" The Mars Pathfinder team developed 25 new technologies with a slightly understaffed, slightly underfunded team.

- Do not become so immersed in grand "strategy" that you forget that strategy is just a fancy name for a related set of tactics. Tactics require something to actually get done, and fast.

- Plan "enough" up front, but do not fall into analysis paralysis, which occurs when the survival brain starts to worry about failure and prevents the executive brain from thinking about success. Consider improvisation part of the formal plan. Improvisation is the planning you do when you learn enough to know what you actually have to do to make something work.

- Eschew focus groups in favor of real-world evaluation of what humans are doing in their natural element.

- Remember that all humans have a natural instinct to build. Building physical things such as shelters or emotional things such as relationships, humans come alive when they are constructing something bigger and better than themselves.

- Interview new hires six weeks after they have joined the company. By then, they will have enough context to understand the business and can still see it with new eyes. Get their perspective on new approaches before they become "grooved," worn into the mindset that "we've always done it this way."

- Make innovation practices part of what you do weekly, not monthly or quarterly. Boldly display innovative success and innovation in progress, and meaningfully reward success, particularly that which comes from people helping other people and teams.

11

Only the Emotionally Intelligent Need Apply

After outstanding leadership, HAPIE companies require outstanding employees, those who are *adaptive, enthusiastic, and emotionally intelligent*. Emotional intelligence, a phrase introduced by Salovey and Mayer in 1990 and taken broadly into the world's consciousness by Daniel Goleman in his 1995 book *Emotional Intelligence*, is an individual's capacity for self-awareness, self-control, and empathy. Standard IQ tests measure one facet of intelligence, best described as reasoning capacity. In addition to concerns about cultural bias, IQ tests do not measure judgment, the ability to learn from experience, or the ability to adapt to change, three common definitions of "intelligence." Goleman gives the example of the straight-A dental student, a bookworm and introvert, who after graduation was far less successful than the B student whose personal skills and rapport with patients led to a thriving practice. In its study of successful leaders, Talent+ has found that the average academic grade of three-star generals is one full point below that of one-star generals. Even in fields requiring raw brainpower, people with moderately high IQs and other capabilities have been as successful as those with higher IQs. In truth, all of us know "brainiacs" whose lives did not measure up to their intellectual prowess because they lacked the emotional intelligence to interact with others.

As Goleman documented, the capacities of successful people to manage themselves and their relationships with others optimize overall team performance. Half a dozen researchers have come up with different formal definitions for emotional intelligence. Ours is simple. Emotional intelligence is the *active* management of your thoughts and feelings to bring out the best of your own abilities and to create positive interactions with other people. This aptitude may be more important than raw intelligence in giving a person the capability to succeed in life and at work. In addition, emotional intelligence can be improved during a person's lifetime, whereas IQ appears to be relatively fixed by the mid-20s. Emotionally intelligent employees are those with the following attributes:

- They look forward to working. They think positively about their work relationships and work projects. Work holds a relatively high place in their overall life priorities. They have appropriate pride for their contribution to work and for what the organization does.

- They know their strengths and talents and lead from them. They continually strive to enhance their skills through experience, learning and training.

- They take personal responsibility for their actions and for finding meaning in their work. They believe that their employment is a matter of choice—theirs and their employers'. They focus on what is right with the company and build on that.

- They use constructive and energetic language. They emphasize what they appreciate about work. Their language challenges themselves and others to grow. When they speak of the company history, they tell stories that are positive and inspirational.

- They often go beyond their job role and responsibility. They never utter the phrase "It's not my job."

- They thrive in environments in which change is common and they show resilience in the face of setbacks and down times.

- Their pleasure in being at work is obvious to visitors and other outsiders.

- They represent the company well both on and off the job.

Hiring emotionally intelligent employees should be the first step, but most HR processes are not geared to achieve that result. Most companies base their hires on some kind of standard personality test, two or three references, and one or two personal interviews. Astute HR managers and hiring managers can account for a lot, but unless the company systematically looks for emotional intelligence as an important qualification, the hiring practices will still be hit or miss.

Using many more interviewers can help weed out those people who look good on paper and who might have the personal skills to "snow" one interviewer but not to perform well on a team. Microsoft's hiring process is notoriously difficult, involving five or six interviewers who grill candidates in a variety of ways. Gauging the emotional intelligence of the prospect usually comes in questions designed to measure teamwork, but it cannot be said that the company is directly trying to ascertain emotional intelligence versus intellect or professional skills in computer science or marketing.

One hiring manager made a point of asking candidates to describe the hardest thing they had ever done. Most would talk about business projects, and from the descriptions the manager could usually get a good sense of the person's ability to deal with setbacks, to work with other people, and to look for nonobvious solutions when reaching a dead end. One candidate, however, said that the hardest thing she had ever done was to care for her dying father. She described in cogent, feeling detail how she had juggled her work against her father's physical decline, how she had handled the often-infuriating medical system when he was no longer able to do that for himself, and how she had kept her family together despite all the stress on herself. She got the job. It was not because she had a convincing sob story. It was that in discussing the situation, she gave proof of courage, resilience, and the capacity for multitasking and growth that are earmarks of success at any company. She also showed a depth of humanity and compassion for others that any company could use more of.

Accenture's interview process is specifically designed to weed out candidates who are emotionally immature or nonemotionally cognitive. As many as six to nine different people, including both analysts and partners, might interview a candidate. Accenture also asks

H	Humble, inclusive, visionary, inspirational, and heartfelt leadership
A	**Adaptive, enthusiastic, emotionally intelligent employees**
P	Profit for all who contribute to the company's success
I	Invigorated stakeholders, vendors, and clientele who serve as first-line marketers
E	Engaged, constructive community citizenship

Table 11-1   Elements of a happy company. This chapter concentrates on adaptive, emotionally intelligent employees, the A in the acronym HAPIE. Happy companies seek to hire employees who are emotionally intelligent. Happy companies shape leadership methods and processes to improve the emotional intelligence of the organization, aiding company performance.

behavioral questions such as the one about the toughest problem the person had to overcome and what techniques and competencies the person used to overcome it. The company has learned that if you ask enough times, you not only learn whether someone is truthful, but also whether the person is emotionally aware. In asking how the person created a solution or managed out of a bad situation, the goal is not so much to identify skills as to obtain as many perspectives as possible on how the prospect relates to other people. Encouraging candidates to tell stories of their own experiences in the context of solutions and emotional responses reveals the full human being. In short, the interview process should ask for stories rather than data and look for experiences as well as skills. This approach determines whether emotional as well as technical competency is part of the person's makeup.

Another important indicator is a question almost never raised by companies about a prospective employee: Does the candidate share the same values as the company? One bond among Endo Pharmaceuticals' initial employees is that they all found emotional meaning in their work. Alleviating suffering was an important value. Most of Endo's original employees were in their mid-40s and had the emotional maturity to understand the needs of someone else. Endo's challenge is to ensure that in hiring its next generation of employees the company can find younger people with the same altruistic impulses, which are as necessary to Endo's continued growth as scientific skills. Waggener Edstrom's highly personal interview process is designed to uncover personality traits that map to the PR company's values of collaboration, curiosity, innovation, integrity, passion, and respect.

Before an interview, a recruiter at State Farm Insurance asks job applicants to read up on the company's founding, which goes back to G. J. Mecherle, a farmer from Myrna, Illinois, who took a job with an insurance company after his wife fell sick. When Mecherle complained about the insurer's practice of charging poor rural farmers the same rates as better-off but higher-risk people in Chicago, Mecherle was told to shut up or to find other work. So in 1922 he formed State Farm Insurance, which has become one of the world's largest financial institutions by following the principle of treating your neighbor right. Today's State Farm recruiter quizzes job candidates about this history, looking for the 30 percent or so who light up at the story of the simple farmer who sought to treat his fellow citizens the way he wanted to be treated. State Farm has learned through the years that agents who care only for the monetary rewards do not succeed. Caring for other folks in the community is a prerequisite for success, not a nice addition to the package. The recruiter is looking for new leaders who embody the same values as Mecherle, people who can carry the company's culture into the next generation through a basic personality trait, that of a giver.

When It is Not Good to VERB-alize

Outside of establishing emotional intelligence as a major hiring criterion, companies do not have the time, resources, or organizational focus to take existing employees and build them into emotionally intelligent individuals for general purposes. As a result, most organizations are either emotionally intelligent or they are not, depending on the quality of their hiring, training, leadership, and culture. This situation leaves the majority of companies to struggle because their leadership and culture suppress emotional intelligence, fail to develop emotional intelligence, or hire and promote employees who lack emotional intelligence. One mid-level manager joined a start-up company in a new field with great hopes, but within two years the negativity and infighting of the culture had drained him of enthusiasm and initiative. Financial reasons caused him to stay for several more years, by which time he hated his job, the people in the company—and himself. "I went into that job as an 'A' employee," he said. "I came out a 'B' employee and maybe a 'C' person. I could not stand who I had become."

This marketing executive had become a VERB, an acronym for people suffering from one or more of the attitudes of Victimization, Entitlement, Rescue [by others], and Blame. Whether high or low in the company, whether manager or staff member, all too many employees slide into one or more of these attitudes, the result of ongoing conflict that activates the survival brain and reinforces its negative tendencies. Try to "fix" any one of these behaviors, and the employee either loops endlessly within one behavior (especially in victimization and blame) or slides from one to another (especially *from* victimization to blame). VERBs typify dissatisfied, disempowered, and stressed employees such as the executive who by the time of his departure had become perhaps 20 percent victim and 80 percent blamer.

Victims are the "poor me" people who do not take responsibility for their behaviors. Everything is always the other person's fault. Reinforced by politics, a litigious society, and our own fear-based psychology, victimhood is rampant. *Victimization* brings with it *entitlement*. Immature, narcissistic human beings come to believe that the world owes them something. Entitlement has many faces, from the able-bodied young person who would rather not work, to rich kids whose excessive material possessions keep them from developing a sense of self, to labor unions that demand more than companies can afford, to overindulged CEOs who take salary increases while cutting labor's pensions. When life becomes challenging, the entitled individual needs to be *rescued* by someone or something else. The need to be rescued makes such people passive. Like Vladimir and Estragon, who spend an entire play waiting for Godot (who may offer them work), they expect a new boss or a new job or new situation to make a difference in their lives. Waiting for rescue, entitled people do little or nothing for themselves. Like the two men in Beckett's play, their motto is "nothing to be done." People suffering from entitlement develop insatiable appetites. The result is *blame*—blaming someone else for making us a victim, for not providing our entitlements, for not rescuing us ... from ourselves.

It is not only lower-level employees or those in drudge jobs who wear the red badge of VERBiage. The marketing executive who succumbed to VERBs was one of the half-dozen most senior people in the company. Sophisticated engineers often blame salespeople for not being technically capable enough to sell their products and customers for misusing or misunderstanding the products. One such designer sniffed that it was not his fault that some people were not smart enough to use his invention. Chris Argyris of Harvard has found repeated instances of what we call VERB behavior among the smartest, best-educated, and most-talented professionals in organizations. He says that "defensive reasoning" keeps individuals from examining their own behaviors and shortcomings and often interferes with learning. No matter how much one company tried to get a consulting team to examine ways to improve its performance, the team members insisted that all their problems were the result of unclear goals, lousy leaders, or stupid clients.

All well-articulated VERBs!

Argyris's view is that many high-level professionals have a deep-seated fear of failure, which their intelligence enables them to conceal. An unwillingness to confront their own shortcomings means that often a company's real issues are not exposed and addressed. At one company, the CEO threw a victory party for the 40 executives involved in a Total Quality Management (TQM) project that saved considerable costs in 9 areas. Argyris learned in talking with the supervisors, however, that the goals had been easy to meet because all of them had known of the inefficiencies for years. Neither the CEO nor the managers could see, never mind address, the lack of accountability for the supervisors that had let underlying Cain-and-Able conflicts stymie the company for so long.

Like many other problem-solving approaches, TQM fixed the first level of problems, what Argyris calls the "single-loop" questions, ones that deal with superficial issues, but it did not address the "double-loop" questions that challenge assumptions, the motives, and rationales behind the superficial problem. Double-loop questions require emotionally intelligent employees capable of examining their own thoughts and behaviors. At Toyota, employees are taught to ask "five whys" to avoid a single-loop solution. They ask "why" five times in succession to dig ever deeper into issues to ensure that they get to the root cause and do not address symptoms only or fall into blame mode. Toyota's view is captured in the word *hansei*, roughly translated as "deep reflection." Toyota considers one of its primary management challenges to be getting its young engineers to think deeply and reflect on issues and consider all options rather than dive in to make immediate changes. Traditionally, makers of luxury cars made them quiet through heavy soundproofing. At the time, Toyota already had the finest part tolerances of any engine, yet asking the "five whys" led Lexus engineers to make further dramatic reductions, quieting noise at its source rather than masking the problem.

Many employees have a fear rooted in their not being good enough for their role. Poor management reinforces that fear—and sometimes plays on it. Fear behavior kicks employees into VERBs. VERBs turn people into catastrophists who see only the negative in every situation or who do all they can to mask their own inadequacies by pointing the finger at someone else. The question for companies is how to get from such typical behaviors to behaviors that are emotionally intelligent.

Build Emotional Intelligence as Part of Strategy

Major strategic initiatives can become the trigger to a long-term, company-wide process that can create and grow emotional intelligence at all levels, beginning at the top and moving through the ranks. Take a typical corporation that brings in outside management consultants to help determine its strategic direction and the likely growth that the direction would bring. That process would give the corporation a five- to seven-year overall plan. From the "what" comes the "how"—how could the company organize itself to meet its new goals? These goals might include the desire for 20 percent growth and for becoming a global rather than a national player. The company could then bring in experts specializing in development of an organizational strategy, which would develop a proposed structure to carry out the plan along with an outline of the leadership and behavioral traits the company required to succeed in the direction. Thus the business context would frame the processes and competencies that the company would need from its people and the context in which emotional intelligence would need to be exercised. In fact, major corporations have followed exactly these steps.

From this point, a company develops profiles that measure the emotional intelligence of its senior executives to determine the personal competencies that already exist within the organization and to determine what new competencies might be needed. A relatively new tool, the Benchmark of Emotional Intelligence (BOEI, pronounced "boy"), takes personal profiling further by assessing the emotional intelligence of the organization as a whole, as well as that of individuals or combinations of individuals. Developed by Steven J. Stein, the BOEI measures 7 factors of organizational emotional intelligence with 14 subfactors: organizational responsiveness, optimism and integrity, coworker relationships, top management leadership, supervisory effectiveness, teamwork, and so on (see Figure 11-2.) Providing analysis by individual, department, job category, location, length of service, or other custom categories, the BOEI can ascertain performance, productivity, morale, profitability, and a host of other factors relevant to corporate well-being. By its nature, the BOEI reflects both emotional intelligence and overall employee satisfaction, because high BOEI scores across the board typify a generally happy workplace, and low BOEI scores reflect the opposite.

Among the general lessons coming out of his research, Stein has found that worker satisfaction, long assumed to be the key to productivity, accounts for only about 9 percent of overall productivity. People can be quite happy in their work, but the work must be strongly connected to the company mission before job satisfaction relates to productivity. Stein has also found that compensation is not an important motivator except as it relates to fairness within and without the organization. Compensation can become a flashpoint for other areas of dissatisfaction, however, because pay is one area where employees can particularize their overall distress. Group cohesiveness and trust among co-workers and between co-workers and management account for a great deal in organizational emotional intelligence and overall employee satisfaction.

Generally, the BOEI shows that upper-level management reports the highest satisfaction and believes that the company as a whole shows the highest organizational responsiveness. These results should not surprise, because these individuals have more responsibility, control, compensation, and perks than people lower in the organization. Mid-level managers are the group most affected by stress and

Sample BOEI Results

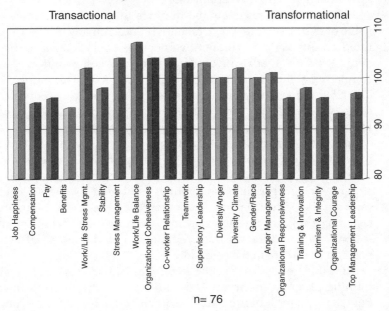

n= 76

Figure 11-2   This chart shows the 21 categories measured in the BOEI, ranging from transactional issues, the everyday interactions that affect perform-ance, to transformational issues, the issues related to direction, leadership, and culture. This chart shows how low scores related to an uncompetitive benefits package on the transactional side (left) undermined employee confidence in transformational areas such as optimism and integrity, organizational change, and leadership (right). (Copyright 2005 Multi-Health Systems Inc. All rights reserved. Used with permission. www.emotionalintelligencemhs.com)

whose work lives and personal lives are most out of balance, the result of balancing demands from above with supervision of those below, as well as perhaps longer hours in the quest to move up in the organiza-tion. The attitudes of line staff vary considerably from group to group and organization to organization, largely as the result of leadership above.

By establishing a benchmark of emotional intelligence, the BOEI can be combined with other tools and programs—leadership training, relationship-building seminars, employee training sessions, and other workshops—to measure progress as a company develops its leaders and employees. Usually part of an overall consulting program, the BOEI serves as an immediate diagnostic tool if one group by category (for example, sales and marketing or warehouse staff) falls well below the company average in certain areas.

How management treats the findings ultimately determines the value of this or any other instrument. At one company, the BOEI identified an inflexible, uncompetitive benefits package as a particular item of concern that also was affecting employees' confidence in the company's ability to tackle difficult major decisions (see Figure 11-2.) The CEO immediately engaged senior managers, had feedback sessions with employees, and quickly revamped the benefits package, lifting morale and restoring confidence in the company's courage, adaptability, and integrity. At another company, the BOEI identified problems in the customer service department. Further investigation uncovered a personality conflict between one employee and the supervisor and possibly preferential treatment by the supervisor toward other direct reports. The organization began a training and coaching program for supervisors, which included feedback from subordinates, and the frustrated employee found a more satisfactory position elsewhere in the company.

At a third organization, the BOEI was intended to help create a training program to improve the functioning of four departments. Low BOEI scores indicated that the organization had difficulty understanding and using emotions. In follow-up, all four departments heavily criticized management. Having decisions made for them with no input or feedback was a particular reason for alienation by the information technology department. When presented with the results of the BOEI, management did not believe that the employees should be unhappy. They viewed the departmental negativity as childish. The managers simply sat on the reports. They did not present the results to the departments or individuals or otherwise act on the findings. As a result, the atmosphere of distrust increased. The situation was a classic example of defensive managers—fearful of examining their own leadership style and abilities—reinforcing VERB behavior in employees. Another Cain-and-Abel conflict came one step closer to exploding.

Personality Profiles and Behavior

Once BOEI has been used to take the emotional temperature of an organization, other steps can improve the emotional intelligence—and therefore performance—of individual employees. Such assessment tools have been developed by Richard Boyatzis and Daniel Goleman, by Reuven Bar-On, and by George West, to mention the best known. Other profiling tools have been around longer to provide the individual with something of an objective view of his or her own behavioral style and some simple tools to help the person better relate to others in the organization who have different styles of interaction. Of the many models, the most commonly used ones are based on the Myers-Briggs Type Indicator (MBTI), which was initially developed to help the U.S. Navy find crew members who would not freak out in the claustrophobic confines of World War II submarines. Beginning with personality preferences such as introvert or extrovert, MBTI models create a number of basic types, usually 8 or 16, but sometimes as many as 72. The types can theoretically create enough different combinations to describe every person uniquely. Often, the models use color schemes to show which personality types are relatively compatible (similar colors) and which ones are not (clashing colors). For example, a person with a directive style might be bright red, and an observer might be cool blue.

MBTI-based models and most other models describe "what" the person is in terms of personality style, the person's preferred method of operating. A more-effective model also describes motivation—*why* the person has that particular style. Understanding their underlying motivation takes employees one level deeper into self-awareness. The motivational model goes back to psychologist David McClelland, whose seminal paper in 1973 argued that raw intellectual ability, as measured by IQ, was not an adequate predictor of whether someone could do a job well. Hundreds of in-depth interviews of successful executives about their work styles led McClelland, his then-colleague Richard Boyatzis, and others to develop 19 (later 21) broad competencies for businesspeople. (Successful female leaders in U.S. companies had almost identical competency profiles as successful males, except that women were less confrontational.)

Over time, the competencies were aligned with three underlying motivations: achievement, affiliation, and power. Still later, George West, in collaboration with Alastair Robertson, added a fourth motivation: autonomy. Although everyone has a mix of all motivations, tests consistently show that one motivator is primary and another is secondary, so that two motivations tend to dominate in each individual. Profiling can evaluate the strength of the motivations, the default behaviors that run with those motivations, and the likely blind spots that accompany those motivations. A person who is high in achievement and high in power can be a powerful change agent, for good or bad. A person who is high in power and affiliation can be a great leader, but sometimes for personal rather than organizational advantage (because such a person can be good at manipulation). A person high in achievement and affiliation can make an organization hum or can become bureaucratic, a talker rather than a doer in the effort to make everyone happy.

Although it is simplistic to think of Tom as an "achiever," Dick as an "affiliator," Hannah as a "power person," and Sally as an "autonomous person," each motivator is powerful enough to be described separately. For the achiever, it is achievement of and control over the work that matters. For the affiliator, it is the relationships. For the power person, it is the ability to have a significant impact and to influence others. The power motivation may manifest itself in one of two ways. Socialized power is that which is used for the greater good of the business, community, or social entity, to create win-win solutions. Personalized power may appear to be socially charismatic but is actually used in service of the power-motivated person's individual needs, something the group typically finds that out later in the process when "win-lose" shows itself. Autonomy provides the motivation for someone to step away from society's dictates, a necessary component for an innovator. Autonomy comes with two facets, independence and coexistence. Valuing the freedom to be a free spirit, someone high in independence refuses to accept the rules of others. Someone high in coexistence is protective of another's right to be different; someone low in coexistence can have the attitude of "my way or the highway," particularly under pressure.

Each motive group (which in combination makes the overall motivational profile) has unique strengths. Achievers want to fix things, to learn, to do things better than anyone else. Regardless of the issue, achievers want to create solutions in a controlled way. They find and present facts and figures. They seldom look or act stressed (unless things are getting out of control). They work out stress by figuring out solutions for the next day. In fact, an achiever's response to stress is typically that it is just another challenge. Constantly seeking contingency plans and thinking about what-ifs, they are seldom surprised. At their best, they present potential practical remedies to any situation and ask for others to help. Affiliators need to cultivate and maintain social networks, to have friendly contacts and avoid conflict. Their golden rule is usually "treat others as you would like to be treated." Affiliators develop relationships throughout the organization to help find solutions. Their empathic ability enables them to cultivate a broad network outside as well, including regulators, politicians, and important members of the community. They know who to go to—including achievers and power people—and how to connect to generate resources and support. Their reaction to situations is to call their buddies as a vehicle for fixing the situation. (Their ability to divine the real message regardless of the actual words makes affiliators good diplomats, but the U.S. government does not use personality screening to find the best candidates.) Power persons seek status, recognition, and the ability to influence others. The core value for high power-motivated people is "change." They use their ability, personal presence, and their oft-present significant persuasive powers to create a shared reality, build coalitions for change, and drive others to achieve what they want. They are skilled at motivating people and energizing an organization. They can push organizations onward through sheer force of will. Autonomous people have a strong need to chart their own course through the universe. These free-spirited souls want to invent, to accomplish something different, to explore, to meet life on their own terms.

All four profiles also have their blind spots and dark sides. High achievers need focus and structure to get the clarity they need for control, and so can become burned out by too many relationships. Used to outthinking everyone around them, achievers can become very bossy and can talk down to others. Achievers who cannot complete a goal can fall into analysis paralysis or continue to butt their head against the wall rather than use relationships to go around the obstacle. Affiliators are burned out by having too many goals versus relationships. Affiliators who are blocked by the loss of an important relationship tend to react personally, first withdrawing, then trying to soften up the perceived blocker, and then attacking the individual on a personal level. (A favorite target is a secretary, who first is rendered incommunicado, then receives flowers, and then invectives.) Power people who feel their power base being threatened may start screaming and firing people or may laugh quietly while undertaking a counterattack. Rule breaking by autonomous persons can wreak havoc if they feel stifled by organizational processes, group-think, or excessive conformity of any kind. Their ability to be a team player is often questioned.

McClelland discovered that successful entrepreneurs showed a combination of high achievement (to complete the invention), moderate power (to influence people to invest or to buy), and low affiliation (to not let anyone get in their way). In contrast, high achievers struggled in senior positions in large corporations, and successful corporate leaders were most likely to be motivated by power. For example, high achievement in the intricacies of finance can lead someone into the position of CFO, but the same achievement profile could cause the new CFO to become a detail-oriented micromanager. A successful CFO must use power to effectively influence other senior executives and must coach rather than direct his or her direct reports. This is an extreme example of the difference between a great manager (achiever), who can deliver on projects and programs, and a great leader (power person), who can unleash the energies of the entire group.

Because each strength of motive creates the default of a distinctive style of interaction, the different motives (and combinations of motives) can easily collide. If a high achievement-motivated person works with someone similarly motivated, "intellectual gregariousness" cuts in; both work together to achieve the task. However, if one achiever perceives lesser qualities in another, control issues may get in the way and a cold, antagonistic work relationship may result. "Task demands" of any sort can spook an affiliator, who might go into a shell like an abused spouse. Conversely, relating and being included is the need of the affiliator. Tapping into this motive pays dividends. An achiever can see an affiliator as lacking focus or discipline for calling a lot of meetings and wasting valuable time in chatter. A family business was nearly torn apart because of clashes caused by one brother being an achiever and the other an affiliator. It took counseling for them to understand how to work together to get the best of both motivational approaches.

Similarly, achievers have an instinctive suspicion of power people, and affiliators fear them. It is easy for both groups to perceive almost any actions of a power person as forceful and arrogant. A power person suffered this perception at a hospitality company, where treating people nicely is the formula for success and the business had a number of affiliative executives who got along well with most others. This executive team had a serious problem with the one executive, whose abrasive criticisms of many of their efforts made others suspect him of having a personal agenda. His motivational profile showed him to be a person of high power, high achievement, and low affiliation, exactly the kind of person to rattle an internal culture that centered on niceness.

When the executive chose to discuss his profile with the group, he explained that his aggressiveness was the result of his seeing the team use politeness as a way to duck hard issues and to let many ideas pass without a rigorous review. He had challenged them, he said, to help the company make more robust decisions and to better serve customers. When the others realized that his goals were the same as theirs and that his power was directed toward improving the company, they recognized that he made the perfect devil's advocate. Rather than fearing his comments, the executive team began to use him as a positive force to "tear apart" proposals to ensure that all plans were thoroughly vetted.

All businesspeople can run into style traps by not seeing how their style impacts others or how the style of others impacts them. If you know your motivational profile, you can develop the emotional intelligence to accommodate the needs of people not like you, improving the likelihood of successful collaboration, while at the same time developing "with the grain" of who you really are. For example, achievers can learn to solicit feedback from others before presenting a solution to the team as a *fait accompli*. At the very least, you will get others to buy in to your plan; at best, you will gather additional good ideas. Affiliators can tighten the "talkie" aspect of their interactions, can reduce the number of meetings, and can give others the option to meet, make the times more convenient, and start and end the meetings on time. Power people can do more than build up their team's ego and ask them to accomplish the impossible. They can lend power to the group by encouraging them to rely on the leader's position to help obtain the resources they need. As with the hospitality company, they can drive the organization to higher standards. Autonomous people can learn that giving up some of their independence might provide others with *more* independence and be better for the company in the long term. If you understand your work style, you can work from your strength to help your organization. Most people have the emotional intelligence to succeed if they have a common language by which to make sense of different world views. Motivational profiles provide this language.

Base All Changes on Strengths

One of the things that practitioners of positive psychology have learned is that trying to fix people's problems is a waste of time, not to mention the patients' money. Only about one in three people improve from traditional psychological therapy. Of those who do improve, only 15 percent improve because of psychotherapeutic technique. Most improve because of their personal relationship with the therapist or because of reasons unrelated to therapy, including the passage of time. B. F. Skinner's discovery half a century ago that positive rewards were more powerful than punishment should have led psychologists to focus on the affirmative. But traditional clinicians, coming from the perspective of traditional medicine that psychological problems are diseases to be cured, have sought to isolate the illness and try to fix it.

Positive psychologists have found much greater success in building from an individual's strength. One example is a career woman who did not become pregnant until the age of 43. Try as she might, she was not an empathetic, "maternal" mother toward her child. Rather than seek to work through her guilt and feelings of inadequacy—or find some childhood trauma to explain her emotional coolness—her psychologist focused on her strengths: her organizational skills, her intellectual understanding of child development, her genuine desire for her child to flourish. The woman evolved into a competent, confident parent with a happy child. Another example is the businessman whose family life was a disaster. His wife brought him to counseling because he was not empathetic enough. She confessed that he had never been empathetic while they were dating or early in their marriage, but she felt that their problems could be solved if he developed this ability now, 20 years into the marriage. The husband was respected in business as a great organizer, and he was famous for running his company by memo. Rather than try to remediate a weakness (lack of empathy), the counselor asked him to write a proposal that would reorganize the relationship. It took six drafts, but the executive took the first step in healing the family rifts by writing a memo telling his wife everything that was in his heart. Eventually, the family reestablished a functional relationship, and most of the individual psychological ills of the parents and children faded away.

Similarly, people in the workplace need to build from their strengths rather than seek a personality transplant. A bright and capable young man with a strong work ethic nonetheless was showing considerable signs of stress. He suffered from sleep problems, he felt that he was going through the motions at work, and he had mood swings that created personal conflicts. A friend asked him where he found his passion, and he confided that he found his passion in inventing things. His friend offered some advice. Rather than wait passively in the hope that something might bring his inventions to life, why not pursue them actively as a career? Encouraged, the young man discussed his ideas with family members, found further support, and began to develop a business plan. In short order, he was running an entrepreneurial start-up company. When he began managing his life from his strength—his inventive personality—his sleep problems, mood swings, and personal conflicts were history. His strength became his source of meaning, optimism, and professional achievement.

Another reason for building on the personal strengths of employees is that leaders cannot always lead in the manner you might want them to. Even if their overall intellect, integrity, and capability are outstanding, their personal style might clash with yours or they may have long-engrained habits of behavior that drive you crazy. Being human long before they were leaders means that they are as likely to err as anyone else. Great businesspeople introduce bad products and fail in new markets. Great generals lose battles. The higher a person is in the organization, the greater the scope of the mistakes will be. Rather than taking the position that they have no control over what the business is doing (a VERB-al response), all employees need to be the anti-VERB, responsible for their own behavior, their own performance, and their own teams, even if everything else is falling apart around them. The concept is captured in a single sentence from Talent+ about personal responsibility: "Each person is the CEO of his or her own life." Managing yourself begins with understanding your strengths and going from there.

Organizations as a whole also have to know their strengths and build on them. Michael Treacy and Fred Wiersema explain in *The Discipline of Market Leaders* that the most successful companies choose a single "value discipline" and design their organization and their business strategies around it. The three disciplines are operational excellence (such companies as McDonald's and Wal-Mart), product leadership (such companies as Lexus and Sony), and customer intimacy (such companies as Starbucks and Nordstrom's). Market leaders not only seek to establish dominance in a particular discipline but also to improve on it year by year, building on strength. They invariably falter when they stray from their strengths. McDonald's focused so much on growth in the 1990s that its trademark cleanliness and consistency suffered. Mercedes fell out of the "must-have" category in automobiles when its product quality failed to keep pace with Japanese and American luxury brands. Upscale retailers suffer when they start treating their high-end clientele superciliously.

A trained consultant or coach can uncover the personal aspirations of anyone—CEO, manager, employee—and where the person wants his or her career to go; can obtain a profound understanding of what drives that person and how that inner drive can take the company in a positive direction; can develop a motivational profile and a map of influences and determine what those influences say about the person's style; can help the person read the lay of land—read the personalities of the team—and learn which club to pull out of bag in terms of behavior to motivate different people. For example, appealing to a power leader's spiritual side can help the leader act in a way that is good for the company and community while helping ensure that the leader does not fall into a reactive pattern of personal power grabs. A coach would determine what activates that leader's higher values and build from there.

The ideal outcome of self-awareness is to align your strengths and your work. That congruence creates energy and passion. Conversely, a lack of alignment between motivations and job creates stress. Stress can bring down an achiever with conflicting or unclear goals, or an affiliator with orders to downsize the organization, or a power person who has been reassigned out of the power base, or an autonomous person running a bureaucracy. Passion is a perpetual-motion machine, frictionless and self-renewing. Stress is the friction that comes from a lack of alignment between capabilities and assignment. Stress can burn out the individual and it can destroy the engine of an entire organization. Passion and frustration are both culturally contagious. Aligning the person with work ensures that positive energy rather than negative energy surges through the culture, reinforcing other positive traits and behaviors.

Because each person is unique, such strength alignment, whether personal or through questionnaire-based programs, is an individual process. Although any time is a good time to start, the most effective way to integrate such programs is at the time a company begins a major initiative. At such times, the need to understand existing strengths (and gaps) is strongest, the need for emotional intelligence and strength alignment is highest, and the case for employee development is most compelling. Just as increased interaction among the many parts of the brain led to a quantum leap in consciousness in humans versus other species, the energy level and the flow of information in an emotionally intelligent company leads to organizational results that are far greater than the sum of its individual human capabilities. A cadre of emotionally intelligent employees can reshape the organization and tap into the whole-brain function of the entire organization. What remains is how the company can engage in a positive, energizing manner and reap a meaningful return in the process.

The Square Peg Who Destroyed the Round Hole

An entrepreneur who had successfully built a number of companies called a consultant to announce that he was about to buy a "small" business for his son to run. The consultant suggested that the right course might be for the son, who was in his early 30s but had never held a job longer than 6 months, to work in the field for a couple of years to determine whether he would have the interest and skills to run the business.

"Can't wait," the businessman replied. "The current owner wants to retire, the company is on the table, and the price is right!"

"The price is right only if the job is a good fit for your son, the employees, and the stakeholders," replied the consultant, who was unable to talk the businessman out of the purchase.

Three months later, the consultant received a frantic call from the father. "You need to get out here before I kill that kid!" The consultant flew out and quickly ascertained the chasm between the new president's skills and the skills needed to run the operation. "Would you talk to him?" the father said. "I'm not sure I could fire my own son."

Leaving the issue of dismissal to the father, the consultant agreed to a heart-to-heart talk with the young man, who knew exactly where the conversation was going. He had become enamored with the status and perks of office. He could not listen to an assessment of his shortcomings. In a moment of spontaneous anguish, he blurted out, "But I like being president!"

Treating the job like a favorite toy that he was unwilling to relinquish, the son refused to resign. The father refused to fire him. The business failed a short time later. This classic example of the misalignment between the demands of a job and the capabilities of the person ultimately cost dozens of people their jobs.

12

Return on People

Reaping a "meaningful reward," an important goal of for-profit businesses, is usually understood to be a reasonable payoff for the money, effort, and time that go into creating the enterprise. A meaningful reward can also signify psychological or moral values associated with the reward as well as the size of the reward itself. This sense of human moral value, of intrinsic importance, energizes and engages employees, who in turn work harder and more effectively on the company's behalf. This chapter explores the steps needed for companies to engage employees, to reward them appropriately, and to improve the companies' overall financial performance by thinking about profit in its broadest sense.

What exactly, then, is the "profit motive?" A speaker at a retail business meeting asked the audience whether they were in business to make money. All the hands in the room went up to signify "yes." He

H	Humble, inclusive, visionary, inspirational, and heartfelt leadership
A	Adaptive, enthusiastic, emotionally intelligent employees
P	**Profit for all who contribute to the company's success**
I	Invigorated stakeholders, vendors, and clientele who serve as first-line marketers
E	Engaged, constructive community citizenship

Table 12-1 Elements of a happy company. This chapter concentrates on profit, the *P* in the acronym HAPIE. Happy companies measure return on people as well as return on investment. In particular, a high return on people creates a high return on investment.

then asked, "So all of you are in such easy businesses that the money just rolls in, without any work on your part? You're just there to count the cash?" When the audience looked at him blankly, he explained. "All the people who I know in retail work very, very hard. They are working six and seven days a week. They don't get a lot of time off. They have put up their own money, mortgage their houses, take a big risk. If all they wanted was a decent profit, they would take a nine-to-five job and invest their money in something safe. They would get a little less return for a lot less risk and a lot less aggravation. Why are you really in business?"

Answers came pouring out. Most people had a passion for their particular retail niche: automotive, clothing, food service, stationery and gifts, whatever it might be. One young woman had turned her love of all things Barbie into a very profitable mail-order business. Others in the audience enjoyed making all the operational pieces of retail come together or enjoyed puzzling out the best merchandising schemes. Others lived to interact with customers, taking joy in finding hard-to-get items for them. Some reveled in being in charge, managing employees, keeping the books, and generally running the show the way they wanted to. (Note the mix of achievement, affiliation, power, and autonomy among the motivations.)

In other words, the speaker said, you are not in business to make money. You are in business to pursue a dream. Money indicates whether you have succeeded. If you are in business only for profit, you probably do not have sufficient motivation to carry out the grueling work needed to succeed. Or you will succeed by becoming a money-grubbing SOB that nobody wants to work for. Which is it for you?

Few if any of the most successful companies in the world say anything about profit in their mission statement. Making a profit is a given, but making a profit is not what the companies are about. People and companies that begin and end with profit quickly slide into a scarcity complex and target fixation. They begin to act as if profits represent their last meal before starvation rather than an indicator of their relative success in achieving a vision. Fear does more than lead to fraudulent accounting practices or to pumping up short-term profitability by cutting longer-term investments. Manipulation of abstract numbers is bad enough, but fear and target fixation also quickly lead to the manipulation and abuse of human beings. Before long, employees become not a major part of the company's generative process but cogs in a machine. Humans become defined in terms of output and nothing but. If they resist being treated as an output device, they become a problem to be dealt with.

Sometimes the devastating results of thinking of people in terms of output can last centuries. The economic rational for slavery in the United States created a fear-based culture that brutalized its African American population, created animosity between the North and South that infected every other national issue, and directly led to the Civil War. Ultimately, whatever profit the South had earned in 246 years of a slave economy was wiped out by war's destructiveness, which left the region reeling—undercapitalized and suffering repeated agricultural busts—for another 100 years.

The notion of "human as output device" also led to abysmal working conditions and child labor with the advent of the Industrial Revolution, to the abuse of coal miners and other workers in the early 1900s, and to the use of soldiers as cannon fodder in many armies, up to the very present. The international community did not formally abolish slavery until 1926, and pockets of forced servitude—not to mention sex slaves—exist today throughout the world. Sweatshops still pop up like poison toadstools in developing countries as companies seek ever-less-expensive manufacturing sites for products ranging from clothing to consumer electronics. Some of America's most respected businesses have at times availed themselves of sweatshop products, looking at the price tags first and human considerations only when called to account by human-rights watchdogs.

Profit fixation can be dangerous not only to workers, but also to consumers who buy a product whose vision came through a lens of fear. One example is the well-documented decision of the Ford Motor Company not to provide adequate safety for the fuel tank of its Pinto sedans in the 1970s. Ford discovered the fuel-tank problem in preproduction. Every test above 25 miles per hour resulted in a ruptured fuel tank. However, the company put the cost of retooling the production line at $137 million, while the cost of likely lawsuits was estimated at $49.5 million. Under pressure by then-President Lee Iacocca to enter the small-car market, achieve weight and cost objectives, and meet deadlines, Ford decided to leave the gas tanks as they were—even though the company owned a patent on a safer design that was used in other small cars.

Target fixation not only caused Ford managers to go blank on higher moral concerns, but it also led to wishful thinking that made the company unable to ask a few obvious worst-case questions, such as the following:

- What if the projected death rate is too low? Actual deaths were somewhere between 500 and 900 rather than the projected 180, largely because higher-speed accidents vaporized leaking gasoline and caused cars to explode.

■ What if an outsider examines a burned car for a grieving family and explains the inadequacy of the design, which let bolts rip into the fuel tank in rear-end collisions? It took a very short time before "recon men," experts who reconstruct the causes of accidents, reported the reasons for the fires to potential plaintiffs and the lawyers eager to represent them.

■ What if the trial verdicts are bigger than anticipated and the $49.5 million estimate for lawsuits is low? One civil verdict alone totaled $126 million, almost equal to what it would have cost Ford to fix the problem. (The jury picked that number for a reason.) Also, corporate misconduct was so blatant that Ford was brought up on criminal charges in one jurisdiction.

■ What if even one publication gets hold of internal documents? Someone leaked a complete set, leading to exposés not only of Ford's shipment of a car known to be dangerous, but also of the company's efforts to delay new federal collision standards that would have forced a redesign of the Pinto rear end.

One moment of thoughtful reflection about the long-term consequences would have led to the decision being reversed. Yet a hard-charging president drove a group of profit-squeezed managers into target fixation and problem solving. How squeezed? A one-pound, one-dollar piece of plastic, which tests showed would stop the gas-tank puncture, was considered too heavy and too costly. The result was a short-term decision to cut corners on a life-and-death issue in a way that made no economic or moral sense and left the company's reputation in tatters.

But wait, there's more.

Today, Ford is the primary provider of law enforcement vehicles in the United States, with its Crown Victoria police interceptor. When three Arizona police officers died in fire-related accidents in four years, the city of Phoenix called Ford to find out whether there were other reports of fires involving the vehicles. Ford said it had no knowledge of any problems. In fact, the Florida Highway Patrol had called Ford six months earlier with the same inquiry. It now turns out that between 16 and 30 police officers have died in fire-related accidents that may have been caused by placement of the fuel tank behind the rear axle, where it is vulnerable in rear-end collisions. Ford insisted that the accidents were quite rare, "occurring under very high-speed, high-energy impacts," although a casual observer might think that "very high-speed, high-energy impacts" are exactly what police cars should be designed to handle. Eight states and a number of cities have sued Ford.

Epilogue: The plastic part was added to 1977 Pintos, enabling the model to pass new rear-end collision standards. Ford has settled some lawsuits involving the police interceptor. Under growing pressure, the company added fire-suppression systems to police vehicles in 2005—but refused to provide them to any organization involved in suits against it.

In stark contrast was Johnson & Johnson's reaction to the Tylenol crisis of 1982. When cyanide-laced Tylenol capsules killed seven people in Chicago, Johnson & Johnson removed all of its Tylenol capsule products from the shelves, stopped production until it determined that the capsules had been tampered with after being placed in stores, and put up a $100,000 reward for the persons responsible. (The perpetrators were never found.) When another attack occurred in 1986, the company discontinued the capsule form of the product entirely, replacing it with a caplet form in tamper-resistant packaging. Although the company took a $100 million charge for its efforts in 1982, the quick, principled response on behalf of its customers solidified Johnson & Johnson as the leading company in personal health care, and Tylenol regained its position as the number one analgesic. It is no coincidence that the company's response radically differed from Ford's. Robert Wood Johnson, the founder of Johnson & Johnson, preached as early as 1935 that corporations had a responsibility to their customers, employees, and community as well as to stockholders. His thinking was considered radical for the day, but Johnson understood that putting the customer first meant profits would come in good order. His corporate credo, published in 1943, has been the reference point for all progressive companies since.

Creating a Return on People

If profit is to be an important but not singular measure of a company's success, consumers, society, and the market need to find a way to measure more than the short-term dollars and cents that companies produce. Analysis needs to include some sense of a "return on people," as well as return on investment. Yet in the United States, only the military has any explicit sense of a "return on people." The military has always evaluated battle strategy in terms of casualties, and the likelihood of excessive casualties would lead to a prudent general to try another tack. Generals who suffered excessive casualties on a regular basis would be relieved.

Today, the military takes that concern a step further, using intelligence, technology, and unorthodox warfare specifically to minimize the number of troops needed and the dangers they face. A typical air raid historically would require big formations of bombers to fly directly over a well-defended target, costing many aircraft and the lives of dozens of crew. Today, stealth aircraft, cruise missiles, and smart bombs can take out equivalent targets with little or no danger to air crews. Combined operations between air and ground forces enable small, expert teams to take out military objectives that in the past would have required massed forces and large casualties.

Compare the explicit goal of the military to take objectives with the minimum harm to its people—and how that approach shapes everything from recruitment, budget, equipment, technology investments, to training—with the way most civilian businesses take their "warriors" for granted and think about turnover after the fact, if at all. Whereas every military decision is informed by the potential human cost, business analysis focuses on hard financial metrics with no concern at all for the people creating the results. Return on investment is usually calculated as return on assets (a company's profitability relative to its total assets) or return on equity (the assets created for every dollar invested). Earnings per share and market capitalization are also common measures of a company's value. Other fundamental analysis includes such metrics as asset turnover, collection ratio, inventory turnover, debt-to-asset ratio, debt-to-equity ratio, interest coverage, and working capital ratio. With no measure of the possible harm to people in creating these financial results, analysts and the market in general are in the position of rewarding a businessperson for killing the goose that lays the golden egg.

Based on the notion of "efficiency," the only common people-related business metrics suffer from the danger of measuring only the output level. The efficiency ratio, normally noninterest expense divided by total income, tracks how much money it costs to make a dollar. A ratio of 0.60, meaning it takes 60 cents in expenses for a company to earn a dollar, would be high. A figure of 0.50 would be good, and 0.30 great. The primary expenses would be salaries and benefits, so a high ratio would indicate relatively high expenses (for example, bloated salaries or high health costs) or low revenues. Either way, the company produces revenue inefficiently. Another measure, management efficiency describes revenue per employee and income per employee. For example, the S&P company average in 2004 was $342,000 in revenue per employee and $26,000 in net income per employee.

However, it is relatively easy for an unhappy company to "improve" efficiency by overworking its people for several years, creating better results, but also creating burnout that causes a later exodus of highly skilled people. Or companies can systematically rid themselves of older employees, not because of poor performance but because salary and health costs are higher than for younger employees. A similar profit spike and burnout can occur in companies that bill by the hour, explicitly or implicitly requiring high billable percentages with no consideration for training, professional development, or the mentoring of others. Banks can underprovide for loan losses and sell assets for short-term gains. A product company can improve short-term profitability by reducing R&D and marketing expenses. *All of these actions have been done to make results look better.* When the increased output is real, employees are harmed through overwork, with casualties defined as illnesses, disabilities, and terminations. When the output is the result of financial manipulation, employees are harmed when the CEO skips out with his or her big incentive-based salary package, leaving employees to suffer the long-term damage.

Even when the goal is not to pump up short-term profits, the people-as-output approach can have deleterious effects. At most law firms, associates are on salary until they become partners. One law firm, however, salaried its associates for only the first two years. After that, they were effectively on commission. The system was brutally efficient at rewarding successful lawyers and weeding out the rest, but one side effect was that lawyers tended to take very little vacation time, and no one in the firm did pro bono work except the less-experienced employees on salary.

Measuring Human Factors

In such a climate, some method is needed to measure healthy output and strong performance, the maximum amount of work that an employee can produce while remaining positive and upbeat—as opposed to being wrecked or chased off by the workload. After all, roughly 75 percent of the market valuation of the S&P 500 is represented by intangible assets, such things as employee knowledge, customer relationships, patents, trademarks, copyrights, and brands, rather than tangible assets such as property, plant, and equipment. In other words, the market recognizes implicitly the value of people-centered intangibles. CEOs are aware that they need to retain employees who represent their companies' human and intellectual capital. In discussions at the annual World Economic Forum in Switzerland about the most important issues they face, leading CEOs say that they should be measured by how much they retain talent, by how much they build a company's intellectual capital, and by how much they can develop the company's employee knowledge base.

Yet current financial measures either fail to account for intangibles or treat them inconsistently. For example, if you develop technology, you show only the expense incurred; but if you buy technology, you record it as an asset based on the price paid. Enron was able to hide losses because intangible sham deals, in which expenses were spirited off company books, were difficult to differentiate from legitimate intangible deals. Some companies have good or bad quarterly or annual reports not on the tangible matter of how many products they produce and sell but on the intangible matter of how they play the energy and currency markets. Southwest Airlines has a 50 percent market premium over competitors because of its leadership and positive employee relationships. Intangibles matter. So do the people who create them.

Speaking of "return on people" is becoming fashionable. No one has come up with a good definition, except for organizational characteristics we have already discussed: good leadership skills and communication, good hiring decisions and working conditions, an innovative culture with a lot of collaboration and information sharing, and engaged and optimistic employees (in a word, HAPIE). HR managers use "return on people" to try to help organizations develop more humane internal practices. Consultants use the concept to sell their services. The better consultants try to do more than measure employee satisfaction, going the extra step of finding ways to tie satisfaction to actual business results. What remains is attempting to measure not just how much cash it takes to produce a dollar, but also how much it takes in terms of blood, sweat, and tears. Or, more preferably, how much energy, sweat, and laughs it takes.

Emotional Intelligence by the Numbers

Despite $56 billion a year being spent on business-related education and training each year, the percentage of good managers has increased only slightly, from 10 percent to 12 percent, according to psychologist Richard Boyatzis. There are two reasons for the lack of progress. The first is the mis-focus of teaching programs. Business schools teach rational analysis but not teamwork and cooperation. If any school has even thought about teaching emotional intelligence, the idea makes them squirm with embarrassment. Also, few on-the-job training programs seek to raise a company's emotional intelligence. The second reason is that CEOs do not examine the question of whether a quantifiable return can come from a qualitative trait. However, more and more research shows that emotionally intelligent employees provide quantifiable returns—staggeringly good returns. Therefore, let's begin at the beginning and work some numbers.

Roughly 70 percent of all people who quit their jobs do so because they dislike their boss. By happenstance, roughly 70 percent of all people who are fired are fired because they cannot get along with other people. So, the overall proportion of people who leave because of a lack of emotional intelligence by boss or employee is close to 70 percent overall. Most estimates put replacement costs for employees at between one third a person's salary to two times salary, depending on position. One company has measured the cost of replacing someone at just under $100,000, an organization average that would roughly equate to the cost of replacing a mid-level executive.

Assume that a company with 1,000 employees has a turnover rate of 20 percent (a figure that would be average or low in many fields), and 70 percent of the lost employees (140 people) leave or are fired because of the employee's or manager's lack of emotional intelligence. At $100,000 per employee, the direct cost of having emotionally immature employees is $14 million annually to this mid-size company. Recall from Chapter 6, "The Lesson of the Salmon, or Why Happiness Beats Going Belly Up," that stress, most of which comes from poor personal interactions, accounts for 19 percent of absenteeism, 30 percent of disability costs, and 60 percent of workplace accidents. Adding the costs of stress from the unhappy environment and you can conservatively guess that the true costs are more than double the $14 million, say $30 million in round numbers.

Assume further that by investing $1 million annually to improve the emotional intelligence of its employees, the example company was able to reduce people-related departures and terminations from 140 to 100 people and to reduce its ongoing stress level by a comparable amount. This roughly 30 percent drop in turnover would reduce direct costs by $4 million and would reflect lower total costs of at least $9 million. The program would offer a 4:1 direct return and 9:1 total return.

Although the numbers are hypothetical, they are also probably conservative. SAS Institute, the largest private software company in the world, has a turnover rate of less than 5 percent, compared to a 20 percent industry average, with savings of at least $85 million annually, according to one study. Microsoft's turnover rate of half the industry average saves it between $250 million and $500 million annually, assuming a replacement cost of between $50,000 and $100,000 per employee. Waggener Edstrom has a turnover rate that is half the average of the PR industry. Costco, the discount chain that considers long-term employee retention a competitive advantage, has a turnover rate half the industry average and one fourth that of Wal-Mart, whose biggest competitive weakness today is employee turnover. (The company's employee situation is borderline schizophrenic. People who might never rise above cashier at another chain have the opportunities to become department or store managers or higher, and Wal-Mart celebrates successful employees in a variety of ways; however, the company also loses 46 percent of its associates each year and faces major employee lawsuits.)

The Phelps Group, which measures retention in terms of length of service, has an average tenure that is more than twice the industry average. Longer tenure leads to employees who are capable of providing better customer service, which supports the company's above-average client retention rate, and also cuts recruitment costs more than half. ?What If! has lost only two or three senior people in eight years. Anthem is at the median among health insurance companies for involuntary turnover and is below the twenty-fifth quartile in voluntary turnover, an indication of its success in keeping the employees it wants. ScriptSave's turnover is lower than average for typical call-center environments. In fact, pretty much all the companies positively profiled in this book have turnover rates below the industry norm. Savings created by emotionally intelligent behavior—by reducing turnover and the costs of stress—go directly to the bottom line as increased profitability.

As with health-care, prevention is a good deal less costly than cure. However, hiring and developing emotionally intelligent employees is about more than reducing costs, which is a form of (legitimate) problem solving. Having emotionally intelligent employees is a way to reinvent a company. Think IDEO in contrast to a typical company developing products or Toyota in contrast to a typical manufacturer. Such companies create innovative products and treat customers in totally different ways than typical companies do. At the Canyon Ranch resort in Arizona, which has a number of wellness programs, a parking attendant once detailed the car of a guest who was in a smoking-cessation program so that the guest would not be tempted by the smell of cigarette smoke on her drive home. Ritz-Carlton hotel guests who ask where the gym is receive more than directions; they are personally escorted to the gym by employees. If a guest is unhappy about a room or service, any employee is authorized to make up to $2,000 in compensation. Hampton Inn has a similar policy. If a guest is unhappy for any reason, any employee can offer a free night's stay. In addition to making employees feel that they have a say in their company, these programs also enable companies to identify areas of improvement.

Emotional intelligence can directly create profit opportunities. A Waggener Edstrom account executive had a biotech client, AVI Bio-Pharma, in need of two things: capital, and a way to test new antiviral drugs. Reading about zoos plagued by the West Nile virus, the Waggener Edstrom executive had an inspiration: Could AVI test its serum in a zoo and possibly save the birds? The question ultimately led to a test in the Milwaukee Zoo. Ten of 11 untreated Humboldt penguins died, but all 3 of the penguins lived who were treated with AVI's "antisense" therapy. These and other clinical trials led to press coverage that turned AVI BioPharma into a recognized player in the effort to find a cure for SARS, and to an infusion of $22 million in private capital. These results occurred because the PR account executive was engaged and proactive about the client's business.

An emotionally intelligent workforce can also have ripple effects across an entire region. Despite higher wages and competition with states in the American South that had offered hundreds of millions of dollars more in tax incentives, Canada's Ontario province won a new Toyota auto plant because of the quality of its workforce over the competing states. Toyota did not focus on cost savings but on creating the highest-quality vehicle possible.

New Measures Grapple with Intangibles

In the last two years of the dot-com boom, a fear of being left behind caused analysts to throw money at Internet companies in the hope that at least one investment would succeed. This market stampede, which gave hyper-inflated values to dot-com firms with barely discernible business plans, led to a search for new measures to find nontraditional but legitimate reasons for a high stock value. The first measures were more sophisticated versions of gauging output and cost, such as determining the cost of equity as well as debt. (The belief by investors that a company's stock price will rise creates a cost pressure on management.) Kevin Gregson of Sherwood Solutions, a business advisory firm, has taken the idea much deeper to try to predict both financial and nonfinancial drivers of stock prices based on actual investor decisions to buy and sell rather than on analyst recommendations.

By studying actual changes in stock as the result of various business actions—financial results, product releases, partnerships and alliances, patent applications, and so on—then rationalizing the results through advanced statistical methods, Gregson has found that activities directly related to emotionally intelligent employees have a far more profound impact on stock price than quantitative results. For example, an $11 billion biotech company that increased its cash by $1 million saw a $7 million increase in market capitalization; a $1 million increase in earnings led to an $11 million increase in market cap. These tidy increases were dwarfed by a single financial alliance, which raised the market cap by $911 million, and a single drug trial that reached the clinical test stage, which raised the market cap by $611 million. Conversely, a single discontinued trial caused a market cap reduction of nearly $3 billion (see Figure 12-2).

Sample Results for *ABC Company*
Market Cap of $11.4B *(Positive Operating Cash Flow and Positive EBITDA)*

Independent Variables	Change in the Value Driver of...	Leads to a Change in ABCs Market Cap of...	Confidence Level
Cash and Equivalents	+$1M	+$7MM	>99%
EBITDA 2000	+$1M	+$11MM	>99%
Acquisitions and Investments	+$1M	+$23MM	>99%
2000 Revenue > $10MM (Y/N)	+	+	>99%
Revenue 2000 > Revenue 1999	+	+	>99%
Number of Phase III Trials	+1 Trial	+$611MM	>99%
Number of discontinued Phase III Trials	+1 Trial	-$2,955MM	>99%
Concentration of Pipeline Trials by Therapeutic Areas	+5 Nervous Trials *	-$905MM	>99%
Number of Alliances per Partner Since 1991	+0.27	+$695	>99%
Number of Marketing Alliances Since 1995	+1 Alliance	+$580	>99%
Number of Financial Alliances Since 1995	+1 Alliance	+$911	>99%
Number of Commercialization Alliances with Large Pharmaceuticals Since 1995	-	-	>99%

*Already concentrated in nervous trials

Figure 12-1   Most financial analysts and investors carefully study financial data to try to determine the value of a stock and the future of a company. However, subjective activities that directly tie to emotional intelligence have far greater impact on actual stock performance than financial results or similar objective data. The market intuitively understands the value of intangibles, but few analysts scrutinize intangibles as carefully as they do numeric returns, or hold management accountable for activities that would improve or detract from human performance. (Source: Sherwood Solutions, www.shrwood.com)

Although it may seem self-evident that the success or failure of a major clinical trial would drive a biotech stock up or down, this is the first time that such changes have been benchmarked against traditional metrics or that other "people indices" have been quantified. Of the three biotech companies that Sherwood profiled—large, medium, and small—the people indices, not the financial indices, were the things that made or broke the company. Every major industry and every major company can develop comparable people indices. They relate to product and service development, to customer service, to all the things companies actually *do*, versus what they report every quarter. By knowing which of several people indices have the most impact on business, companies will know where to put the effort. A biotech company might focus on marketing alliances without knowing that financial alliances create nearly twice the impact on stock performance. The opposite results might be true for a computer company or automobile manufacturer. Managers can change only what they can measure. Yet so far, few managers—or investors—measure any meaningful people indices. They do not yet get the fact that emotional intelligence underlies the greatest gains a company can make, and the lack of emotional intelligence underlies the greatest losses.

Valuable as the Sherwood approach is in proving the value of people-related metrics, value-driven analytics requires a discrete industry group with enough publicly traded companies to create a credible statistical model and an industry group that has a substantial amount of publicly disclosed nonfinancial information. Many companies and industry groups fall outside those bounds. But meaningful statistical data is available to confirm that high emotional intelligence yields startling financial results.

Here are a few:

■ A survey of 3,000 companies by the University of Pennsylvania showed that an investment of 10 percent of revenue on capital improvements yielded a 3.9 percent rise in productivity, while the same investment in people yielded an 8.5 percent increase in productivity.

■ Companies with the best people practices provided a 64 percent total return to shareholders over a 5-year period, more than 3 times the 21 percent return for companies with the weakest practices, according to Watson Wyatt, a research firm that has studied more than 750 companies across the world. (For details, see the section "Rewards and Recognition" in Chapter 13, "Engage with People.")

■ In the book *Practice What You Preach: What Managers Must Do to Create a High Achievement Culture,* David Maister showed that professional services firms with great people practices demonstrated financial results far above the average. The 5 highest-scoring offices in his survey had results, in order, as follows: 52 percent above the index average, with profit doubled in 2 years; 47 percent above the average; 73 percent above the average, with profit growth double the average; 169 percent above the average; 300 percent above the average. (See the "Attitudes Drive Profits" section that follows for details.)

■ In another study, the University of Michigan Business School found that companies with strong organizational virtues such as trust, integrity, optimism, and compassion had a higher level of profits than organizations that are not perceived to have those virtues.

Do the math.

Attitudes Drive Profits

Studying 139 offices of 29 professional services firms in 15 countries and 15 different lines of business, David Maister showed that offices with positive employee attitudes were more profitable than other offices. The clincher is that the book *Practice What You Preach* shows statistically that it was the attitudes that drove profits, not the other way around. Office size, firm size, the nature of the business, and geography made little difference in overall performance. *Financial performance was directly related to the level of emotional intelligence in each office.*

Maister compiled one set of questions that gauged the emotional health of each office. Separately, he compiled the financial results of the offices, producing a financial performance index that consisted of four underlying measures: profit margin, profit per employee, two-year growth in revenue, and two-year growth in profits.

Results showed that small increases in emotional intelligence generated geometric increases in financial performance. For instance, a 10 to 15 percent increase in quality and client relationships *caused* a 104 percent increase in financial performance. A 10 to 15 percent increase in employee satisfaction *caused* a 42 percent increase in financial performance. A 10 to 15 percent increase in professional standards *caused* a 40 percent increase in financial performance.

Return on Intangibles Is Tangible

If this chapter proves nothing else, it proves that leaders need to think about people metrics as seriously and as rigorously as they do about financial metrics. Upbeat, positive employees create an enjoyable place to work or improve customer relations and generally create good feelings around them in the workplace. But the more important contribution is that emotionally intelligent employees directly and substantially reduce costs and increase revenues. For these reasons, companies need to begin measuring return on people. Like the military, companies need to factor in the human cost of achieving objectives, and leaders should be held accountable for unreasonable losses in personnel, which in business manifests itself in turnover and health costs. Conceptually, the approach is to create a set of positive people indices and divide them by a set of negative people indices and reward leadership on the basis of the resulting number and how it changes over time. A simple example would be revenue per employee divided by turnover. A more-complex example might be revenue per employee times employee satisfaction times R&D spending times training spending, divided by turnover and health costs. If two companies have equal revenue per employee, the hidden costs to that revenue will become apparent when the negatives are factored in.

Such measures would provide investors with a better long-term gauge of a company's growth prospects and would provide an organization's board of directors with insight about management practices that could be sabotaging the company's future as opposed to building substantially toward that future. Proper board governance of senior management on people practices and ethical behavior is itself a prime indicator of company success. A 1999 *BusinessWeek* study showed that boards providing the greatest oversight of management averaged 51.7 percent in shareholder returns, against an average of 12.9 percent returns for companies whose boards provided weak oversight. Institutional Shareholder Services' 2003 study on the quality of management governance and board oversight showed that the top 10 companies had returns of 6.5 percent and 7.9 percent for 3-year and 5-year returns, whereas the bottom 10 had returns of negative 0.2 percent and negative 4.0 percent for 3 and 5 years, respectively.

Although profit is the honest reward for a mission well done, excessive focus on profits occurs when human beings mistakenly equate the loss of money, power, status, and prestige with self-preservation. Taken far enough, this fear can override reason, ethics, morality, and law. As always in business, this fear is self-defeating. Profits come when you align the right people in the right roles, give them the right direction, and provide the right (meaningful) work. This is why the focus should not be on pursuing profits, but on finding the right people, creating a people-friendly culture, and establishing the measures to ensure that employees are properly led and managed. Investment in human capital creates a real return.

Understanding your role and accepting accountability creates a natural discipline. To revisit some previous exemplars, Toyota says that with employee understanding, you need few controls; Muirhead of the Mars mission says that the greatest success comes by putting responsibility directly on people, not on rules and policies; and Jim Collins says that having people who are disciplined means you do not need much hierarchy. A large multinational company that went through the processes described in this chapter was able to change its culture from leadership by intimidation to leadership by inspiration. Morale and productivity increased, and absenteeism and turnover decreased by 50 percent. Those changes will ultimately improve the bottom line.

A people approach actually requires more courage than management by process, hierarchy, or objective (where an objective might be achieved by cutting corners). Maister and the University of Michigan found that when trust and respect between management and people are high, financial performance rises. What finally resonates about return on people is that the choice is not between people and high profits. Being good to people *causes* high profits. The corollary is that leaders must have the guts to practice the professional and ethical standards they so often preach. The average and stellar offices in Maister's study preached the same standards. The difference is that the stellar offices lived the standards. In particular, they hewed to them in difficult times. These actions sometimes cost them short-term business, but the increase in employee confidence and trust generated greater long-term business results.

13

Engage with People

Waggener Edstrom's CEO, Melissa Waggener Zorkin, has a unique way of describing the accountability she expects from her associates at the public relations firm. "Sign your own work," she says. She wants the quality of work to be so high that employees will proudly affix their signatures to what they produce the way artists attest to their responsibility by signing their paintings with a flourish. Signing your own work requires employees to be highly engaged; yet highly engaged employees are the exception. According to the Gallup organization, only 29 percent of employees are "actively engaged" in their occupation. The rest are getting by, painting by number rather than producing originals. Such employees are highly unlikely to want to sign their own work.

With so much to be gained from emotionally intelligent employees, organizations have a vested interest in engaging the typical unmotivated employee. Much of the lack of engagement comes not from worker laziness or ineptitude but from management indifference. In studies done in 1949 and again in the 1980s, the two highest priorities for employees were to be appreciated and to know what was going on. In fact, four times as many employees at major corporations say appreciation is a very significant motivator as say salary is a very significant motivator. Yet the output orientation of management leaves many employees cold. In the cold, cruel world of business, it is interesting how often the word *appreciation* appears. Four out of five people who quit their jobs say that the reason is lack of appreciation. Not surprisingly, most of the ways that companies can engage employees involve appreciation, and all of the ways help the bottom line. The first several of these ways are general approaches and general attitudes. The last two are specific programs designed to connect employee energy to a company's financial results.

Generating a good return on people begins with the simplest of notions: listening to employees. Earlier we saw the example of the e-mail-compulsive executive who sometimes checked his e-mail while in meetings with employees. Other executives sometime read the newspaper or answer phone calls (which are seldom "must answer") while an employee is attempting to communicate an important point. Despite a decade of talk of "empowering employees," it is amazing how many companies still function from the top down. All 20-odd corrupt companies mentioned in summary in Chapter 1, "The Naked Ape Dons the Designer Suit," were run from the top down, from the small manufacturer to the multibillion-dollar multinationals. This top-heavy power concentration confirms the rule that "power corrupts, and absolute power corrupts absolutely." Even companies well short of criminal behavior create problems for themselves by failing to recognize that empowering people is not a phrase to put on a slide presentation but a demand for a major recasting of top-down management behavior. Most efforts at reorganizing, reengineering, realigning, or otherwise remaking organizations fail because of employee resistance, which occurs when employees do not understand how the company's goals relate to their jobs, when employees believe that companies do not listen to their issues and concerns, or when employees do not have confidence in management's motives and ethics.

As innovation begins with the simple step of putting a diverse group of people physically together, employee empowerment begins with the simple act of listening. At Toyota, the organizational structure has employees at the top, not managers. Even *Marketing Warfare*, the high-tech marketers' bible in the 1990s, insisted that strategy should evolve from the "mud of the marketplace;" that is, developed

H	Humble, inclusive, visionary, inspirational, and heartfelt leadership
A	Adaptive, enthusiastic, emotionally intelligent employees
P	**Profit for all who contribute to the company's success**
I	Invigorated stakeholders, vendors, and clientele who serve as first-line marketers
E	Engaged, constructive community citizenship

Table 13-1   Elements of a happy company. This chapter concentrates on profit, the P in the acronym HAPIE. If a high return on people creates a high return on investment, organizations must have strategies to engage employees to create those high returns.

from the bottom up, not from the top down. The fact that a bottom-up, pull-it-to-us approach of communicating with employees has a much greater chance of success than a top-down, push-it-on-them approach is more than enough reason to justify the tremendous courage it takes for those in a position of power to contemplate letting go of some of that power. Rocco Fiorentino, CEO of United Financial Services Group, specifically builds corporate culture around the coaching and enabling of his employees. He does not see the leader's role as being to drag employees along or make decisions for them. He wants them to be one step ahead of himself. He expects associates to make the best decision possible with the available facts. He encourages people to talk with each other as well as to him. He would rather have his team make 10 decisions, and 1 or 2 of them be wrong, than to have only 1 decision be made because that is the only decision he as CEO has time to get to. Following this philosophy, his last business, a food-service operation, became the number two profit center in the chain within two years. He was even prouder that employee spouses came to him and said, "What a change in my husband's life. He's not stressed out all the time now."

When in Doubt, Over-Communicate

Listening to employees comes in many fashions. ScriptSave does extensive, anonymous surveying of its employees on such topics as how the company is doing against its mission, on general satisfaction with work, and on whether management "walks the walk" in how it treats employees. The company solicits feedback on what employees believe are the two or three most critical issues ahead. ScriptSave publishes all the results, good or bad, so it cannot hide any blemishes. CEO Lori Bryant considers herself personally accountable to keep employee satisfaction high. Like ScriptSave, Waggener Edstrom also commits to "over-communicate"—a word used by both companies—regarding vision and direction, and then surveys employees to determine whether they understand the company's direction and their own role in the company reaching its goals. The surveys are not designed to determine whether employees are "happy" per se, but whether the company's values and missions are getting through. The organization's effort to inform employees provokes a high level of energy and commitment from associates.

Jim Collins recommends an employee council that is ongoing and multidisciplinary, including regular employees as well as key executives, to fully engage the collective on important matters. The Phelps

Group, an integrated marketing and communications firm in Los Angeles, puts together task forces of people from different disciplines for short periods to address issues such as recruitment, development, and accountability. Anyone can attend task force meetings as long as he or she contributes, and the teams post meeting notes on the company intranet. The task forces present their results to the entire agency to get additional feedback. Joe Phelps says that the 50-somethings on the task forces learn as much from the 20-somethings as the other way around and that the interaction energizes both the grizzled veterans and the new hires. Phelps, who wrote the book (*Pyramids Are Tombs*) on cross-functional organization, encourages his different client teams to self-organize, although he retains final say on assigning team leaders and coaches. Talent+ has self-managed teams so that decisions are made as close to the action as possible. At Wal-Mart, associates from each store choose their own representatives to attend the company's annual meeting and report back, and employees sit on the company's pension and profit-sharing committee. At IDEO, one of the most innovative companies on the planet—it has led *BusinessWeek*'s list of product design firms for five consecutive years—individuals are allowed to choose their own projects *and their own team leaders*. In this process, various potential leaders describe the kind of projects they want to do and their working styles. Employees submit their requests for teams. Almost always, people get their first choices. Every couple of years, IDEO shuffles teams and leaders. People have the opportunity to move around, and leaders have to reestablish their credentials.

Training is another way to engage people, but it must be substantive and directly linked to work or professional development. For example, much of Waggener Edstrom's training is scenario-based. New PR hires are formed into teams, given a client situation, and asked to devise a PR plan. Ranging from unusual product releases to corporate crises, the scenarios are based on experiences that actual account teams have faced in the company's 20-plus years of existence. The results are then critiqued by experienced staff. New employees quickly become indoctrinated into the ways the company thinks, acts, and reacts in a variety of practical circumstances. In addition, the company has 150-plus training programs that are routinely revised according to company goals and tailored to meet specific needs of employees. Whenever a new corporate initiative is introduced, the training team is expected to develop new programs to support it. Finally, the company has a continuing education fund of 2.5 percent of salary each year for outside training.

In addition to formal training, Waggener Edstrom does a great deal of "in the moment" training, built around an individual's actual working day. For example, instead of sending an account executive to a class on client management, the person's mentor debriefs the executive immediately after a client call or meeting to evaluate what went well and what did not and how the executive could improve next time. Senior executives are expected to spend 20 percent of their time in teaching and training others from all parts of the agency. The individuals being mentored define how they want to use the senior executive; the senior executive is committed to have a good understanding of the person's business and to maintain an ongoing dialogue. Every one of the company's most senior staff has five or six people to mentor, including the CEO, Melissa Waggener Zorkin. Training and personal development come together directly in business. The company makes up-and-coming executives a part of presentations to potential clients. If the agency wins the business, the executive becomes part of that new team. This concept, known as "action learning," enables promising newcomers to work on real problems rather than on theoretical issues. The employee gets more valuable training; the business gets immediate business value.

Using a Balanced Scorecard

Because managers can change and improve only what they measure, companies must begin to measure performance against people indices with the same depth and consistency traditionally reserved for tangible goals and objectives. Historically, managers have been held accountable for financial and operational results and sometimes for customer-focused results. Very seldom are managers held accountable for people results. One manager, in a 30-year career spanning 5 companies, was never given a single measure related to his staff's development. His last company in theory provided 360-degree reviews (reviews from subordinates, peers, and superiors), yet he never received a single comment about his managerial style as opposed to his operational or financial performance. Sad to say, this experience is typical.

In the 1990s, Robert Kaplan and David Norton of Harvard developed the concept of balanced scorecard, which takes into account the human dimension as well as the financial and operational dimensions of work. Adding people indices to traditional management measures has three goals: to make leaders accountable for developing the people who worked for them (developing emotional intelligence); to drive all of the strategic goals and objectives deep into organizations; and to link all measures (financial, operational, customer, and people) to one another. The scorecard raises an important point. The purpose of the people goals is not to improve employee skills and capabilities in some generic, if self-affirming, way but to link the tasks, competencies, and skills of all people directly to the company's other objectives. This approach is both a cold calculation, to ensure that all employee efforts are geared to a strategic objective, and a warm aspiration, to show employees how their contribution fits into the company's strategy and *therefore has meaning*. The scorecard enables employees at all levels to see what skills and competencies they need and the rewards they can receive for obtaining them. It provides context and impetus to training and professional development. (See Table 13-2.)

Strategic Objective	Measure	Target
Maintain high quality of staff	Retain highest-rated staff	Reduce unwanted terminations 20%; 100% retention of highest-rate staff
Improve hiring	Hire best and brightest	Hire 66% of first choices
Improve staff quality	Training programs	Develop specified set of courses; 100% employee completion of courses
Improve cooperation, trust, teamwork	Internal satisfaction	10% increase in satisfaction; increase number of cross-functional teams
Improve work environment	Internal satisfaction	10% increase in employee satisfaction
Improve productivity	Compress delivery milestones	10% improvement
Improve safety	Reduce accidents	15% decrease for staff, 25% decrease for customers
Exceed customer expectations	Customer, peer, staff, and management satisfaction	15% increase

Table 13-2   Companies traditionally develop strategic and tactical goals for financial results, customer satisfaction, and their market discipline (product excellence, operational excellence, or customer intimacy). Outside of HR, however, few companies develop people-based metrics or hold managers and executives responsible for improving their return on people. This chart provides sample metrics applicable to most levels of management in most businesses. Such a chart would also include columns showing who measures the result (VP, HR, and so on), how the result would be measured (statistics, surveys, and so on), and what strategic initiative the objective relates to. (Chart based on a balanced scorecard by Sherwood Solutions. Used with permission.)

Publishing everyone's scorecard, up to and including the CEO, creates transparency that enables all employees to see the connection between their work and everyone else's. It also creates accountability, because all employees can see that their efforts are required to achieve the interconnected goals and objectives. Finally, the scorecard improves governance by creating discipline and fairness in the organization's reward system. Employees can see the basis on which everyone will be rewarded (although not the rewards of others). The secret to the balanced scorecard is to create a clear line of sight between an individual, a manager, a department, a division, the CEO, and the board. A clear line of sight between the employee's job and the company's purpose is an individual's single greatest motivating factor.

Driving new strategies is an important use of the balanced scorecard. The Rockwater organization, which manages undersea construction, and the National Reconnaissance Organization, which operates America's spy satellites, have used the balanced scorecard to create a new and single value proposition for customers out of many differing internal views. Sherwood Solutions' use of the balanced scorecard with a number of clients is best illustrated with results from the Intrepid Museum Foundation, which operates the Intrepid Sea-Air-Space Museum on the Hudson River in New York City. Using the balanced scorecard, Intrepid reinvented itself from a "mom-and-pop shop" to a contemporary nonprofit organization that could achieve operational break-even, broaden its brand, and become a "must-see" destination. The basis for transforming the Intrepid's internal operations, assessing staff, and managing performance, the new approach led to major organizational restructuring, numerous senior staffing changes, an integrated marketing campaign, and educational offerings woven into the fabric of city schools. In 3 years, the Intrepid went from a $35 million organization with 450,000 annual visitors to a $57 million organization, most of that in capital improvements, with 700,000 annual visitors. Business operations increased from $5.4 million in fiscal 2002 to $10 million in fiscal 2005, an 80 percent increase in 3 years.

In general, the balanced scorecard has been used to drive corporate goals and objectives down into organizations so that all employees at all levels have a set of deliverables that map back to the company's strategic efforts. To take it a step further, companies should also create deliverables that tie directly to company values. Every year, for example, CEO Waggener Zorkin lays out how Waggener Edstrom expects to live its values of collaboration, curiosity, innovation, integrity, passion, and respect. Every team and individual develops goals specific to those values. Under integrity, for example, the company decided to "open the kimono" with its clients about its internal cost structure. One reason was to eliminate any client concerns about billing practices. The other was to educate clients on ways to eliminate wasteful practices, which in public relations means projects that consume a number of billable hours but return little value. The result of the change was greater trust and partnership with clients.

Under the value of collaboration, support of other team members and other teams has a major role in employee reviews. Under the value of innovation, one year the company's "dreaming team" of brainstormers developed a point of view about how the agency could develop a public relations strategy for engaging the emerging group of influentials who produced online Web logs (blogs). In sum, the agency made sure that employee behavior reinforced company values—not undermined them—in obtaining desired corporate and financial results. It is no coincidence that in 1 year Waggener Edstrom won separate national awards as the best public relations agency and as the best place to work while also adding 31 new accounts and increasing revenue by nearly 20 percent. In the same time frame, it was also named vendor of the year by its largest client.

Making Appreciative Inquiries

Seeking employee input requires some cautions. If you set up a system in which the primary purpose is to allow employees to bitch and moan, you reinforce the VERBs—victimization, entitlement, the need for rescue, and blame. For example, a poorly designed system of suggestion boxes frequently become *complaint mortars* for firing gripes at management, serving little purpose but to vent hostility. The inherent fearfulness of human nature combined with the fear-inducing nature of most business cultures means that employees focus on problems and blame others for them. This inherent fear is why employees are often bipolar in their reactions to work situations. They love to be empowered as long as management takes responsibility for their actions. They love change as long as they have the security of doing things the same old way. They want to be entrepreneurial as long as they are they are protected from risk. Managers reinforce this ambivalence by their own behavior. A weak manager might over-coach, never letting a subordinate get to the point of formulating a decision. A forceful manager might rush in at the last minute to change a decision that a subordinate has already made.

Bespeaking a lack of confidence, both attitudes create *learned help-lessness* in employees. The concept of "learned helplessness" goes back to Martin Seligman, who showed that animals put in unwinnable circumstances became passive. Dogs were placed in cages on an electric grid and received shocks randomly. They had no options or alternatives to the shocks. Unable to escape the shocks, over time the dogs ceased trying. Then, a redesign had the shocks occurring only in part of the cage. New dogs that received a shock jumped to the back of the cage where they were safe. But animals that had been conditioned to shock after shock made no effort to find relief. They had been taught by circumstances to be helpless.

Learned helplessness occurs in business more often than you might think. Individuals create it when they react to new ideas by saying "that's not how we do it around here," conditioning new employees not to question process and just "get along." Mid-line managers often do it in a panic just before their team is going to present to senior managers by redeciding issues at the last second. Entrepreneurs of new companies and CEOs of old-line companies create learned helplessness all the time when they turn over the reins to their replacements and immediately undercut their authority.

Proper leadership and culture can overcome learned helplessness. Wal-Mart once had a money-losing store in a low-income Texas neighborhood, and store managers had a defeatist attitude about the employee pool. Sam Walton, however, ascribed "low-quality workers" to bad management. He had the department managers meet with successful managers in that district to learn how they ran their stores and managed their employees. In addition, Walton offered employees financial incentives when theft was reduced and rewarded employees who busted theft rings. Before long, the store substantially improved business. A Cleveland clinic was plagued by poor service after buying a hotel to house patients coming for heart treatments. Rather than deal with the learned helplessness of the staff, the clinic took them to a successful four-star hotel and showed them how it was being run. Like Wal-Mart, the clinic encouraged people to envision the possibilities.

Learned helplessness often occurs in mergers and acquisitions, when the acquiring company treats the acquired company as damaged goods. In one such merger, the acquired bank had been in trouble, and most of its leadership was let go. At the acquiring bank, a limited number of people were allowed to work on the merger, so that after the merger few people had any understanding of the situation at the acquired bank. The loss of the old leadership and the standoff attitude of the new leadership left the remaining employees at the acquired bank with their heads down, unwilling to act. The acquiring bank overlaid cultural problems on top of financial problems.

Compare this approach with the one that Anthem used in acquiring health-insurance companies. In addition to creating broad-based integration teams that fine-tuned the merger process, Anthem also looked to understand what the other companies were doing well that could serve as a best practice for the existing Anthem units. Anthem's use of as many employees in mergers as possible created a broad expertise within the company about best practices.

Partway through one acquisition, Anthem's Ben Lytle heard that his team was perceived as being haughty. Meeting with the group, he reminded them how they had felt two years earlier. "I want you to remember what it felt like when other people were inspecting *your* numbers, *your* processes, and *your* way of doing things," he told them. "Look at it from their perspective. How do you think they feel?" He reminded the team that their goal was not to acquire an "entity" but to retain the talent and the subscribers—people. The merger team proceeded more empathically, and the acquisition was completed successfully.

The Anthem example shows how quickly humans can forget the importance of emotion and positive behaviors but also how quickly that memory can be reconstituted through positive leadership. The acquiring bank could have come into the second bank with a compassionate rather than condescending tone. They could have engaged all the employees to find out what had worked well before and what had not. By incorporating the good practices into the combined operation, they could have improved their own processes, as well as cemented the cultures instead of leaving them fractured. What the bank needed was a process that would enable them to pull positive energy and positive ideas out of their employees while avoiding the trap of fear-based negativity, whether of management or other teams and departments or (in this case) outside groups. Such a process exists. Mentioned before in passing, appreciative inquiry is a formal business change process that engages employees in "conversations that matter" to find, develop, and spread the most positive aspects of a company throughout the organization. It is a pleasing antidote to practices in which employees have to "swallow whole" the decrees of remote management.

Originated by David Cooperrider, Srivesh Srivastva, and other colleagues at Case Western Reserve University, appreciative inquiry has been expanded over the past 15 years by Diana Whitney, president of the Corporation for Positive Change and founder of the Taos Institute. Appreciative inquiry is designed on the assumption that our questions make a difference. The questions determine what we learn and what we create together. A key component of Cooperrider and Whitney's approach is that they understand organizations not as mechanistic systems but as organic living entities to be grown and nurtured. They believe organizations can find answers to their questions within themselves, their history, their tradition, their best practices, and—most important—within the thoughts, ideas, and perceptions of their own employees. The function of appreciative inquiry is to discover from these elements what gives life to the organization.

Implicit in appreciative inquiry is the concept that queries have direction. Ask a negative or "deficit" question and you will most likely fall into a downward spiral of lower and lower energy and motivation. Ask a positive or "constructive" question and you will most likely lead yourself toward an expanded vision of your potential. Whitney describes the affirmative process as creating an upward spiral of energy, enthusiasm and performance, a "Pygmalion effect" in which our images and stories of the potential future influence our present performance. The language we use and the stories we tell ourselves and others create a gravitational effect on our behavior. Here is another example of the difference between problem solving and opportunity seeking.

Affirmative inquiry begins with an affirmative topic, a subject of strategic importance and something that employees want to see flourish in their organization. For British Airways, one of the first topics to be proposed in an appreciative inquiry engagement was lost baggage, a major problem for all airlines and an inherently negative theme. Coaching from consultants led employees to rethink the issue and to begin to express their desires in a positive way. Eventually the employees framed the topic as the aspiration to provide an "exceptional arrival experience" for passengers. (This is not the opposite of "lost baggage," which would be "found baggage"—a problem-solving technique to create a more efficient system for luggage retrieval.) This broader, positive line of inquiry ultimately led to a task force of 40 people from 18 locations—union and management, technical and nontechnical—to set in motion changes that would improve the arrival experience for everyone, with or without bags.

After investing the time and thought to identify and properly frame topics of importance, an organization is ready to launch into the "4-D steps" of the appreciative inquiry process: 1) discovery of best practices; 2) dream of the future possibilities of the organization; 3) design of an organization that will enable the realization of the company's dreams; 4) and destiny, capitalizing on all of the successes of the process to date and supporting the self-organizing realization of the dream. By the time destiny is implemented, the organization is ready to begin discovery anew, using all of the insights generated the first time through.

The focus of discovery is the appreciative inquiry interview, which is initiated by appreciative inquiry consultants and which cascades through an entire organization as employees are trained in the process and begin to do interviews. The goal is to interview as many employees and stakeholders as humanly possible. Using techniques to keep interviews from turning negative and reactive, interviewers seek to uncover all that is best about the organization, whatever that may be. The focus of dreaming is to create a larger vision of the company's role in the world, to define a *calling* rather than an occupation, and explore how that might change the company's view of itself and its future. At Hunter Douglas Window Fashions, this dreaming led to the idea of programmable window coverings that could display any scene a person wanted—a beach at sunset, a mountain lake at sunrise, family photos. This idea led to the insight that the company's core competence was not window fashions but the technology to create window fashions. Within a few years, Hunter Douglas was working on "smart shades" that would automatically go up or down based on weather conditions.

Design creates a set of "provocative propositions" about what the organization can be and defines the necessary social architecture to carry out the change agenda. This design is not the action plan for change, though the design implies the action to be taken. The social architecture may be traditional or newly made, but it needs to fit the dream. When Avon Mexico undertook this process to improve the working relationships between men and women, it realized that cross-gender cooperation did not occur through training programs but day-to-day work. As a result, Avon Mexico created new organizations with men and women sharing leadership responsibilities. Another company's dream of job security led it to create two businesses that ebbed and flowed on opposite cycles. Rather than lay off employees seasonally, the company could transfer them from one business to the other. Another company wanted to give autonomy to teams, so it created a structure that hired families as separate self-managing teams. *The right social architecture simplifies both planning and the implementation of the plan.*

Destiny establishes a series of inspired actions to explore all the ways that new ideas and ideals can be achieved. From the steps thus far, a number of exciting ideas will have emerged. This phase gives employees the opportunity to design their own ways and means to implement the ideas. By relying on volunteers from within the ranks of the company, the process sets free employee energy and creativity. Often, the teams choose their own leaders outside the regular management structure. The organization supports the process by providing senior leaders to assist, by coordinating among teams, and by communicating the results.

Hunter Douglas's approach makes a solid point. Appreciative inquiry does not turn employees lose willy-nilly to pursue random areas of interest. Nor does it put employees in charge of the organization. Leaders are always closely involved, and the change topics are ones that matter to management as much as anyone. For example, 1 of the 14 change topics at Hunter Douglas was eliminating mandatory overtime. Many employees dislike mandatory overtime because it disrupts their nonwork activities. Managers dislike overtime generally because of the cost and mandatory overtime because of the friction it creates with employees. Driven by employees and guided by management, the appreciative inquiry process led to cross-training and improved planning that virtually eliminated mandatory overtime within eight months. Later, additional planning enabled people to work four 10-hour days with 3 days off, a schedule preferred by all. *The process works because the people seeking the solution are the ones who gain the most.*

Appreciative inquiry, which is much more sophisticated than this brief run-through might suggest, combines many of the elements intuitively used by innovative companies in creating, designing, and implementing their work and developing their organizational structures: open communication, cross-pollination, positive psychology and culture, and complete employee engagement. Appreciative inquiry can also be applied successfully to help organizations weather negative periods. Like other airlines, British Airways faced severe cutbacks after the 9/11 terrorist attacks dramatically cut air travel in 2001. Having used appreciative inquiry before, the airline engaged employees again rather than dismiss them en bloc. The result was that some employees volunteered for sabbaticals, took part-time positions, job-shared, or retired. The net effect was to reduce the number of forced terminations and to give employees as many choices as possible in an otherwise impossible situation.

Similarly, Waggener Edstrom's loss of a major client once threatened the jobs of 62 people. Rather than terminate the team as most companies would have done, Waggener Edstrom asked the employees for their ideas and their help in defining their own future.

Although the company did not formally follow the appreciative inquiry process, the intellectual and moral approach was the same: engage the affected people directly in a positive way. Some team members asked to join other teams, even those in different industries, and were given the training to do so. Others were put to work on internal projects for which there never had been enough time, such as improving the company's marketing programs and its external Web site. Still others were eager to develop new business and help the company diversify its client base.

Subsequent business wins enabled the company to rebound, with revenue coming in 2 percent higher than the previous year. The company turned a profit, although senior executives did without their bonuses. Transitioning the team was not painless, however. Unable to adapt to available roles, some people ultimately were terminated. Yet the company salvaged the jobs of more than 50 skilled professionals, whose retention laid the foundation for significant growth in future years through new business development. The agency also sent an uplifting message to all of its hundreds of employees: We cannot guarantee you work, but we will stand behind you as much as is humanly possible.

By creating the conditions that unleash human power, appreciative inquiry provides a mechanism by which potential human energy is converted to kinetic human energy. As with the other approaches described in this chapter, appreciative inquiry leads to meaningful financial results. Using appreciative inquiry, Lovelace Health Systems reduced nurse turnover by 30 percent and Hunter Douglas took turnover to a 6-year low. Nutrimental Foods in Brazil showed a 66 percent increase in sales, 422 percent increase in profitability, and 42 percent increase in productivity. In just 5 months, Roadway Express reduced dunnage costs 31.6 percent, skid costs by 66 percent, and airbag costs by 53 percent—in addition to the $10,000 savings a month through elimination of overloads.

Appreciative inquiry's twin pillars—appreciation and inquiry—give it unique strengths over other processes for organizational change. Early in the evolution of appreciative inquiry, Cooperrider believed that "inquiry" was the most important aspect of the process. It was only later, when researchers began to understand the power of positive emotion on higher brain function, that he realized the importance of appreciation in individual and organizational vitality. Positive questions amplify an organization's positive core, but it is appreciation that enables people to see what it is about the organization that energizes and inspires them.

Rewards and Recognition

The final step in engaging people is that of rewards and recognition. It is not possible to cover every possible compensation program, but it is worth making a few points. Many companies have performance-based incentives that reward employees for good tactical performance. Approaches such as the balanced scorecard ensure that performance and incentives such as profit sharing and bonuses map to strategic objectives. Chemical Bank, BC Hydro, CIGNA, and Mobil have used the balanced scorecard to eliminate programs that did not directly tie to strategic goals or that underperformed against those goals. Such changes enabled them to put more people and resources into those programs that did map to strategic goals. The Intrepid museum's use of the balanced scorecard aligned and clarified people's roles and responsibilities with strategy, making it easier for leadership to see whether managers and employees had the skills they needed or were able to develop them within a reasonable period of time. It was then a short step to determine appropriate rewards.

Clear rewards and accountability generate 16.5 to 21.5 percent growth in annual shareholder value, according to Watson Wyatt, the research firm that has done extensive surveys worldwide. Watson Wyatt also found that companies with a clearly articulated reward strategy have 13 percent lower turnover than other companies. Practices such as a lack of hierarchy, employee input into company processes and decisions, and high trust in management deliver a 9.0 to 21.5 percent increase in shareholder values. Overall, Watson Wyatt found that companies with the best people practices provided a 64 percent total return to shareholders over a 5-year period, more than 3 times the 21 percent return for companies with the weakest practices. Like Maister, Watson Wyatt shows statistically that it is the enlightened people practices that drive success, not success that drives enlightened practices.

Like the social architecture, rewards should reinforce the mission and culture. Bonuses can be used to reinforce individual performance, as GE and Microsoft do in skewing bonuses and other rewards to top performers. Or bonuses can be used to cement culture and teamwork. Talent+, for instance, gives equal-sized bonuses to all employees regardless of salary. Doug Rath, the CEO of Talent+, believes that every employee contributes to the success of the company and therefore should share equally in the bonuses, a radical departure from a top-down, command-and-control approach that rewards only the powerful.

A great example of tying the rewards to values and mission comes from The Phelps Group, the communications firm. Joe Phelps's ownership and profit philosophy go back to the questions he had when he worked for someone else. What happens to the business if the CEO gets hit by a truck? What happens if the CEO sells after I have worked hard to help build his business? Phelps's response was to ensure that his employees are protected in either eventuality. In addition to normal compensation, the associates receive half of the total profit of the business each year. Of their 50 percent share, associates receive half in cash and half in stock. In a dozen years or so, as Phelps likely begins to consider retirement, the associates will own the majority of the business. The stock plan also ensures that the employees benefit if Phelps ever sells. Further, if he should die, a company-funded life insurance policy would enable the business to buy back any remaining stock from his wife so that employees will then own the company outright.

Not every company leader is in Phelps's position, but every company and every CEO can ask Phelps's question: What happens to employees if the leadership dies or goes away? What happens if the company sells? Companies that actually believe in their people will ensure that employees benefit in such circumstances. Each company's answers will lead to different approaches to compensation. The appropriate schemes will not only benefit employees and improve long-term retention of the company's most valuable assets but will also improve profits. Jeffrey Pfeffer of Stanford has found that managing people in ways that build high commitment creates returns of 30 to 50 percent.

Proper recognition can also lead to improvement in the bottom line. One study has shown that timely recognition can lead to 70 percent better products and services and a 65 percent increase in productivity. ScriptSave provides recognition by the usual awards for such things as length of service and monthly leadership, but its most interesting method consists of "bravo bucks." The fake currency, which comes in denominations of $1, $5, and $10, is used by employees to reward other employees who pitch in to help overloaded workers. Bravo bucks get handed out every day for any number of conceivable reasons: for adeptly handling a major cross-functional assignment, for making a phone conversion painless, for successfully managing a Medicare audit, for spending extra time with a confused customer on the phone. When an employee reaches $300 in bravo bucks, the employee receives a day off and a $100 gift certificate. Other awards are given when the employee reaches the $300 level again.

Recognition comes in many ways. Avis Rent a Car Systems uses "virtual bucks." People can post a recognition of other employees on the company intranet, with the recipients receiving plaques or gifts. When a Wal-Mart associate trimmed shipping costs by $500,000 a year by figuring out how to deliver new-store fixtures on company trucks rather than on separate freight lines, she not only received a bonus but was brought to a Saturday-morning management meeting to be celebrated in front of everyone. In a hospital with 60 percent turnover, the laundry manager had only 5 percent turnover. His secret was hanging up photos of high-achieving employees along with a paragraph describing what they did. Likewise, Talent+ seeks to "catch people doing the right things right." Praising employees on the Mars project was a specific goal for Muirhead, whose formal summary letter commended his team for "performing miracles on demand."

Return on people has a number of dimensions. The first is that the greatest return on people occurs when every employee from the CEO to entry-level staff align with the company's strategic initiatives, can see how their efforts relate to the mission and those initiatives, and receive their rewards based on how they perform relative to the mission and those initiatives. The second is that proper alignment requires that in addition to traditional metrics everyone have a "people" scorecard similar to Figure 13-2. The third is that recognition—a company's direct statement of appreciation—can have as powerful effect on performance as any effort at reengineering. The last is that listening to and engaging with employees in positive ways can transform companies. Listening and engaging can be part of daily business culture, an organic outgrowth of the personalities and values of the leaders, but often many current business cultures need to be galvanized through positive change processes such as appreciative inquiry.

Typically, business leaders fail to recognize their people for one of three reasons. Geared to wait until problems occur and then jump on them, a leader simply does not react to success and is surprised to think that she should. This is the boss that says employees get all the recognition they need in their paycheck. Or, a leader's own personal deficits cause him to fear that an underling might show him up. Or, a leader fears that praising employees too highly might give them too much leverage in negotiating compensation.

Such fears are short-sighted for many reasons. First, employee talent is more crucial than ever and will become more important because of the imminent departure of Boomers to retirement. RHR International estimates that most companies will lose half their senior management in the next six years—this, after much of middle management was gutted by layoffs in the 1990s. Companies need to retain and develop the talent they have. Further, these negative reactions fail to see the motivating power of recognition and the explosive power of a positive culture. This fearful mindset is exactly what causes organizations, despite protests that their people are their most valuable asset, to treat people as output devices or as interchangeable cogs in a more valuable machine.

The numbers in this and the previous chapter present irrefutable evidence: A *real* commitment to people has a far greater financial return than a commitment to things—processes, plans, policies, capital investments. This attitude is not about supporting blind equality among all people in an organization but rather about respect for contributions to the finished product by employees and the value created by all those who contribute. People are the only assets that generate profits. All other assets are derivative. It is high time that companies begin acting on this hard-nosed financial fact.

14

Doing Well and Doing Good

So far, the discussion has focused primarily on internal matters: the attitudes and behaviors of corporate leaders and employees. It is time now to look outside. There is one final difference between ordinary business organizations and ones that are truly exceptional. The truly exceptional companies engage in positive ways with the world beyond their own walls. This strategy has two elements. The first is developing *invigorated stakeholders, vendors, and clientele who serve as first-line marketers for the company*, the *I* in HAPIE. The second is becoming an *engaged, constructive community citizen*, the *E* in HAPIE.

A traditional hierarchical organization not only creates a rigid structure up and down the organization, but also inside and out. The command-and-control scheme not only creates an "us versus them" mindset between leaders and followers, but also between the organization and those on the outside—customers, community, and other stakeholders. Outsiders come in only with permission and only if they pose no "danger." The image that comes to mind is a fortified castle run by an imposing commander and his highly efficient army. Exceptional organizations, on the other hand, have no walls between themselves and the outside world. There is more of a semipermeable membrane that, as in biological systems, protects the integrity of the cell but allows the passage of critical nourishment. Warren Bennis has observed that leadership in the twenty-first century will be transparent. If this is one component of excellent leaders, it must be equally true for the companies they run. In business, this nourishment comes as information. The emphasis, however, is not on "disembodied" information such as sales numbers and trends, spreadsheet data, or formal customer surveys. In addition to these usual sources of information—the safe data that would be allowed into any organizational fortress—the emphasis is on interaction with real people and the serendipity that occurs when people inside and outside a company can freely exchange ideas and experiences.

To reemphasize again, the "open-arms" approach is not some namby-pamby, let-it-all-hang-out approach that avoids the discipline of business. By extending decision making to a larger and less-controlled group, the approach requires more discipline. It also requires emotional intelligence rather than management dictates to glean and implement the best from the feedback without the process disintegrating into chaos. The principle is best illustrated by how an American auto company dealt with parts suppliers versus the way Toyota does.

The U.S. company dreamed of creating a world-class supply system that would be the envy of the industry. However, most of the suppliers were more efficient than the company itself, and the feedback from 25 parts suppliers was for the manufacturer not to build an expensive supplier development center but to get its own house in order. The project was killed during a cost-cutting crisis, and the company did not take the outside advice to improve its own people and processes or to learn about the suppliers' processes so that an efficient, integrated system could be created between the manufacturer and suppliers. Instead, the company demanded ever-lower prices for parts to force efficiencies on the part of its suppliers—the other guys.

This approach is by no means unique. It might be described as the current American standard for lowering costs. One of the largest manufacturers in the United States demanded a certain percentage in costs reduction from suppliers each year for four years. One supplier proposed several simple design changes that would achieve the

H	Humble, inclusive, visionary, inspirational, and heartfelt leadership
A	Adaptive, enthusiastic, emotionally intelligent employees
P	Profit for all who contribute to the company's success
I	**Invigorated stakeholders, vendors, and clientele who serve as first-line marketers**
E	**Engaged, constructive community citizenship**

Table 14-1 Elements of a happy company. Engaging with all stakeholders and with the community are the last steps that a company must take to become truly exceptional.

reductions, but the manufacturer declined because the manufacturer would have had to do some short-term work to incorporate the changes. The supplier also had to use materials from other approved suppliers, one of which was single source. The manufacturer refused to approve a second source (more work still). Before long, an emergency caused the second supplier to increase prices, more than offsetting the reductions agreed to by the first supplier.

Companies ranging from manufacturers to software companies are using such strategies as online "reverse auctions" to get the lowest possible bids from potential vendors. These are all examples of target fixation. Although having vendors bid prices lower and lower may be efficient and cost-effective for commodities, the approach also keeps vendors at arm's length, presumes that vendors have no expertise to add, fails to adequately factor in quality as well as price, and eliminates any possibility of developing joint strategies that might create breakthroughs rather than incremental gains in deliverables. If the manufacturer in the second example had worked with all suppliers to create simpler designs throughout the complex machinery being produced, the result would have been a lighter, more-efficient, higher-quality, more-easily-maintained product. Customers would have been happier, and the overall cost savings would have been considerably higher.

Forcing suppliers to cut prices is premised on problem solving ("costs are too high") rather than on opportunity seeking ("find better ways to work together"). In contrast, Toyota works directly with its suppliers to improve the efficiency of the companies' combined efforts. As demanding as the company is, Toyota also teaches suppliers the Toyota production system and works to create processes that improve efficiencies on both sides. If a supplier has a better way of doing something, Toyota does not hesitate to make the process its own. Toyota has often seen 100 percent improvement in efficiency after it has trained and integrated suppliers, and annual surveys of suppliers regularly place Toyota number one in such categories as trust and opportunity and as one of the top three companies in promoting innovation among suppliers. Toyota's attitude creates incredible loyalty. When a major fire ravaged one of the company's few single-source suppliers, 200 other vendors rallied to create a replacement brake part within 48 hours.

In developing its new vision, Hunter Douglas Windows Fashions sought feedback from 400 employees from all over the company plus 100 outside stakeholders, including vendors, customers, and community members, to help the company understand what it did best.

Hunter Douglas asked vendors what made it a good customer; it asked customers what made it a good vendor; and it asked community members what made it a good citizen. The answers of the stakeholders helped shape the company's strategic questions about its future. IDEO, the design firm, has so successfully engaged its stakeholders that now as many companies seek out IDEO's expertise in creating a constructive corporate culture as solicit the company's wonderful designs. All software companies respond to bug reports by customers, and many companies have sophisticated electronic systems to sort, categorize, and prioritize problems. SAS, the largest privately held software company in the world, goes further by actively meeting users once a year. In contrast to the usual dog-and-pony show intended to sell customers on the next generation of products, SAS creates a forum in which SAS's top software developers can meet with users and technical peers from the world's largest companies to brainstorm new ideas for innovation.

According to Duke's Wesley Cohen, corporate creativity depends on a company's "absorptive capacity," its capability to soak up knowledge and innovations from outside the company. The University of Chicago's Ronald Burt has shown that long-standing interactions between employees and customers improve profitability by increasing the number of "productive accidents"—the serendipity that comes from positive human dealings. The goal for companies is to identify all stakeholders and ascertain how they might be used to extend the company's knowledge of itself and its environment. Many stakeholders function as first-line marketers. They have such a high regard for the company that they want to tell others of their positive experience. Other stakeholders, knowing the company has their best interest at heart and desirous of seeing the company's continued success, freely provide input to the company on ways to improve products and services. Still others may be the company's sternest critics. Like competitors, they provide the company with an opportunity to learn.

In other words, just as happy companies engage everyone inside the company in brainstorming and idea creation, they also engage people outside the company, whatever their role, to make the organization better. Wal-Mart has engaged stakeholders to be marketers and has also engaged stakeholders who are critics. When the company first went public, Sam Walton flew bankers and investment firms from New York out to northwest Arkansas, with the goal of them meeting the Wal-Mart's managers and understanding the company's dedication and integrity. Many years later, after intense criticism for the scale of its super centers and some of its employment practices, Wal-Mart's current CEO, H. Lee Scott Jr., began to meet with people who, as he put it, "don't have a natural love for Wal-Mart," including politicians who would meet with him only in secret. Conceding that Sam Walton had had a "wonderful capacity for criticism" whereas his successors at the company have been defensive, Scott now sees listening to critics as a new way to be entrepreneurial. As one example of its new response to complaints, the company simplified its packaging on toys, saving 230 container loads in space, a huge amount of energy—and more than $1 million in shipping fees in a short period of time. There is more the company could do, of course, but the doors at Fortress Wal-Mart appear to be creaking open.

Becoming a Community Citizen

Last, and probably the least appreciated of the HAPIE traits, is that a company needs to be an engaged, constructive community citizen. Most companies of any size contribute to civic or charitable causes, some quite substantially. Many companies match employee contributions to charity. Many companies allow or encourage employees to take time off for community activities of one kind or another. Regardless of the level of involvement, however, most companies treat their charitable work as a matter secondary to their primary role of generating profits for the benefit of shareholders and employees. We take a radically different view. We believe that to succeed, companies need to be highly engaged in their communities and to make community involvement a central part of the corporate mission.

The reasons are many, but the primary one is that serious engagement with and for the community is the single most important way in which a company can develop and retain its heart and soul. With the constant reminder of good in the world and good that the company itself can do, an organization is far less likely to be sucked into a state of fear and aggression than if its only focus is on competition and profits. The positive experiences and the positive mindsets that result from community service help buffer the constant pressures of business and the tendency of those pressures to drive an organization into a state of fear and reactionism. Positive experiences reinforce the whole-brain function that leads to improved creativity and business thinking.

Consider again our friends at Enron. Like people, companies talk about what is important to them, and a company's annual report is a good place to find out what matters to a corporation's senior executives. Enron's 2000 annual report, the last, pre-collapse report (the last one available as of this writing), bragged that the company "continued to outdistance the competition" with a return of 89 percent versus a negative 9 percent for the S&P 500. The results, which purportedly put the company in the "top tier" of the world's corporations, were false. In the same report, on its "Values" page, the company claimed to work "openly, honestly, and sincerely," another false claim. The company's true nature came out in a single phrase. "Enron is laser-focused on earnings per share"—the profit obsession that destroyed the company. Nowhere in the annual report did *stakeholders*, *community*, *charity*, or any variation of these words appear. The word *employee* appeared only in the usual summation of costs.

Granted, the annual reports of many companies are no-nonsense financial summaries that have brief and fairly technical management discussions. Few in fact touch on civic or human matters. But as every company's most important statement of its mission and business, the annual report provides a snapshot of the company's culture and the underlying psychology of the executive staff. Failure to talk about the "softer side" of business reveals a soulless mission and a sterile culture. Companies that do not care enough to mention civic activities very likely have no soul to speak of, or their soulful activities are buried at low levels. Either way, such companies are ripe for fear-based derailment that leads to short-term thinking and ethical lapses.

Contrast the typical "just the facts, ma'am" annual report with the annual report of Accenture, the largest publicly owned consulting company in the world. By any financial metric, Accenture is one of the most successful enterprises in the world, and the company lists its achievements with a good deal of pride. At the same time, the CEO's letter to shareholders in the 2004 annual report discusses an ethical work environment, ethical behavior toward clients, and the importance of trust in the organization. The annual report devotes three full pages to Accenture's social initiatives, which range from multi-country food-relief efforts to technology-based teaching programs to workshops that help female entrepreneurs in underdeveloped markets. Accenture also promotes its community efforts on its Web site, including development partnerships that make high-quality advisory and consulting services available to charitable organizations, and support for VSO, an organization that sends people to share their skills and experience to help fight poverty in local communities in the developing world.

These programs are just the tip of the charitable iceberg. The company also supports hospitals, colleges, the National Junior Achievement Organization, the Boys and Girls Clubs of America, local and national orchestras, opera companies, ballet and dance, theater, sporting events, and schools. Many of these activities are hands-on. Accenture technical talent develops software and contributes hardware to many children's organizations around the world. Accenture employees donate community service time to Habitat for Humanity, food drives, and other social programs. They provide business apparel, shoes, and accessories such as briefcases and computers to help people in shelters get a start on a career. They help women jettison their dependence on welfare by supporting and directing them in achieving career goals. Every year, Accenture analysts, consultants, managers, and partners adopt a school, serving as tutors, contributing books, supplies, cash and equipment, and painting and rehabilitating classrooms in need. Employees participate in a Principal for a Day program, during which they mirror the activities of the actual school principal and then report out at a general session to the local school board on what works in the schools and what needs improvement. In total, approximately 8,300 Accenture people participated in 160 volunteer programs in the United States, adding up to more than 41,000 hours of service.

A culture that values the external stakeholders is also likely to value the internal stakeholders. The last several chapters describe the many ways that companies can nourish and grow the careers of individuals, but Accenture's treatment of its staff is noteworthy here in a different context. When a managing partner in Accenture's New York office became chronically ill, she received time off with disability with no pressure to return to work. The leadership and employees took interest in her treatment, recovery process, and her need for future financial security. By her own account, the people at Accenture went out of their way to offer social support, aided her in finding the best medical care, advised her regarding financial planning and taxes, and made sure to include her in group e-mails on updates inside the firm. Being treated as part of the "family"—a big family of nearly 100,000— helped the manager stay on track mentally, emotionally, and physically; and the support contributed significantly to her recovery. One of the hallmarks of a happy company is that those associated with the organization think of it as family.

Timberland Company is another firm that places social involvement high on its corporate priority list. In the same year that Enron's annual report was blank about its role in the community, Timberland's 2000 annual report celebrated the fact that the company generated more than $350,000 for nonprofit organizations and that it was the first U.S. business to complete a youth corps project. To commemorate reaching the $1 billion revenue number that year, Timberland launched a sabbatical program enabling select employees to take off as much as six months of paid leave to work full time on charitable causes. The company continues to promote its community causes as a central feature of its mission. A special Web site dedicated specifically to community service, www.timberlandserve.com, includes a searchable database of more than 30,000 volunteer projects. As a company that began by making boots and expanded into a variety of outdoor wear, Timberland has taken its passion for the outdoors and for conservation to build a much broader community—read "potential customer base"—than it could have done any other way. People believe in the company because they believe that the company shares their values. Nothing expresses this concept more than Timberland's own statement of values, which displays anything but a win-at-all-costs mindset:

- Offering the consumer a company to believe in and get involved with

- Offering our employees a set of beliefs they can stand behind

- Offering the community help and support at all times

- Offering shareholders a company people want to buy from and enjoy working for

Some companies go well beyond the annual report to discuss social commitments. The Starbucks Corporation provides a "Corporate Social Responsibility Annual Report" that measures everything from its efforts to buy coffee from socially responsible growers to its energy consumption and recycling efforts to its purchases from female and minority vendors. In addition to contributing more than $440 million in cash and software to more than 5,000 schools and nonprofit organizations to promote workforce development and lifelong digital literacy, Microsoft issues a "Global Citizenship Report" that details the company's efforts to become a better citizen worldwide. It also has engaged PricewaterhouseCoopers to assess its business practices and citizenship activities, and SustainAbility, a consultancy on economic, environmental, and social accountability and sustainable development, to help the company better engage nongovernmental organizations in a number of countries. Both Starbucks and Microsoft solicit comments from the general public on ways to improve as corporate citizens.

Taking Corporate Social Responsibility

To become socially responsible in a way that changes a company, you need to insist on substantive involvement at all levels, particularly senior executives, up to and including the chairman and CEO. Ceremonial activities such as charity auctions do not suffice, however much money they raise for worthwhile causes. No doubt Houston's society pages were filled with photos of the Lays and Skillings at charity events during Enron's glory days, but such public rituals had little to do with the corporation's internal way of life. For the Enron-World-Com-Adelphia axis of evil, charitable activities were outside the core corporate culture. They did not reflect the companies' real values. Nor did they ever serve to positively change that culture. For community engagement to stick in the company itself, executives at the most senior level must be personally engaged in corporate programs.

In turn, these programs must also engage the rest of the company in a meaningful, tangible way. What matters in community work is not how many dollars your company contributes to charitable causes or how many employees participate in community events on company time. The issue is not the size of the financial or in-kind contribution. Beyond the good done in the community, the issue is whether these activities become part of the company culture and *positively infect* the attitudes and behaviors of corporate leaders. Altruism in and of itself is a good thing, but from a self-interested standpoint, a good leader wants community involvement *to positively affect behavior inside the company* as well as outside, in the community.

This concern of corporate lip service to community activities applies to all companies, not just the nefarious. Even actively engaged companies can suffer a slip between intention and result. One company participated in the United Way "loaned executive" program, in which one or two company executives worked for United Way each year while remaining on company salary. This was a tremendous gift to the community, and the executives who served did a uniformly good job. However, none of the company's most respected executives ever participated. Only "B team" executives took the time. After a while, no "A team" executive would have considered the step, for fear of being branded as a B-teamer—or worse, in this hard-edged culture, of being branded a "softie." Good as the program was for the community, for the company it merely reinforced the notion that "real" men and women remained chained to their desks, working fearsome hours on behalf of a do-or-die culture.

Companies obtain substantive involvement in the same way they obtain any other desired behavior. Community involvement must be part of the reward system. At Accenture, new employees are expected to immediately begin working on community tasks, and promotion often depends on such involvement. At higher levels, 10 to 15 percent of a partner's compensation is based on community-facing activities. Employees at State Farm Insurance, which has social programs similar in scope to Accenture's, routinely report their community activities during their personnel evaluations. Although treated less formally than Accenture's, such activities probably account for 10 to 15 percent of a State Farm employee's review as well. Anthem's "reward" comes before the actual hiring, in that the company gives a close look to community service in applicant resumés on the belief that community work signals maturity and shows that individuals are here not just to take, but to be part of the fabric of where they live.

Rewards should be secondary, however, to the inherent value of the program itself. The community activity must mean something to you, the CEO or senior manager. Charlie Horn, the founder of Script-Save, underwrites medical services for the indigent for the same reason he founded the company, to reduce medical costs. Joe Phelps uses his organizational expertise to advise the Los Angeles PBS station (KCET), the Junior Blind of America, and the City of Hope (a cancer-treatment center) on management issues.

Timberland's primary customers are young adults, so its core community activities relate to young people. Young people are also the primary demographic for Ben & Jerry's Homemade, Inc., famous for their cheekily named frozen desserts, so Ben & Jerry's works with nonprofits around the country to operate a dozen shops that hire disadvantaged teens. Store profits are used to support the nonprofits' other programs, but the jobs themselves may be the greatest benefit to struggling young people. Grocery stores tend to support food drives for the needy. ScriptSave, which is in the business of reducing prescription costs, provides emergency medical funds for low-income families and supports the American Diabetes Association. Toys R Us is a major corporate sponsor for the Marine Corps' annual Toys for Tots campaign.

If you think your organization is too busy for major corporate charitable activities, every year the Marines manage to provide nearly 20 million toys for 7.5 million needy children in nearly 500 communities despite their day jobs fighting battles in far-flung locales.

Extraordinary corporate responses to hurricanes Katrina and Wilma provide a context for the way that companies can shape ongoing charitable efforts toward their expertise. According to the *New York Times*, biotech company Amgen concentrated its $2.5 million in relief efforts on dialysis and cancer patients. GE donated a mobile power plant in addition to cash. Emigrant Savings Bank deposited $1,000 into the accounts of nearly 1,000 customers in hard-hit areas. Papa John's employees handed out thousands of pizzas. Georgia Pacific sent 65 truckloads of its consumer goods. UPS and Yellow Roadway provided logistical support to relief efforts. Intel kept 200 employees on payroll while they volunteered. Wal-Mart, which had trucks rolling immediately after Katrina, ultimately delivered more than 100 truckloads of goods, made its buildings available for relief efforts, and gave $17 million in cash.

Interlacing community involvement with corporate enterprise works best if the original mission of the company demands it. Starbucks' initial mission statement had as one of its guiding principles to "contribute positively to our communities and our environment." That statement has driven the company's involvement in educational and environmental programs from the beginning. State Farm's prototypically all-American story shows how underlying social values can become part of the culture and can ultimately spread through future generations as part of revered history that continues to shape the company. The story of Mecherle, the founding farmer, is repeated timelessly at State Farm. New employees hear it and read about it. Old employees embellish on it. After more than 80 years, it is part of the company mythos. "Like a good neighbor"—and the more current "We live where you live"—are not advertising taglines but statements of company intent. Corporate staff are encouraged to become involved in the community, as are agents, who are technically independent contractors and run their businesses as they want. One company employee said he naturally joined a local service club when he was first hired because all of the current employees and agents were involved in similar ways—an example of the pull of positive culture.

Specific activities need to be geared to the company context. In the 1990s, some high-tech companies were criticized for having few employees involved with local governments and agencies compared to other companies. The implication was that the new generation of entrepreneurs was greedier and less civic minded than the older generation. In actuality, most of the high-tech companies were small, the businesses were in start-up mode, and the leaders had young families. They were not in position to do as much as executives who were a generation older and much more established financially.

At the same time, up-and-coming executives can find a way to contribute. They might not have time to serve on the school board, but they can volunteer at schools. They can have their kids help collect donations for the needy or deliver food to shut-ins, or serve food at local homeless shelters. All agencies are eager for volunteers, even those with limited time. Company engagement can help provide a focus and give an extra impetus to such endeavors. For example, most companies have annual picnics. As the company grows, such corporate activities disappear because of logistics related to size. That limitation goes away if the fun activity is building a house for Habitat for Humanity, or cleaning up a local neighborhood, or painting houses for the working poor. Rather than a limiting factor, increasing company size becomes a more and more powerful tool by which to serve the community—as Accenture, Timberland, State Farm, and others have found. Many companies also have "ship parties" to commemorate release of a product to market. Instead of a pizza-and-beer festival for employees, the employees could provide food and beverages for a needy segment of the local populace. The company's joy becomes the community's joy, and the employees feel a double dose of pride and accomplishment in both their product and community.

Begin with Values, Interests

If you do not have an existing community project that is central to your company's mission, begin with an inventory of your own personal values. Take a good look inside to identify the causes and issues that you most care about outside of work. Identify those causes that you would work hardest to change or improve—if only you had time. You might want to help kids, the environment, or the disadvantaged. You might want to support school athletic programs, restore a stream, improve trails in cash-strapped national forests, get behind the local Special Olympics, put up a house for Habitat for Humanity, encourage voter turnout, or reverse the downhill slide of schools. Instead of viewing your company as the major impediment to doing good because of the time commitment business already requires, see the company's personnel and resources as the most efficient and effective way to achieve that good.

Another approach is to research model programs that other companies have already put together, including the companies mentioned in this chapter. Finally, open the issue of charitable activities to your employees. They may have great ideas on projects that could fit with the company mission, or ones that achieve substantial results with relatively modest demands on the firm. A company that distributes parts to several manufacturers in the construction industry hires homeless people, a program that helps citizens in dire circumstances and also reduced the distributor's turnover. The program began through the efforts of a single determined employee.

"Related to business" also can mean taking a company or industry weakness and flipping it into a strength. This is an area of potentially powerful differentiation that requires careful examination by every organization. Automobiles are one of the major sources of pollution in the world, so Toyota has launched a worldwide initiative to make its entire organization as "green" as possible. The company has led the development of fuel-saving hybrid cars, is using recycled materials extensively in its vehicles, and is committed to making future generations of all of its vehicles either low-emission or ultra-low emission vehicles. The company does not stop with its rolling stock. The company's new sales and financial offices in Torrance, California received environmental awards for using materials from scrapped cars and 90 percent recycled materials throughout. The facility runs on one of the largest privately owned solar arrays in the United States. Although costly in the short term, the bold pro-environmental steps by Toyota position the company positively in the long term with consumers. As Toyota says, "Caring for the Earth. We think it's good business."

Intersection of Social and Corporate Goals

"At Timberland, we act on the belief that doing well and doing good are not separate activities. In fact, our commitment to social justice is a part of how we can earn our living. It's how we create real, sustainable change in this world."

—Jeffrey B. Swartz, president and CEO, Timberland

"During the early days at Starbucks, we were determined to create a company with a heart and a conscience—one that would continually deliver shareholder value while touching people's lives and enriching the human spirit. ... Our ongoing success will always be measured by how well we balance our fiscal responsibility with our goal to enhance the lives of those whom we serve and who serve us."

—Howard Schultz, chairman, Starbucks

"Corporate citizenship is about good business sense, enlightened employment practices, and a commitment to make a difference in the communities in which we operate. ... We focus on projects that have measurable outcomes and sustainable benefits [in educating people, alleviating poverty, and crossing cultural divides]. .... We seek to support initiatives, either global or local, where our contributions will build sustainability rather than dependency."

—Accenture, 2004 annual report

"The decisions that are good for society may ... hurt the bottom line for a moment, but it may come back in another form in the long term. I basically think all these monies are well spent. I don't consider it as a cost but as a good investment. ... It's good for society at large, it's good for business, and it's good for the company."

—Ewald Kist, chairman, ING Group

"The poor represent a 'latent market.' ... Active engagement of private enterprise at the bottom of the pyramid is a critical element in creating inclusive capitalism. ... Free and transparent, private-sector competition ... can transform the 'poor' into consumers."

C. K. Prahalad, *The Market at the Bottom of the Pyramid*

How companies can act responsibly in their community is limited only by imagination. In one town, fly-fishing tour guides provided educational classes for children on the ecology of rivers and the life cycle of fish. In another town, a small machine shop helped a troop of low-income Boy Scouts manufacture their own pack frames for a 50-mile hike, giving the troop practical experience and pride of ownership in their accomplishment. Daniel Lubetsky, a socially conscious entrepreneur, created an export company in the Middle East that involved Jews and Muslims with the specific intent of having people from both cultures work together. The company, PeaceWorks, which Lubetsky says is a "not-only-for-profit business," later expanded operations to have Christians, Buddhists, and Muslims work together in other countries.

Even better than engaging the community in a way *related* to business is to make the social engagement *part* of business. ShoreBank Pacific was the first commercial bank in the United States to create a lending practice centered on environmentally sustainable community development. Investment houses are developing environmental specialties. California's public employee retirement system and the

Investor Network on Climate Risk, a coalition of investors, are investing heavily in environmental companies. Individual and institutional investors are pressuring companies to do more for the environment, and American companies feel compelled to be more environmentally sensitive in countries that signed the Kyoto environmental accord, particularly because the United States did not sign. Companies are beginning to turn agricultural waste into diesel fuel, burning used motor oil and cooking grease as fuel, using vegetable oils instead of petroleum-based ingredients in their products, and making chemicals from otherwise wasted petroleum byproducts.

Creative companies look to underserved markets as potential growth markets, and tapping some of those markets is socially responsible as well as good business. The ING Group has joined with other Dutch insurance companies to insure, at affordable premiums, people with diabetes and other serious medical conditions. Silicon Valley venture capitalists are beginning to see the value of socially responsible start-ups, such as Pionetics Corporation, which raised $6.4 million to develop purification systems to help eradicate waterborne disease in underdeveloped countries. The nonprofit Initiative for a Competitive Inner City says that 364 companies that have gone into some of the most distressed inner-city neighborhoods in the United States are seeing extraordinary growth, an average of 866 percent in the 5 most recent years. The results stem from an eager and willing workforce, generally good municipal services, and proximity to highways, airports, and nearby wealthy markets.

Finally, organizations can "walk the talk" by committing a fixed percentage of corporate revenue to charitable activities, the secular version of tithing. Tithing traditionally has meant 10 percent, but economic realities make the number lower for businesses. Ben & Jerry's gives 7.5 percent of its pretax revenue as contributions to eligible nonprofit organizations. QuikTrip, which operates convenience stores and travel centers in nine states, budgets 5 percent of its net annual profits. One percent is the standard that a number of companies use, including The Phelps Group. Patagonia, the outdoor wear company, has contributed 1 percent to charities since 1985, and company founder Yvon Chouinard also co-founded 1 percent for the Planet, a group of more than 175 companies that pledge 1 percent of their net profits to environmental causes.

Cancer Treatment Centers of America (CTCA) goes further with the 1 percent concept. Rather than contribute the funds to outside agencies that may or may not properly run clinics for the poor, CTCA combined the 1 percent investment with volunteer efforts by its own health practitioners to create its own high-quality clinics for the poor.

Its commitment led to more-effective, less-costly ways to deliver medical services for all patients.

Other organizations may not have a mission that fits directly into specific charitable areas such as the environment or health care. The underlying message of CTCA's efforts, however, is that *tithing feeds innovation*. The secret is to find community work that stimulates innovation within your particular organization. As State Farm shows, many entrepreneurial opportunities result not from new products and services, but from openings created by existing companies that treat their customers in an unneighborly manner. *Looking to do good in business itself is one way to discover new markets*. C. K. Prahalad, the teacher and author, shows how almost any industry can create a successful business model by going after the poorest markets in the world. In *The Fortune at the Bottom of the Pyramid: Eradicating Poverty Through Profits*, Prahalad demonstrates that the poorest markets have the greatest potential because they are the largest markets in the world—four-plus *billion* people! In rebutting many of the assumptions about the lack of viability of the "BOP" market ("Bottom of the Pyramid"), Prahalad argues that the greatest change required is one of mindset—seeing this market as a business opportunity rather than a social obligation.

Normally, companies design products for the top of the financial pyramid. These products are then modified somewhat to sell to the bottom. However, this approach creates an implicit cost structure that puts most products beyond the reach of the poor. To succeed, companies must reverse their usual procedure. Companies that innovate from the BOP *up* rather than from the top *down* can show a 10 to 200 times cost advantage, putting their products well within reach of this huge emerging market. Such innovation creates a sustainable win-win scenario for the new consumers and the businesses alike. As the result of research by Prahalad and others, Hewlett-Packard, DuPont, Monsanto, and other companies have established venture funds to pursue this market.

What Goes Around, Comes Around

Doing good for the community does good for the company itself in multiple ways. First and foremost, such efforts generate community respect and trust that help the company grow in good times and survive in bad times. The importance of a strong bond with the community extends beyond the local community and beyond shareholders and customers to the public at large, at the local, state, national, or international level—whatever constituencies might one day affect a company's overall operating climate. Whether the issue is expansion plans, legislation that affects the company or industry, or a business downturn, consumers are more likely to support an organization they have seen doing good around town or around the world. When companies make mistakes or even release a poor product, people are more likely to give that firm the benefit of the doubt long enough to rectify the problems. The ING Group is convinced that its socially responsible behavior has made the company more welcome in new communities and has helped its business take hold as it has expanded worldwide. Strengthening the company's standing in every community and showing that ING is a reliable partner thus benefits the company and its shareholders in the long term. Accenture believes that integrating itself into the fabric of the communities it serves by "showing up and lending a hand" has a similar indirect but positive impact on its business in the hundreds of communities where it has offices.

In addition, employees involved in the community often learn a great deal, developing new skills, new insights, and new perspectives that can be used to broaden the company's vision and to develop new practical ideas for their teams. Innovation often comes from examining an old situation in new ways, and community engagement is one way to refresh tired eyes. Timberland reports that community involvement not only reinforces feelings of purpose and accomplishment, but also provides another opportunity to develop employees as professionals. Another benefit: Employees out in the community meet other talented people, and your employees' presence out there will cause some number of gifted outsiders to gravitate to your firm.

In addition, the employees who go out to the community receive as much positive energy as they give. They return that positive energy back to the company. Their recharged spirits light up the moral and psychological climate within the hallways. Company leaders and employees (even those who do not directly participate) feel better about themselves and the company, knowing that it stands for something more than making money. Like all people, they perform better when they feel that they are part of something bigger than themselves or their own immediate needs. However subtle the community's appreciation may be, or however subtly individuals may respond, the positive reinforcement has an effect. Leaders and employees become more positive themselves. The warm glow of altruism increases their energy to take on the difficult tasks of work—the positivism helps individuals see hard work as an interesting challenge rather than as a difficult grind.

Remember, this positive psychology not only activates the creative centers in the brain, but it also helps the creative centers to remain consistently activated. Just as stress triggers chemical reinforcement of the body's biology that drives continually more fear-based behaviors, positive activities trigger chemical reinforcement of the higher brain centers, tending to lock in creative functioning of the whole brain over time.

Doing good's positive atmosphere and positive vibes create the kind of company in which employees want to work. With fierce competition for highly skilled employees—the very creative and high-functioning employees that can separate a business from the pack—all major companies want to be listed among the best places to work. Accenture has been named one of the top companies to work for by a variety of magazines, including the *Times* of London, *Working Mother* magazine, *Black Collegian* magazine, and *Fortune*. Timberland has been cited as one of the best places to work by every major polling organization (including seven straight years by *Fortune* magazine) and has also received any number of major humanitarian awards. It has also won major design awards and other industry awards, a testament to *the quality of people* it is able to draw because of its values and because of *the positive environment it creates* for employees through its community efforts.

Some cynics may claim that community programs are designed to create more future customers for the company or to provide "cover" for other corporate activities that may not be so positive. Outsiders— or cynical insiders—can read positive or negative intent into any program, according to their bent, but cynicism is irrelevant as long as the public or the disadvantaged benefit. If some teenager buys boots from Timberland because of the company's community program—then good for Timberland (and for the conscientious young person). Improving child safety seats and eliminating dangerous intersections may help reduce State Farm's automobile claims, but the claims go down because death and injuries go down, and that is a social good. It is a big stretch to say that rehabilitating an inner-city school will create, a decade from now, a customer for Accenture or Microsoft, or that providing funds to the poor for medical treatment will lead to a new ScriptSave customer down the road. If these are the ultimate results, so much the better, because the programs will have provided a far greater benefit to society in the meantime by lifting someone out of poverty. If you do good, Mother Teresa said, some people will always question your motives. Do good anyway. The conversation is not between you and "them" but between you and your conscience.

Stimulating the Biology of Hope

If nothing else, community-facing programs provide a clear indicator of a company's moral compass. Consumers are becoming acutely sensitive to every aspect of company behavior, whether it is the source of goods, prevailing wages, or corporate presence in repressive nations. More and more consumers select products on the basis of a company's environmental or political positions. The corporate debacles of recent years also have changed the social and cultural landscape. Consumers expect more from businesses than "same old, same old." It is no longer sufficient to be a passive "good guy" or "good gal" in the corporate world, running a clean shop and generating a decent return. Today, it is important for profit organizations to become actively involved with causes of merit to convey to all stakeholders that those at the helm embody ethical values and that those values are central to their corporate culture.

Most business leaders would probably desire to keep a low profile, doing whatever good they can personally, quietly and without fanfare. But the power of the organization can be an order of magnitude greater than uncoordinated individual efforts. Brought to bear on specific needs and challenges of the community, business-driven philanthropy can make marked differences in the lives of the average citizen, thereby endowing the company with a more essential quality within the community than a company that provides only jobs and revenue, as valuable as those two things are in their own right. Giving back to the community also helps cement—and in some cases restore—consumer trust in the business community, scarcely a bad thing. Finally, citizens themselves need to be inspired. Their confidence in business and society as a whole rises when they view the business community as a constructive and contributing force, when they see business doing the right thing.

Determining whether social consciousness and good works are part of your culture's soul is both simple and mysteriously difficult. Obvious signs of the affirmative are the participation of senior executives, the number of the company's active social programs, the ability of employees at least occasionally to do volunteer work on company time, and the number of employees who belong to various community organizations.

A checklist (such as the one that follows) provides a minimal outline of how to view charitable activities, but you cannot create programs simply to satisfy a check box, in the annual report or in the minds of company leadership. A company can have good programs and still suffer corporate misdeeds. While Adelphia employees were supporting Little League baseball teams, the Special Olympics, the Humane Society, and food, clothing, and blood drives all over the country, the Rigas family was systematically looting the firm. Do-gooding at the employee level does not provide inoculation against misdeeds at the corporate level. However, inculcating altruism into the highest levels of the company, and making community partnership an integral part of corporate culture, creates a positive atmosphere. Like quality or innovation, social consciousness cannot be added on. It must be built in to. In this way, it has the power to transform people and organizations. When everyone from the CEO down in a company walks the walk with regard to virtuous conduct in the community, personal and organizational tendencies toward honesty are positively reinforced and knee-jerk tendencies to dishonesty are damped out. Notices of your company's social deeds will appear in the annual report not as an effort to impress stakeholders but as a natural consequence of who and what the company is. Profit remains critically important. However, profit must share the limelight with making a difference for the better in people's lives, both inside and beyond the walls of the organization. Those happy companies of the twenty-first century not only understand this but live it every day.

Accenture, Starbucks, State Farm, Timberland, and other companies have found that social consciousness in their culture has inspired and motivated employees and made them proud to be part of the organization. Good deeds also create a psychological climate that improves professional creativity and innovation. A sustained positive environment creates physical changes in the neurobiology of individuals—what is called the biology of hope—that help reinforce creativity and innovation. Corporate service to the public is one of the most overlooked ways to create and maintain such a culture and climate. Many companies subscribe to the belief that if they are doing well they have an obligation to do good. There is another equally compelling truth. Doing good provides the changes in the hearts and minds of employees—both physically and metaphorically—that companies need in order to do well.

Follow the Spirit, Not the Letter, of the Checklist

To assess your company's community efforts, consider the following issues, which are meant as a reality check rather than a checklist to be completed:

- Is the CEO passionate about the company's community programs? Are all senior executives engaged in meaningful, as opposed to ceremonial, ways?

- Are a number of employees engaged in the company's community programs or engaged in programs of their own choosing that the company supports?

- Do you try to discover new markets by seeking new ways to be "neighborly" to untapped customers?

- Are there new markets to be found among less affluent groups, if only you looked?

- Do the company's reward systems reinforce community programs and reward those who participate?

- In addition to helping the community, have the programs shaped (or reshaped) the people and culture of the company in a positive way?

- If your company went away, would it be missed—not because of the jobs it provided but because of the positive role it has played in the community?

15

Tools for Building Constructive Culture

Tool use is one of the defining characteristics of humanity. Whereas a few other species use simple tools in simple ways, and chimpanzees *make* and use simple tools, human beings and our predecessors have been making and improving tools from the earliest days of our existence. It is possible that proto-humans began to use tools—bone and stone applied in their natural state—as soon as they began to walk upright, about 3.6 million years ago. It is quite likely that Lucy, one of our oldest known hominid ancestors, used stone tools 3.2 million years ago. Archeological evidence shows that by 2.5 million years ago proto-humans were shaping stone and bone into points to make them more effective. Stone flakes created by such shaping are often telltale signs of early human sites.

For most of those three-plus million years, tools expanded the range of physical effort. Bones and stones gave way to copper, iron, and steel, which eventually gave way to titanium, carbon fiber, and nanotubes. Tools helped us travel farther and faster, build ever-larger and more-complex structures, live in less-hospitable environments, grow more and better crops, create ever-more complex societies, communicate in ever-more persistent ways, and—sad but true—fight ever-more vicious wars.

Along the way, tool making and brain development became interlocked; development of one helped spur development of the other. Finally, tools began to expand the capability of mental effort. From simple calculating devices, computers have evolved to help humans unravel the structure of DNA, develop new medicines, fashion new materials, create working models of the ocean and atmosphere, predict voting patterns, and investigate the earliest and hottest moments of the evolution of the universe. Tools also enable us to understand how we think and act as individuals and how groups think and act collectively. Just as we cannot directly examine the lives of our ancient forebears and must rely on indirect evidence such as archeological examinations and observation of contemporaneous people who live in similar environments to try to understand their behavior, we also cannot get inside our own brains to directly dissect our every thought and emotion. We can, however, apply behavioral tools to help us understand ourselves and create awareness of those elements that we want to examine more fully and, in many cases, plan to change.

Tools for understanding and, therefore, intervening in behavior have been applied in organizations for a long time. Freud's revolutionary application of ego analysis and Jung's appreciation of the spirituality of the human consciousness created an understanding of the importance of self-awareness and self-understanding in the effort of people to change their behaviors. Jung's initial two psychological types, extrovert and introvert, led directly to the behavioral models that have evolved with greater and greater sophistication since World War II and that were summarized in Chapter 11, "Only the Emotionally Intelligent Need Apply." Different chapters have discussed some of the more important tools, the ways they are applied, and the business results that the tools help create. Happy companies make use of behavioral tools to sync up the vision, mission, strategies, and business behaviors and align rewards with those behaviors. This chapter describes the actual process flow for using such behavioral tools, with some additional examples of application. The goal of behavioral tools is to align the organization around positive values to achieve superb business results.

Companies can initiate the use of tools at any time, but most do so at a moment of change: when management seeks to launch a new strategy, when earnings slide or plummet, when a new CEO arrives, when the company is sold or merged, and other organizational life-changing events. Highlighting individual as well as organizational competencies, the tools enable investigations that help organizations make decisions about their ability to manage change, engage in a new strategy, or target new markets.

The Step-by-Step Way to Prosperity

There are three standard models for tools: ones targeting individuals; ones targeting groups, from teams to divisions; and ones targeting systems, which could be the company as a whole or the industry. For simplicity, this chapter breaks the tools into personal and group tools. Although coaching can benefit all individuals, the process usually begins with the leadership team, because these individuals have the most power and the most influence and their issues generally define issues throughout the organization. Different coaches use different terminology, but in essence the purpose of the process is to provide the following:

1. **Values analysis**. Understanding of leadership's values and how values underscore success

2. **Congruence analysis**. Degree to which the values of the team align with the leader and with each other

3. **Energy assessment**. Understanding of stress points and antici-pated trouble spots for transitions

4. **Cultural assessment**. Leadership profiling and feedback of cul-tural awareness

5. **Co-definition of future**. Validation of operating principles and shared definition of the team's future

6. **Leadership development**. Creation of programs to improve capa-bilities of the leadership team, in conjunction with the recruit-ment of new talent as needed

Although some overlap exists between personal and group tools, in general the first three steps are personal and the last three steps are group or systems tools, depending on the scale on which they are applied (See Figure 15-1).

Values analysis and congruence analysis normally begin with a profile of the senior management team. We recommend the previ-ously described motivational profiling, but a number of other person-ality profiling tools exist. The profiles provide two benefits. First, by understanding the personalities of the people on the team, the coach can better understand the best way to work with the individuals and to design effective change processes during the coaching engagement itself. For example, if the profiles show that seven people are moti-vated by achievement, two by affiliation, and one by power, then to make meetings meaningful for the majority, the achievers, the coach

Process Flow to Align Teams

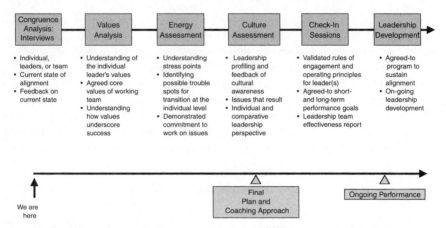

Figure 15-1 Beginning with the individual, then the team and culture, a collaborative process is needed to align any leadership team to achieve more effective decision-making and partnership behavior. The six-step process is covered in the text in detail.

would make the meetings highly structured, task- and decision-oriented, and anchored in the discipline of punctuality. The coach would also provide enough interaction and sharing to satisfy the affiliators and would act in such a way as to affirm the status of the power person. If the team were all affiliators, on the other hand, the coach would know to allow a great deal of give and take, with less concern for the clock.

Second, and more important, the profiles provide insight into how individuals relate to others on a personal level and how the team can best function together. With permission, the coach reveals the profile for each of the participants and explains the communication style for

Online

For further reference, the book's Web site, www.h2cleadership.com, contains a complete set of tools that are useful for evaluating the current status of behaviors for individuals and teams. The tools provide a rich sampling of programs, demonstrating the types of programs that organizations can develop to build on the strengths of individuals and teams for better overall corporate functioning.

each person. At Dell, for example, chairman Michael Dell and CEO Kevin Rollins chose to reveal their profiles to the rest of senior management so that the team better understood their motivations and working styles. In Dell's case, it helped his colleagues to understand that his occasional romoteness was part of an achievement profile rather than aloofness per se. The leaders also revealed the results of a 360-degree review to encourage the rest of the executives to be open to learn about how they could also improve. The process ultimately was simple and personal. Dell would say, "This is what I am proud of, here is what I want to improve upon."

The next step is a series of interviews involving between 10 and 50 leaders within the organization. Whereas the profiles can be and often are shared, the interviews are anonymous to establish the trust and confidentiality needed for a full airing of all issues of concern. The coach seeks to ascertain how the team functions at the most fundamental working level, such things as the level of commitment that each person has to individual and team goals, whether the team shows demonstrable sponsorship and support for one another, and whether each individual is able to integrate with the other leaders and sustain their ability to work together over time.

To create trust and uncover the quality of personal and business interactions, the coach needs to ensure that the individual understands the importance of the interview, understands the larger purpose and process—usually the creation of a new leadership team or new leadership direction—and the way in which the interviews and tools will be used. Also, the coach needs be certain that the interviewee's personal commitments are articulated, and all background issues and concerns are identified. Typical questions would be:

- How does the leadership team support the organization's strategic intent?

- On what key operating principles should the team's long-term relationships be based?

- What business benefits do they expect from the relationship personally and professionally?

- What must be done to ensure full buy-in to these benefits?

- What could get in the way of their ability to sustain their performance and programs over the next one to three years?

- Which key executives may not yet be on board and how could they be incorporated?

The coach would incorporate into the analysis an understanding of the individual motivations and the congruence of values between the individuals. (This is a positive act; traditional organizational development would center on "gap" analysis rather than "congruence" analysis.) The interviews are also designed to turn up congruence or the lack thereof between individuals such as the CIO and COO, or between business units, or between business units and support organizations such as information technology. A large enough sampling of people enables common themes to emerge. The coach concentrates on the two or three most common and most important themes in the follow-up. The interviews should also turn up "undiscussables"—deep issues that are often ignored while people focus on superficial issues. Of course, superficial issues seldom can be resolved while the underlying undiscussables fester. Just about every organization has some undiscussable: the boss's tyrannical style, which no one wants to confront; conflict between individuals that the team pretends does not exist; favoritism, cronyism, or nepotism somewhere in the company; a contradiction between what leaders say and what they do or what they ask of others and do for themselves; and so on.

To reinforce the position taken already, the interviews may well turn up problems, but the coach should direct the interviews into a positive direction that can lead to opportunity. For example, if two leaders are at loggerheads with each other, the coach would draw out what the individuals believe is the best about the other and use that information as the basis for developing future interactions. Many coaches now use a generally positive approach. The value of a more formal approach such as appreciative inquiry is that the structure itself directs participants toward a positive outcome. The inability of any one leader to recast viewpoints into a positive direction becomes a flag as to whether that person can succeed as part of the new team. As part of the assessment, the coach should also evaluate each leader's emotional intelligence. A lack of awareness by leaders of their feelings becomes another flag for potential risk areas as the program moves forward.

Two issues are worth noting here.

The first pertains to profiles. Profiles are pretty much standard, particularly for executive positions with major companies. The profile belongs to the company but cannot be revealed without the individual's permission. However, motivational profiles do not contain the kind of personal information that might embarrass individuals or put them at a disadvantage if the information were revealed. Any concern about such a possibility is alleviated when the CEO and other senior executives reveal their profiles first. The purpose of these profiles is to get people talking about who they are and how they bring their talents to work. Profiles are intended to institute dialogue and interaction by creating awareness by all the group of their own motivations and the motivations of the others. Profiles may also bring to light short-term issues that a person needs to address, such as a preoccupation with a serious illness or a major family problem that might, as one example, cause a highly affiliative person to temporarily score low in that area. If there is anything in the profile that makes an individual nervous, the coach can ask to disclose only the most high-level components of the profile. The person almost always says yes. Coaches have a professional responsibility to ensure that all profile information is used properly, and are invariably in a position to see that it is.

The second issue is that organizations should not become overly reliant on outside coaches or consultants of any kind. When the need for help with change is evident, the senior-most HR person is almost always involved. Many companies turn to internal resources first. Other times, the scope of the program is beyond capabilities of the internal HR organization. Or there may be internal sensitivities that make it more tenable for an outside party to handle the first go-round. The idea is not call on outside coaching consultants every time some difficult issue emerges. Coaches make executives aware of issues, teach skills in resolving them, methods by which to keep resolving them, and who to call in the rare cases in which more help is needed. Any coaching program should contain elements that enable the company culture to become healthy enough that change programs become self-sustaining, with an internal or external coach occasionally checking on progress. In finding coaches, senior executives should be able to interview several coaching candidates and pick one that best fits in terms of chemistry and experience.

Energy, Cultural Assessments Provide Guidance

Coming out of the interviews are the energy and cultural assessments. In an energy assessment, individuals compare their values, personal climate, and work climate to determine whether their lives are in balance. Individuals first list in rank order the values that are most important to them, the amount of time they spend on those values, and whether the values take energy or give energy. If raising healthy, well-adjusted children is a high priority, but the only time you spend with your kids is driving them to school, then children would be a negative in terms of energy expended—you are not doing enough with them. If doing interesting, meaningful work is a high priority and you spend 60 hours a week at work, then work would be a net positive in terms of energy expended. However, the overall life is out of balance. Individuals craft a personal management plan to put more time and energy into those values, such as children, that they identify as being important but that so far have been underserved. Individuals track their commitment to change through journals or diaries in order not to drift back into an unbalanced personal life. The design and building of positive change in personal and work life serves to reinforce both.

A similar approach is applied to the work climate to identify energy losses and energy gains. Individuals list all of their colleagues, supervisors, direct reports—anyone who has a direct bearing on their work climate—to assess whether the people have a positive or negative effect. Individuals are responsible to determine what they can do to improve their work climate through their own actions, which could range from changing their own behavior toward a particular person, to seeking to have other people brought on or taken off their teams, to changing teams themselves. Individuals' evaluation of themselves is incorporated into the coach's overall evaluation of the people and their teams.

In parallel, the team works together to develop its future, aligning its values and principles to achieve whatever objectives have been set. The team creates a charter that describes in specific terms the mission, scope, and responsibilities of each team that will work on different projects in the new initiative. Simultaneously, individual leadership development programs begin, along with recruitment of new talent that was identified as a need.

When the different change processes begin, a series of check-ins is established in which teams can present deliverables, validate changes and learning that have occurred to date, and develop a new series of next steps. Depending on the scope of the assignments, the check-in/follow-up sessions may occur every few weeks, or every quarter for a year or more, or some combination. The important thing is that a structure is defined for follow-up. Studies show a rapid fall-off of new skills after leadership training, as much as 83 percent in one month for traditional leadership workshops. Marshall Goldsmith cites an example, which he considers typical, after leadership training at a major multinational. Fully 30 percent of the leaders did not do any follow-up on their training. The rationale is that they will catch up with training when they have more time, when things are less crazy. But, business leaders never have more time, and business never gets less crazy. Goldsmith has leaders focus on one thing they can change right now, and measure it every 30 days via feedback from others. He focuses on "feed-forward"—what I can do better in the future, not what I did badly in the past.

From the profiles, interviews, and initial working sessions come an overall characterization of the organizational culture and the management implications of that culture; the predictable issues and stress points that emerge from the personalities and culture; a list of relationship enablers and barriers; a preliminary list of new operating principles and proposed enhancements for achieving the goals. All of these elements become the input into the team's next work session. The focus on this workshop is the governance model going forward. This model includes leadership roles and responsibilities, influence and decision processes, the rules of engagement, near-term performance goals and quick wins, and the launch of whatever leadership training and development is needed.

Aligning everyone on certain operating principles is the essence of the governance model. Operating principles fall into two broad areas: business alignment and cultural alignment. Business alignment consists of such things as establishing agreed-on objective metrics, including financial metrics; establishing clear definitions of roles and responsibilities; and creating mechanisms to push authority and decision making down into the organization. Creating business alignment throughout the organization also involves categorizing desired individual and team behavior in business terms. Examples include defining the role of shipping in terms of desired business results—say, customer satisfaction and profitability—as well as in terms of boxes moved per day; or defining IT's responsibility and performance in terms of business projects and results rather than internal IT operations.

Cultural alignment consists of all the human-centered activities needed to establish the business results. This is an area in which such tools as the Benchmark of Emotional Intelligence (BOEI) can help identify any lack of cultural alignment throughout the organization and in which such tools as the balanced scorecard can create cultural and business alignment at all levels, by tying all behaviors and all results to specific strategic goals. Again, the essence of a balanced scorecard is to cover all aspects of desired behavior, not just the financial or numerical targets. The essence of good cultural alignment is that the organization clearly defines and lives by its decision-making principles. If the principle is to drive decision making to the lowest possible level of the organization, that principle must be adhered to on important matters, not merely the easy decisions.

Tying business and cultural governance together comes through agreed-on Service-Level Agreements (SLAs). In SLAs, each group or department involved in a deliverable develops explicit definitions of what they seek to achieve, what their role will be, and what they can deliver toward their goals and the goals of other teams. Any discrepancies can then be addressed. For instance, customer service might desire all responses to customers occur within 24 hours, but IT, manufacturing, or shipping might not be able to process all requests any faster than 48 hours. Such explicitness helps identify disconnects before they happen and enables a dialogue that syncs up the organization at all levels. The organization might agree on a 48-hour response standard; it might define one set of customer responses that will occur within 24 hours and another within 48 hours; or it might use an appreciative inquiry-style approach to develop major new initiatives to more broadly define and improve customer service, as British Airways did with its "arrival experience." The wording in the SLA creates the business congruence; the honest negotiation of the SLA creates the cultural congruence.

If outside partners and vendors are part of the delivery of any product or service, they should be part of the alignment process as well. From a timing standpoint, this involvement likely will come after the first round of internal alignments, but care should be taken that decisions are not passed on to outside partners as a *fait accompli*. Just as cross-pollination, dialogue and opportunity seeking expose new opportunities within an organization, the same dynamic enables new approaches and creates new opportunities across organizations. It is an act of hubris for one company to assume that it knows more than any of its partners, particularly those partners with more experience in particular areas. SLAs should be developed, agreed on, and adhered to for all parties, inside or outside the formal corporate walls.

How Leadership Programs Succeed

Many efforts at organizational development fail, usually because of a lack of full commitment at the highest level or a lack of follow-through at lower levels. To ensure that a company is fully engaged, companies should take the following steps:

1. Change programs should be anchored in the priorities of participants, should have specific goals, and should have clear, agreed-on outcomes.

2. Because many programs are driven too much by consultants and come across as "academic," the CEO or other senior executives need to "own" the programs.

3. Company leaders must articulate their personal commitment to the program objectives and the agenda of workshops and all check-in working sessions.

4. Key people must be present during critical discussions.

5. The organization's real concerns must be addressed, however painful or awkward the results. This requires real management courage.

6. The program must establish a clear pathway for how and when open issues will be addressed.

7. Participants must be adequately prepared for their leadership roles and receive whatever training necessary.

8. Ample attention must be paid to leadership commitments and action plans that cascade down from the program to every level of management below the leaders.

9. A structure must be designed to address the fact that, without follow-up, new leadership skills fall off rapidly and people revert to old behaviors.

As with any other project, an effort to improve leadership and organizational performance can be derailed in many ways. If individual leaders, departments, or the leadership team as a whole do not buy in to the changes, the effort fails because of conflict or lack of follow-through. Too often, a particular department opts out, citing short-term business pressures, and effectively cripples overall change. Failures also occur when management slams the project in without listening to the rank and file. Many a major change endeavor has failed because of the grudging resistance of employees. A final reason for failure comes when management measures too much, measures the wrong things, or uses the results of measures to punish rather than to learn. For example, if you are supposed to call someone every day to follow up on a certain item, and you do not, the other person should call you. But if the call has little or no value, the second person is more likely to wait and "turn you in" after several days for not calling rather than initiate a call to you. If the organization punishes you for not calling rather than examining the rationale for the call, you will mentally opt out of the process.

Enabling factors for success come out of the personal commitment by the senior leadership, the definition of clear and meaningful metrics, and the measuring and tracking of those metrics. Important human enablers come from establishing clear definitions of roles and responsibilities throughout and ensuring that the change process ultimately involves a representative sampling of all groups and all employees. Living by the defined decision-making process is a litmus test for success, as is management behavior that "walks the walk" in terms of the newly defined way of interacting with other managers and subordinates. As psychological folklore says, it is easier to act your way into a new way of thinking than it is to think your way into a new way of acting.

Success also stems from the understanding that the process is not a one-time destination but a journey of continuous refinement in which the organization constantly seeks to improve. Toyota's mindset in this regard is instructive. Most companies celebrate success when they standardize on some best practice. To use a sports metaphor, they treat the achievement as a touchdown rather than a first down. Toyota views standardization not as an end-all, be-all, but as the starting point for improvement. Without standardization, you have no consistent basis from which to measure results or from which to enact further improvements. Standardizing to achieve the best practice for today gives you a solid foundation for creating improved practices for tomorrow. To continue the metaphor, Toyota puts together long drives. It does not think in terms of scores, but of "moving the chains" with a series of first downs. Each new standard sets in motion successive improvements that lead to another new standard.

Change Process Helps Integrate Distrustful Group

An example shows how business coaching can serve to align an organization around positive values and as part of a strategic plan. A common challenge these days is the organizational disruption that can occur as companies integrate electronic business into their operations. One major company built a state-of-the-art Web site at which customers could change their individual or corporate information, view their accounts, track shipments, pay bills, and so on—the classic self-service use of Internet technology. Before long, hundreds of thousands of customers were successfully using the site. However, as in many such projects, behind the gleaming new Web site were back-end computer problems. Workarounds were needed to make the system appear seamless to users. "Sneakernet"—manual actions—were needed in some cases to move data from one computer system to another. The operational staff performed Herculean efforts to make the system work. Eventually, they achieved all the upgrades and integration needed to make the process digital from front to back, the equivalent of changing the tires while the vehicle raced down the digital highway. Not being celebrated as the e-business team was, the operational team felt that the e-business team had been rewarded for glitz while they had been ignored for substance.

When the e-business leader was promoted to a position supervising both groups, the organization was rife for conflict. Compounding the situation, the new leader was a high achiever with little affiliation or power motivation. This personality meant that the person had less political savvy than usual. He understood the potential friction, but did not know how to deal with it. His perception, in fact, was that the company had set him up for failure rather than giving him an opportunity to create his magic on a larger scale. Fortunately, this new vice president had benefited from coaching before and brought in a consultant who worked through the six steps of organizational change. The interviews uncovered the perspective that the leaders from the operations group admired their new leader but nonetheless saw the reorganization as a demotion for them. They were also nervous about the new leader's management style, which was less personal and affiliative than their previous manager.

The new vice president shared his profile, which set the stage for others sharing theirs. This openness helped align the values of the team. With a better understanding of one another's motivations, the group had enough trust to begin honestly discussing their hopes for the organization and their own futures. The dialogue helped them to understand that they could help develop the climate of the new combined group and define the charter that would define their own reality—their performance measures, the way in which they would treat one another, and their interaction with senior executives, including those above the new vice president. These steps helped solidify the new organization and give it a positive basis from which to start. The process also laid the groundwork for a new strategic plan and the leadership training that would enable it. Without coaching, the team may eventually have found its way to success, but the potential pitfalls and personality conflicts would have been numerous, especially for a new team embarking on major new initiatives. A corollary benefit is that the successful reorganization freed up resources for other new projects. When the newly integrated organization succeeded, several individuals from the team were promoted to run their own groups.

Where the preceding example took many months, the qualities of individuals and the particulars of organizational culture can simplify the process a great deal. At another company, the leader's positive traits were so strong that the initial alignment meeting with the team was largely done in a day, and the interviews primarily served to prioritize initiatives rather than bring to life any underlying personal or cultural issues. This same leader also once turned back a unionization campaign by factually showing the benefits of unionization versus nonunionization, comparing the financial health of his company versus that of the union, and promising to respect the employees' decision, whatever it was. When employees said that "management" intimidated them, he told the employees that they could meet with him as much as they wanted and bring as many buddies as they wanted so as *not* to feel intimidated. The overwhelming rejection of the union was one of his happiest days, he said—not because he had beaten the union, but because his employees had believed in him. It is no surprise that aligning other leaders in his organization with his values was a simple task.

Changing Climate Quickly, Culture Slowly

Implicit in the idea of change processes, positive behavior, and the tools to carry out both is the need to change corporate culture. Despite the desire of many companies to empower their employees, corporate culture often restrains or prevents empowerment. The military, for instance, places a premium on leadership and initiative at every level. However, tradition, command-and-control structures (and strictures), the sheer scale of military organizations, and the potential for catastrophic mistakes sometimes cause the military to replace leadership with leadership substitutes. The organization and organizational processes sometimes create a sense of leadership and direction when none is actually forthcoming, when the underlying message is "take no risks" or "do as you see best, and we will second-guess you."

Furthermore, geographical dispersion and complex, ambiguous, and ever-changing situations such as those on the ground in Iraq and Afghanistan make it difficult for senior commanders to give meaningful direction to junior officers in the field. As a result, junior officers improvise constantly. To achieve the objective, they learn to follow a commander's intent rather than a commander's plan. The macrocosm of military *culture* therefore often differs from the microcosm of military *climate*.

Culture in every organization is the result of history, policy, values, and organizational structure. It is a complex phenomenon embedded in an organization, influencing the behavior of individuals both directly and indirectly. Because of the military's size, the change in overall culture is slow in coming. Officers in the field, however, make changes quickly. They have no choice, if they are to keep themselves and their troops alive. A similar parallel exists in business. The business organization may implicitly state that it wants managers to take risks, but its culture may punish or squeeze out those who do without permission. Culture in large business organizations is slow to change, but climate within smaller groups (subcultures) can change quickly. Unless the leader is an organization's founder, an individual leader cannot easily create or change a culture. Strategic leaders, however, do spend a great deal of time attempting to influence culture.

Within every culture is the working climate, which also results from history, values, and structure but which is also the direct result of leadership. In the Army's case, platoon leaders or company commanders can immediately change the climate by their own personal approach to action. Dramatically different climates may exist in an organization, from gung-ho leaders in the trenches to cautious bureaucrats back at headquarters. Consistent, combined efforts of many individual leaders can change the culture over time. Typically, mid-level managers in volatile markets must make difficult decisions with imperfect information in very short periods of time. Like army lieutenants, they must learn to improvise by acting on the company's *intent*, rather than on the company's rigid plans. Therefore, managers further down the line must be able to initiate change even though senior leadership may not have initiated any themselves.

The purpose of change programs and the behavioral tools that accompany them is to create climates in which fresh thinking and innovation flourish, in which a bias to action exists, and in which senior leaders act as coaches and leave decision making to those who are the closest to and have the best grasp of the situation. The climate is defined by the way leaders treat their people, how people treat one another, the professional opportunities within the organization, and the way in which individuals can contribute—all of the elements that emerge from the six-step change process that began this chapter. A positive climate, particularly one that encourages managers to use their best judgment to act on the company's mission and intent— rather than waiting for someone higher up to make a decision— improves a company's ability to respond to change. By seeding positive climates, beginning with senior leadership and expanding throughout the organization, companies can eventually create a positive culture throughout the organization. Businesses that empower their employees in this way improve their ability to satisfy the company mission, show resilience in the face of difficulty, and attract and retain good leaders.

Positive Climate Indicators

The behavioral tools and the process for change described in this chapter are designed to create a positive climate, an environment that directly affects individual teams in the short run and overall corporate culture in the long run. A positive climate has many traits, among them are the following:

- A spirit of teamwork
- Open, candid communications
- High collaboration, seeking out of advice from others, mentoring
- High employee retention rates
- Low daily absences
- Regularly demonstrated mutual respect
- Commitments that are kept
- High customer loyalty

Source: Greencastle Associates Consulting (www.greencastleconsulting.com)

16

Happy Companies Are All Alike and Yet Unique

What a journey. In about 275 pages, we have traversed the whole of human history and prehistory, explored the sociology of human groups and organizations, examined the inner biology of the brain and heart, detailed the ways that unhappy environments can smack down even the strongest of individuals, and showed countless examples of how traditional but inherently negative corporate behavior can be transformed into positive and more successful behavior. If the path was not always straightforward, the purpose of the expedition was: We wanted to examine business not as some objective activity separate from "real life," but as a major part of "real life" in terms of the time people spend at work, the energy and emotion they invest in work, and the way that work affects them—and they affect work—at a deep and personal level.

We wanted to show how business is fraught with the same feelings and fears that permeate every other human activity. We wanted to show that the way humans are wired biologically makes it easy for human beings in the office environment to react as fearfully as our ancestors did on the open savannah. We wanted to show that however valuable those fear-based behaviors are in actual life-and-death circumstances, they are debilitating and self-defeating in the world of commerce. Most important, we wanted to contrast those behaviors with higher behaviors based on the best of human motivations rather than the worst of fears.

Although human behavior in all matters is subtle, complex, and often unpredictable, we can observe consistent patterns in negative emotions that derive from fear. Because fear is centered in the more primitive parts of the brain, we can be sure that the behavior will be reflexive, reactive, and limited. Because fear short-circuits the higher brain centers, we can be sure that fear behavior will lack the breadth, subtlety, imagination, and humanity that comes from higher thought processes, higher emotions such as appreciation, and higher spiritual values such as compassion.

Fight, freeze, or flee reactions directly cause negative behaviors that show themselves in such actions as greed and accommodation (the fear of not having enough) and the putting down and undercutting of others (the fear of not being enough), or the reluctance to change or embrace new ideas. The fight response leads to turf wars and power struggles—the Cain-and-Abel conflicts within an organization—and to target fixation on competitors and what they do rather than what the company itself is best at. However it may dress up—in arrogance or gamesmanship or anything in between—fear is the little child inside us all pretending to be an adult.

Because economics *ought* to be based in logic and reason, we assume that business is a place of reason and dispassion. Yet business is about relationships. Relationships with fellow employees. With vendors and partners. With customers. With the greater community in which businesses operate. Relationships are as much about emotions as about reason. Because humans easily fall into fear—it is how we survived all these ages—a failure to recognize the importance of emotion can result in fear becoming the predominate emotion, almost by default. When fear creeps in, the brain reinforces fear behaviors at the individual level and soon the culture reinforces fear behaviors at large. The negative feedback loop quickly turns any organization into a fear-driven creature. Because fear behavior is always selfish—what I need right now—and narrow in view—what I see before me at this moment rather than what I can imagine in the future—the results are organizations focused on short-term projects, short-term finances, and short-term thinking. Taken to an extreme, these behaviors become unethical and illegal. Short of criminality are the many, many companies that are dysfunctional: unhappy and generally unproductive.

Positive Company Requires Intentional, Sustained Effort

Leadership through appreciation and vision requires conscious effort and conscious reinforcement until the higher thoughts and emotions become ingrained in personal biology and in organizational culture.

As the late management guru Peter Drucker said, "The only things that evolve by themselves in an organization are disorder, friction, and malperformance." The best leaders set out to create an intentional culture. They do not let culture happen as they pursue dollars. They begin with values and mission. Products, services, finances, and all the rest flow from those two things. Culture is what leaders stamp on an organization, not what happens while leaders are elsewhere attending to "business." Rocco Fiorentino of United Financial Services Group points out that culture is not a fact but a feeling and takes time to create, time to change, and effort to maintain. If we could learn and absorb a culture overnight, that culture would not be deep enough to last. Conversely, when a positive culture takes hold, it becomes self-reinforcing and long lasting.

Happy companies are made, not born. This idea means that organizational structure, management policies, and reward systems are designed to reinforce positive culture. As Amabile's Harvard study showed, there are not two categories of people, creative and noncreative, but two categories of organizations, those that encourage creativity and those that do not. Of the many traits of the happy leader—humility that unleashes the energy of the entire organization, the hiring of people with complementary skills, a hands-on approach to understand the business and to teach others—the three most important are vision, appreciation, and the *deliberate establishment of culture*. On 31 projects through 1997, Toyota worked with its U.S. suppliers to reduce inventory by an average of 75 percent and improve productivity an average of 124 percent. Again and again, however, the company found that U.S. suppliers would not carry forward the changes throughout all their lines and all their systems. The problem was not shop-floor resistance, according to Liker of *The Toyota Way*, but top management. Executives were not committed enough. They had not yet internalized the Toyota approach of "continual improvement through action," or *kaizen*—a cultural mindset.

As for specific practices, innovation comes from a number of beguilingly simple steps: putting people together, focusing on customer needs in the real world, doing real and regular brainstorming, making progress literally visible to all, listening to and engaging with employees—who after all, know what is actually happening with the company in the market—and celebrating success. The particular steps may not matter as much as that the organization specifically takes action to encourage initiative and creativity.

Part of the deliberate culture is organizational development, cultivation of employees, and alignment of everyone's work with strategic goals. These areas must extend beyond traditional training and traditional goals and objectives. Happy companies seek and cultivate emotionally intelligent employees as *policy*, as a conscious strategy, thereby attracting and retaining the best and the brightest talent. Happy companies develop emotional intelligence in day-to-day business activities, seeking a balance of deep reflection on strategy and fast, energetic execution on tactics. Learning is part of the company's DNA, and programs such as motivational profiling, appreciative inquiry, and the balanced scorecard are used to construct a culture that reinforces the values and mission.

Keep Your Eye on the Target, Not the Ball

Happy companies also have profit as one goal, but not *the* goal. Toyota North America's mission is to contribute to the economic growth of the community and country, to the stability and well-being of the team members, and to the overall growth of Toyota by providing value to customers. Ford's mission is to continually improve its products to meet customer needs and to provide a reasonable return to shareholders. In short, Toyota's mission is to help its community and employees. Ford's is to build better vehicles to make more money. This subtle difference in mission creates a profound difference in human response, from the passion that Toyota has for quality to the passion that it has for its customers.

Undoubtedly, Ford has many good people passionate about cars and customers. The difference is what the *entire culture*—all the people, especially top management—believes and how the entire culture—especially top management—acts on that belief. Building a good vehicle and selling it for a fair profit is not the mission for Toyota. It is the mechanism by which to achieve the mission of improving the community. Toyota and most other highly successful companies have long understood a profound moral. You do not have a mission of achieving profits. You have profits to be able to pursue the mission. Psychologically, a focus on profits is a fear motivation. Closely allied with this fear is the need for control. Seldom do you find profit-driven leaders who are also not control freaks. Ultimately, however, you cannot control people. You can only get them to accept the mission and make it their own. Then you do not *need* to control them. They motivate and even inspire themselves.

After companies have achieved competency in basic areas, what separates one organization from another are the "immeasurables," a term coined by Susan Priddy, operations manager for CyberOptics

Semiconductor. Her comments are worth repeating verbatim: "At a certain point in your career, you have reached a good level of responsibility, you are making a fair salary, and you pretty well know what you will be doing in the next 5 to 10 years. So what gets you out of bed in the morning? For me, it is the product being made, the challenges of the position, the relationship with my peers, how the company pursues its vision, and its involvement in the community. It was a bit of a revelation to me, because I had been unhappy in another job for a while and really couldn't articulate why. Once I thought about it, I was very surprised at how much value I put in the 'immeasurables.' Turning 40 had something to do with it. I was looking at life differently. Not just aspects of work but also of friendship, home, spouse, and my commitment to my family. Other friends in my group are having the same reaction to their jobs. There is no soul to their work. They need a value beyond the core job. It is a huge hole for a lot of people. Things you took for granted when you were young and crazy now mean something. Values flow between work and home."

Study after study shows that companies with strong missions and high levels of integrity outperform those that suffer from weak missions or poor corporate governance. An entire generation of industry experts and scholars has reached the same conclusion: Bennis, Blanchard, Collins, Covey, Drucker, Goleman, Goulston, Peters, Senge, and Tichey, to mention the most notable. CEOs have eagerly embraced the processes and practices recommended by the experts but have not necessarily undertaken the underlying shift in values, without which the processes fail to produce much in the way of meaningful change. The reason is the "laser-like focus on profits" instead of the "laser-like focus on values."

To pick an analogy familiar to many CEOs, the company focused on profits is like the golfer focused on hitting the ball hard and far. People whose mission is to smash the ball usually hit badly or erratically. People whose mission is to have a beautiful swing usually hit the ball far and straight—the ball just happens to get in the way of the club. The club is not used to hit the ball; the club is used to get to the target. For companies, the "beautiful swing" is the presence of a meaningful mission and leadership integrity (the backswing) and the proper consideration of their employees, their many other stakeholders, their customers, and their communities (the downswing). With this combination, profits happen like a 250-yard drive straight down the fairway.

A thoughtful balance is the key. The CEO of one happy company said he constantly tuned his profit needs against his need to develop employees and be a good community citizen. He had not built his company out of a profit motivation but to fulfill his passion for the business. He could not afford to work in a company that did not have profits, and he could not stand to work for a company that did not have a healthy culture. Just as a happy person in business is a well-rounded person, with a busy and engaging work life balanced by a busy and engaging personal life, so a happy company is a well-rounded company, with legitimate financial needs balanced by legitimate cultural and community needs.

Too many businesses operate like the individual who once sought counseling for a highly stressful life. When asked by his counselor what he would do with his life if he were better able to manage his stress, the executive said, "Why, I'd work a lot more!" His counselor showed him to the door. "I can't help you," he said. "You're totally nuts."

Given enough financial success, too many businesspeople think only of more. Piling on more financial success becomes the goal in place of the original mission. Like the executive, the firms become "totally nuts" in their profit fixation. This is the start of the death spiral. A typical company profile is a bell curve beginning with the birth, vision, strategy, structure, and management leading the company to the top of its first peak. If the company forgets the birth and vision—why the company was created—the organization becomes stuck in management mode and becomes bureaucratic and reactive. At the top of the first (or successive) curves, companies either reinvent themselves around a positive future by revisiting their birth or they go down quickly.

This need for balance between profit and culture, and the need for rebirth at regular stages in a company's life, brings us back to the HAPIE acronym. (See Table 16-1.) Companies need not be perfect

H	Humble, inclusive, inspirational, innovative, and heartfelt leadership
A	Adaptive, enthusiastic, emotionally intelligent employees
P	Profit for all who contribute to the company's success, with the focus being ROP (return on people) in addition to usual metric of ROI (return on investment)
I	Invigorated stakeholders, vendors, and clientele who serve as first-line marketers for the company
E	Engaged, constructive community citizenship

Table 16-1 Successful companies are ones that are strong in three or more of the areas defined in the acronym HAPIE. The fewer the areas of strength, the more the company struggles. A company strong in only one area invariably fails.

across the board—no one company is—but companies need to be strong in at least three areas to prosper. A company that is strong in only two areas will struggle, and a company strong in only one is likely to fail. A small company had the best employees imaginable, but it had few stakeholders, little community involvement, and a poorly defined business model that led it to misapply those talented employees. The reason is that management lost its vision after the first major product release and began to cycle. By not revisiting its vision, the company could not generate enough other positive attributes to keep going. The company failed, and those terrific employees seeded a number of other successful ventures that had most of the HAPIE qualities.

Enron is a company that began with a great vision, many self-styled "smartest people in the room," but leaders with a pathological focus on themselves and profits led the company to ruin. The Enron example carries across all other sectors, particularly technology sectors in which a high premium is placed on IQ. Companies sometimes overlook transgressions on the assumption that they need these really smart people onboard to succeed. The phrase for this attitude is "the competence deviance hypothesis." The greater the talent, the greater the deviance in behavior that others are willing to tolerate. Obvious examples are sports stars, entertainers, and—within organizations— people who generate a lot of money for their company. People keep prima donnas out of a fear of not being able to find equivalent talent, but in the long run such people often cause far more harm to the organization than they bring benefit.

Here's a secret: Talent and personality are unrelated. It is not required to accept negative traits to benefit from the positive. Either the negatives change, or the person goes. The prima donna believes that talent brings privilege. A mature adult believes that talent brings responsibility. In place of talented but emotionally inept or morally limited individuals, opportunity-focused companies actively recruit people with comparable skills and far more emotional intelligence and integrity. They are out there, if you look.

Among the companies already profiled, Endo has big-picture leaders sensitive to the pain-management market; employees with a passion for alleviating suffering; strong profits because it has minimized R&D and manufacturing costs; and strong community involvement, particularly in healthcare and education. Among the example companies, Anthem, Comcast, IDEO, ScriptSave, Talent+, Toyota, and others are also strong in all five dimensions.

Companies that have most of the HAPIE traits can do extremely well in the marketplace but still struggle in ways, perhaps because of the visible disparity between those positive traits and areas where they are weaker. Wal-Mart pioneered high-volume, low-cost products for the masses, has strong leadership, and is a good corporate citizen in terms of charitable activities, but the company has a mixed record on profits and return on people. Wal-Mart hires and promotes large numbers of people who otherwise might not have any other opportunities, but at the same time it has depressed overall retail salaries and it offers relatively poor benefits to its lower-paid employees. Its large, efficient stores lead to lower customer prices, but the colossal scale and the concrete-block conformity of the stores have also led to their being rejected in some communities.

As a result, a company with tremendous talents has been subject to withering criticisms from some number of citizens and competitors—fears aroused—who can imagine only the worst from it. The company has been scrambling to respond to those criticisms, generally in problem-solving mode. The question is whether Wal-Mart will use its imagination to redefine its mission in a way that makes outsider concerns moot. Two ways would be to re-imagine the physical design and scale of its retail stores and to reestablish the primacy of employees at all levels, which was once a hallmark of Sam Walton's business. Anyone at Wal-Mart who does not understand how Walton would respond to the swirl of issues around employees can read Walton's own biography for gutsy guidance.

Because most other companies also fall somewhere in the middle of the HAPIE scale of perfection, just about all companies have reasons to launch programs that can help them to imagine a positive future for themselves and to build a new mission around that vision.

The Choice, the Whole Choice, and Nothing but the Choice

With the emphasis on the biology and the history of human behavior, one question is whether human behavior and therefore business behavior is "wired"—preprogrammed. Regardless of nature or nurture (genetic traits or environmental factors), humans have choice. Free will, in traditional Western lingo. The more primitive the area of the brain involved, the more limited the repertoire of choice. At the level of the reptilian brain, the responses are almost entirely physical and reflexive—jump out of the way, strike back, freeze until danger passes. At the level of the emotional brain, the choices are more varied but remain limited, reactive, and short term. At the level of whole-brain functioning, the entire suite of human behavior is open to consideration. The executive brain is your logical buddy who steps back and evaluates the situation in rational terms, and the emotional brain is the good friend who advises you how to apply your personal history to new interpersonal interactions. The executive brain tells you whether a specific matter is logically correct or incorrect; the emotional brain tells you whether the situation overall *feels* right or wrong. In addition to synthesizing these inputs and others from the heart and limbic system, the executive brain also coordinates the creative centers.

At any moment, humans can react from any level of the brain. In ethical matters, for instance, people responding from the level of the survival brain zero in on misdeeds and punishments. People responding from the level of the executive brain zero in on redemption and forgiveness. The Old and New Testaments of Christianity illustrate the difference—two books from the same religious tradition, the first punitive and second redemptive, the first born of fear and the second of hope. Albert Einstein, who changed forever our understanding of the universe, also showed keen insight to the human psyche when he said that the only way to solve our significant problems is to go beyond the level of thinking we were at when we created those problems. Perhaps because he spent so much time there, he understood the need for humanity to move to the next stage of consciousness.

Except for the split second when actual life is at risk, humans have a choice on how to act and react. If you choose to react from fear, you live with the consequences. If you choose to react from the whole brain, you live with the consequences. With choice comes optimal management. Wherever they are in an organization, individuals can choose to change their environment, choose to change their attitude about their environment, or choose to opt out of this environment for a healthier one. However difficult the situation, personal mastery is the root of success. The essence is personal responsibility. If people are accountable for their behavior, they are not likely to fall into the VERBs: victimization, entitlement, the need for rescue, or blaming. Their choice is to make the company more productive and healthier mentally or to find another environment in which they believe they can better contribute.

Happy companies also provide as much choice as possible to employees. Motivational profiles and balanced scorecards provide ways in which organizations can properly align people according to their motivations, their abilities, and the strategic needs of the organization. Within this context, decisions naturally move down into the organization. People not only are better motivated, but they have a clearer sense of the context in which to make decisions. With people, teams, and strategy aligned, and employees understanding their precise role in the company, competent people are usually able to make good decisions on their own—with appropriate coaching from superiors and support from peers.

One CEO believed that he encouraged decision making in his organization—what was the big deal? In actuality, he made all the decisions himself. His senior executives were lined up outside his office all week long, waiting to get time with the big boss man so that he could make their decisions for them. He was taking an expensive, talented group of senior employees and teaching them learned helplessness. In contrast is the CEO who sees himself as the coach, encouraging his executives and employees downstream to make all the decisions possible, to take responsibility and to move quickly by following the intent of the company mission rather than following orders from the chain of command. The decisions he reserves for himself are the ones that cross divisions, that require substantially greater resources than budgeted, or that constitute a fundamental shift in strategy.

Even in difficult times, companies should think in terms of choice. Downsizing and outsourcing have been things that few employees have had any say over, and the results have often been devastating to people and communities suffering layoffs. Too often, downsizing and outsourcing are portrayed as strategic choices to reinvent the company when in actuality they are reflexive acts to cut costs, a financially driven decision to reduce headcount, period. Each division manager and department head is given a number of heads to lop off.

How many companies have, like British Air after 9/11, asked employees to participate in the layoff decision to ameliorate the worst of the pain? When Comcast merged with many different companies and when Blue Cross Blue Shield of Illinois merged with Blue Cross Blue Shield of Texas, both organizations brought together individuals from across the companies that were merged to help with the consolidation of positions. Although cutbacks were not eliminated, when people seen as trusted peers were involved in restructuring, the reorganization made more sense to people who were impacted. Or, before layoffs are determined, how many companies have gone to employees in each division, each department, and each team, and said, "Come up with a new vision for your group"? Tell us how you can reimagine your future to create more value (and justify your positions).

This positive change would require more time than taking an axe to headcount, but as happened with Waggener Edstrom when it lost the client and had no immediate work for its large account team, the positive approach would be more likely to position the company for growth than for more shrinkage. GM once went to its plant in Delaware and told the 3,500 employees that the facility would be closed in a few years and there was nothing they could do about it. The plant manager, Ralph Harding, told the workers they could do something about it: They could make GM feel "really stupid." In two years, the plant had the lowest production costs and lowest warranty costs of any GM plant, and dealers specifically requested models built in Delaware. GM wisely decided to keep the plant open.

More to the point, if companies practice choice and opportunity seeking all along, if they internalize the practice of constantly asking positive questions, they are far more likely to stay ahead of the market than otherwise. They are far more likely to constantly develop new products and services, avoiding a bloated organizational structure or the price wars that force companies into reactive downsizing or automatic outsourcing. The problem is not with outsourcing per se. The problem is that organizations create too few new opportunities to engage employees once present-day products make the inevitable transition toward obsolescence or commoditization. Environments that stimulate creativity—and therefore new business opportunities— have little likelihood of retrenching.

Finally, leaders have a personal choice on how they interact with others in the company. Following in the tradition of the humble, empathetic leader, managers at all levels should consider the lesson of the non-alpha horse. In a small herd of horses, the stereotypical alpha horse runs the show, with bites and kicks to prove it. However, when the herd becomes too large for a single horse to control, those horses outside the reach of the alpha horse begin to follow whichever horse leads them to food and water. Often, this is an unassuming mid-pack horse smart enough to find resources and determined enough to obtain them. Formal studies show that other herd animals, such as cattle and bison, follow a similar leadership formula. Bullying and dominance play no role; cattle follow leaders who demonstrate intelligence, experience, and good social skills.

Among primates, a similar phenomenon occurs in times of scarcity regardless of the presence of a dominant male. Research by Robert Sapolsky, a neuroendocrinologist at Stanford, shows that primates at the top of the social order are highly stressed by the need to maintain power, and those at the bottom by the need to survive. The relatively nonstressed animals in between are the ones that show creativity. In Japan, a mid-pack juvenile female macaque named Imo discovered how to wash sweet potatoes and wheat in salt water to remove sand. Eventually, the entire troop of monkeys copied her behavior.

No systematic survey has ever been done, but experience leads us to believe that the most creative, innovative work in a company run by an alpha-style leader is done *out of sight of that leader*, where his or her antics do not reach. Sometimes creativity can occur only away from dominance, in the absence of the arrogant leader. Although several examples come to mind, one in particular is a high-tech company that has always performed better when its CEO was off playing with his yachts and airplanes than when he was behind his desk issuing orders. Dominance is not leadership.

For humans the lesson is threefold: 1) Innovation and leadership can come from anywhere in the ranks; 2) even in times of scarcity, the commonsense leader (horse, macaque, or human) does a better job of providing for the troop than a leader fixated on power; and 3) humans naturally gravitate to those who demonstrate leadership as opposed to dominance. If you want people to follow you, *strive to be the chosen leader*. Understand and exercise the attributes that cause your employees to voluntarily seek you as their leader, which seldom relate to anything like alpha behaviors but usually mean doing nothing more than what is right for the company and the people. This attitude will naturally move you toward empathetic, inclusive, appreciative behaviors.

It Takes More Than Money to Move the Troops

Our survival-based emotional wiring causes people and organizations to rally around problems. A consultant once asked a group of executives how much time they spent on problem solving and how much they spent on opportunity. A show of hands indicated that they spent 90 percent of their time solving problems and 10 percent on new opportunities. Further, they thought this was a pretty good ratio! The assumption is that you have to solve problems to clear the decks for opportunity. In actuality, the more time you spent on opportunity, the less you *need* to spend on problem solving. Also, the focus on problems gears people toward fear. Fear *does* stimulate companies to act, but only in short bursts and only with excessive casualties. In essence, the company races along on an adrenaline high. As with all addictions, the costs are high. Over time, people become inured to fear and fail to respond, fall by the wayside from exhaustion, or burn out and walk away to find something more meaningful. Some leaders may be aware of the costs but do not know any other way to work except through fear. Unless a company is in emergency-response mode, the leaders may not feel that they have a mission or can create sense of urgency.

There is another way, one that achieves comparable results in the short term and healthier and more sustainable results in the long term. Instead of the energy of panic-induced negativity, companies can draw on the energy of the creative and imaginative centers of the human brain. These centers create the same force and vigor as fear, but the energy is a kind of "green power." It is a renewable resource that energizes rather than drains individuals and companies. By not stimulating the stress hormones, it does not send people on boom-and-bust rushes or wear the body down long term. By triggering appreciation, it synchronizes the heart, the autonomic nervous system, and the brain. Appreciation dampens or cuts off the threatening messages from the amygdala and the survival brain. During an epiphany, the amygdala temporarily shuts off. All of the body's energies, mental and physical, are pointed in a positive direction. The difference between panic power and positive power unleashed by appreciation and vision is the difference between the diffuse energy of a light bulb and the focused energy of a laser.

There is a reason that the preamble to the U.S. Constitution does not rattle off a list of problems to be overcome by a common government but rather begins with the first statement in history of a people inspired to create a nation worthy of their dreams: "We the People of the United States, in Order to form a more perfect Union, establish Justice, insure domestic Tranquility, provide for the common defence, promote the general Welfare, and secure the Blessings of Liberty to ourselves and our Posterity, ..." There is a reason that Gandhi—in essence choosing the executive brain over the survival brain—said, "The spirit lies dormant in the brute and he knows no law but that of physical might. The dignity of man requires obedience to another law—to the strength of the spirit." There is a reason that Martin Luther King's speech on racial equality in America was not titled "I Have a Nightmare" and why it did not focus on all the wrongs done to minorities. Instead, it was titled "I Have a Dream" and spoke to the vision of equality for all children. Speaking positively of the future, he inspired a generation of Americans to the call for social equality.

In the darkest hours of 1776, George Washington faced the dissolution of the Continental Army as recruitments expired and all his men were free to leave. Unable to entice them to stay with money, the general told the men that he appreciated their sacrifices, that no one could ask more of them than what they had already faced, but that if they stayed for just one more month they would do something that no other generation of men would ever be able to do, that later generations would envy them for—claim liberty for their friends and families and establish a new nation. Washington's success in convincing his soldiers to stay illustrates the value of the inspirational leader. Notice the traits: an instinctive use of appreciation and vision to give his soldiers an understanding of their higher calling; humility toward his role; recognition of others. Not once did he put himself before his troops or his nation. He declined calls to be made president for life (king) when the war was over. The only time he called attention to himself was when he raced to the front of a battle to try to turn the tide—aides wisely hauled him to safety. His officers wept when he left the service at war's end. His country wept when he died.

Few people have the opportunity to write a new chapter in history, but every business leader, at every level, has the opportunity to write a new chapter in the behavior of a business and do with the organization something more than make a serviceable product. By having a bigger vision of the organization, and using appreciation as a bedrock principle, business leaders can establish a higher level of thought and behavior not only for themselves but for the people they lead. They can accept the mantle of business knighthood and make it part of what they do every day.

They will not be alone in the effort. Kaiser, Zohar, and others are pushing the idea nationally. Consumers, investors, and regulators *clamor* for knightly behavior from business. *Corporate Knights,* a Canadian magazine with a circulation of 150,000, is the first mass-market magazine to focus on corporate social responsibility and the proposition that good corporate citizenship and solid financial performance go hand in hand. Its articles range from the positive financial results of recycling to socially responsible investments to annual listings of the top 50 most socially responsible companies in Canada.

Paralleling these efforts is the Integrity Institute, which was founded to create a standard of measure called the Return on Integrity (still being formulated as of this writing) and to independently and objectively assess and certify corporate integrity, similar to the way in which the Underwriters Laboratory (UL) assesses and certifies consumer products for safety. In addition, software products are coming online to help companies monitor accounting practices, improve fraud detection generally, and to provide anonymous ways in which employees can report ethical violations. The first generation of such packages primarily helped companies deal with reporting requirements of the Sarbanes-Oxley Act in the United States, but subsequent releases are growing more sophisticated. The hope behind all of these efforts is that a small number of people—in this case, dedicated and highly motivated people determined to inculcate organizations with higher ethical values—can create huge swings in the behavior of organizations and society.

Change within the culture of business—and not stricter regulation or clever software—is ultimately the answer to the question of better business. Government regulation may restrain or stop some crooks, although more-complex regulations can also create more places in which criminals can hide, as well as overburden honest businesses. Activist consumers can slow or stymie misbehaving businesses through negative publicity or boycotts. Both categories of actions are inherently fear-based, reactive, and after the fact. The government and consumers should always be alert to protect against nefarious behavior, but the best solution is for the poor decisions and lawbreaking of business never to occur at all. Business needs to evolve to a higher level of responsibility. This book has a simple standard for you to consider. If the United States gave out knighthoods for ethical, people-oriented, community-oriented leadership, would you be on the short list?

Higher forms of conduct come from value-based consciousness. Because values are transmitted through culture, value-based consciousness applies to individuals, companies, industries, entire markets, and the societies in which they exist. High levels of conduct are the only way to ensure consumer confidence and to keep government oversight to a reasonable minimum. The lesson is not strictly about ethics and morals. Economic freedom is closely allied with political and personal freedom. A continuation of corporate misbehavior and corporate extravagance will undoubtedly lead to new strictures, and those strictures could ultimately affect everyone's lives in unexpected and intrusive ways. The constriction of free enterprise would undoubtedly mean the constriction of many other freedoms. Happy companies know that taking individual and organizational responsibility for their business behavior will safeguard the health of their organizations and ultimately will create more wealth for each and every one of their stakeholders.

You should do right for your employees, customers, and stakeholders for no other reason that it is the right thing to do. Another reason is that every business decision has an ethical dimension as well as a financial one. If you lose the ethics, sooner or later you will lose the business.

A Happy Company Is Unique as Each Creative Person Is Unique

In the opening to the novel *Anna Karenina*, Tolstoy said that happy families are all alike; every unhappy family is unhappy in its own way. We would turn the sentiment around. Tolstoy was juxtaposing the external behavior of happy and unhappy family groups. Externally, unhappiness manifests itself in many ways, whereas happiness appears as straightforward joy. Internally, however, unhappy social groups—family, society, or business—are all alike; and every happy social group—family, society, or business—is happy in its own way. The reason is that unhappiness stems from fear, whose many and varied symptoms nonetheless come from a set of limited, reactive, unimaginative, cowardly actions that are easily and often repeated. Happiness stems from courage, which produces appreciation and respect, and which sets loose imagination and creativity among individuals and powerful social bonds among the group.

Paradoxically, the simplistic reactions of the survival brain produce the wide variety of fear-based behaviors explored in this book. The complex, sophisticated, and liberating behaviors of the executive brain produce the simple external affect of people who enjoy being and working together. Underneath the surface, unhappy individuals and groups are cycling through a limited repertoire of reflexive behavior that are identical at the core; whereas happy individuals and groups are constantly expanding their range of thoughts, emotions, and behaviors, learning as they go and building on that learning.

As humans have done through the ages, the more the imagination is applied, the more ideas are exchanged, the more the individual brain develops and the more the group evolves culturally in a positive direction. What matters is not the destination, but the journey forward. After one company discussed the many positive things it was doing, the CEO stopped and said: "If you write this down, it will portray us better than we really are. But it does represent what we strive for." Striving in a consistent fashion to achieve a positive culture is the essence of the matter. The difference between an unhappy company and a happy one is the difference between reacting to what the existing world wants you to do and modeling a new reality—the future that you want—and bringing the world along with you.

Happy companies have the ability to act and react quickly, the ability to thrive in uncertainty, and strength of resilience when times are hard. As the most evolved form of business, they have the internal capability to cope with change imposed from outside or to initiate and sustain change created from within. Among other characteristics, happy companies know that they and their leadership teams are set not just for today, but are ready to take on the journey toward their future. Happy company leaders earn their pay when it comes to change. Alastair Robertson, the motivational profiling expert and principal of Evolve, a change-management and leadership-development consultancy, summarizes 20 years of experience when he says that the only way for organizations to learn how to implement change is for the leaders to lead change themselves. Having someone else within the organization lead change will not work. Senior management involvement is needed not only to create systemic processes throughout the organization, but also because sustainable improvement comes only when leaders and managers can inspire, motivate, and support people to achieve more. This requires great personal leadership.

In both a Darwinian and Tolstoyan sense, all unhappy companies are the same. Unable to adapt, unable to leap forward, they fail sooner than later. Happy companies are happy in their own way, for they all explore different paths. Their imagination—whole-brain functioning led by the executive brain and supported by the emotional brain—gives people in those companies the greatest opportunity for personal satisfaction and growth, the finest prospect of prevailing in tough environments, and the energy and innovation needed to expand into new niches.

What happy companies know, other companies can learn.

Qualities of Happy Companies

- **Integrating vision**. All people have a common and unifying sense of direction and have made a strong commitment to move cooperatively in that direction.

- **Humanizing mission**. The mission speaks to individual and collective values of all involved with the company. The mission allows all participants to create meaning and purpose in their lives.

- **Active philanthropy**. Doing good for the community is a specified and integral part of the company vision and something that the company does every day.

- **Energizing spirit**. A palpable energy permeates the culture. The energy is perceptible in verbal and nonverbal communication.

- **All-around respect**. Everyone believes that all employees regard and honor others as they would like to be regarded.

- **Trust**. All employees have confidence in the competence of others and belief in the capabilities and integrity of management. Expectations are clearly stated and frequently meet.

- **Constructive language**. The stories about the organization and the language used in daily business of the organization are positive in attitude and phrasing. Language inspires individuals, creates strong connections, and helps to build on individual and collective strengths, best practices, and hope for tomorrow.

- **Supportive relationships**. Generosity, kindness, and consideration are elemental. Helping one another inside and outside the context of business is essential. Colleagues collectively celebrate the good times and together share the difficult times.

- **Life-long learning**. The culture encourages all members of the organization to continually stretch their knowledge and skill sets. Training, mentoring, and employee-development programs are a central feature of the culture. As much knowledge and wisdom as possible are gleaned from every experience, and the company has systems by which to collect and publish best practices.

- **Encouragement of risk taking**. Organizations create business contexts in which associates can take risks, make decisions, and occasionally make mistakes. Mistakes are studied for what can be learned and successes are studied for what can be taught others. Organizational structure and processes are geared toward fostering innovation.

■ **Primary focus on opportunities**. The organization constantly seeks, explores, and discovers what energizes and brings life to the organization. Problem solving primarily focuses on the practical implementation of opportunities, not as a way of fixing existing issues.

■ **A climate of appreciation**. The common tendency is for members of the organization to focus on what is right and good with one another and the company. Using the best reality of today as the foundation, everyone imagines and works toward a better tomorrow.

■ **Humor**. When you are up to your rear in alligators, sometimes the best response is to laugh. Leaders and individuals keep in mind that half the fun of business is the fun of business.

■ **Balance between competitiveness and cooperation**. Individuals need competition in order to grow. The best competition is competition with yourself to be better than yesterday and with others inside the company to improve your skills and theirs. The purpose of competition with other companies is to learn what they do best and how this can apply to you and your company. The skills honed in competition need to be pulled into a cooperative effort for the company. All employees understand that cooperation is the secret ingredient to innovation. Individual effort as well as organizational programs emphasize cooperation.

■ **Willingness to extend beyond job description**. All employees at all levels should see as their job the need to do whatever it takes to make the organization run well and grow, as long as "whatever" is ethical.

■ **Unquestioned integrity**. Honesty and fair dealing are the hallmarks of every employee, every team, and the organization as a whole. In every situation, people treat others as honestly and fairly as they want to be treated themselves.

Index

M

MacDonald, Mariann, 138

Mack, John, 81

MacLean, Paul, 26

Maister, David, 202

mammalian brain, 26-27

management

biological approach to business behavior, 19-20

corporate mismanagement, fraud, 1-7

stress, 95

benefits of, 108

corporate culture, 111-127

corporate mastery of, 98-101

heart-mind connection, 101-106

personal mastery of stress, 97

physiological and psychological emotional connections, 107-108

Manhattan Project, 151

manufacturing and sales, 63

Marketing Warfare, 72, 206

Marmot, Michael, 90

Marshall, Ian, 146

Mayo, Robert, 144

MBTI (Myers-Briggs Type Indicator), 179

McClelland, David, 179

McCraty, Rollin, 102

McFarland, Keith, 122

McNeil, John, 145-146

Mecherle, G. J., 172

meditation, physiological effects, 105

Medstat Group study, 99

mental stress, 90

mergers

Cain-and-Abel conflicts, 64

corporate cultures, 126-127

Microsoft

Business Systems Division, 38-40

Global Citizenship Report, 230

hiring process, 171

real-world approach to innovation, 158

turnover rates, 197

visible innovation, 163

mid-brain, 26-27

moral awareness, executive brain, 27

Morgan Stanley, 81

Mother Standard of Care (CTCA), 141

motivational profiling, 247

Muirhead, Brian, Pathfinder project, 122

Myers-Briggs Type Indicator (MBTI), 179

N

Nelson, Don, 50

neocortex, 26

net promoter score, 141

neurons, 26

norepinephrine, 84

Northwestern National Life stress survey, 89

Norton, David, 209

Notes (Lotus), 73

Nucor Steel, 155

Nutrimental Foods, 218

T

U

V

X-Y-Z

Capitalism at the Crossroads
The Unlimited Business Opportunities in Solving the World's Most Difficult Problems
BY STUART L. HART

"Professor Hart is on the leading edge of making sustainability an understandable and useful framework for building business value."
—Chad Holliday, Chairman and CEO, DuPont

Capitalism is at a crossroads, facing international terrorism, world-wide environmental change, and an accelerating backlash against globalization. Your company is at a crossroads, too: finding new strategies for profitable growth is now more challenging than it has ever been. Both sets of problems are intimately linked: the best way to recharge growth is to pursue strategies that also solve today's most crucial social and environmental problems. In this book, you'll learn how to identify sustainable products and technologies that can drive new growth; how to market profitably to four billion people who have been bypassed or damaged by globalization; how to build effective new bridges with stakeholders; and much more.

ISBN 0131439871, © 2005, 288 pp., $27.95

The Enthusiastic Employee
How Companies Profit by Giving Workers What They Want
BY DAVID SIROTA, LOUIS A. MISCHKIND, AND MICHAEL IRWIN MELTZER

This book is about employee enthusiasm: that special, invigorating, purposeful and emotional state that's always present in the most successful organizations. Most people are enthusiastic when they're hired: hopeful, ready to work hard, eager to contribute. What happens? Management, that's what. This book tells you what managers do wrong, and what they need to do instead. Drawing on more than 30 years of employee attitude research, the authors detail exactly how to create an environment where enthusiasm flourishes and businesses excel.

ISBN 0131423304, © 2005, 400 pp., $26.95